A Far Distant Place

ALSO BY DANIELLE THOMAS

Children of Darkness

Voices in the Wind

Cry of Silence

Drumbeat

DANIELLE THOMAS

A Far Distant Place

MACMILLAN

First published 2000 by Macmillan
an imprint of Macmillan Publishers Ltd
25 Eccleston Place, London SW1W 9NF
Basingstoke and Oxford
Associated companies throughout the world
www.macmillan.co.uk

ISBN 0 333 75170 1 (Hardback)
ISBN 0 333 78324 7 (Trade Paperback)

1 3 5 7 9 8 6 4 2

A CIP catalogue record for this book is available from
the British Library.

Typeset by SetSystems Ltd, Saffron Walden, Essex
Printed and bound in Great Britain by
Mackays of Chatham plc, Chatham, Kent

This book has a special meaning for me, maybe because of the circumstances under which it was written and perhaps because I had the most fun researching it, for these and a hundred other reasons.

It is for my husband, Wilbur Smith. We are still marching forward, hand in hand and shoulder to shoulder, my love, and may that continue.

And,

it's also for my niece, Shannon Smith, who has typed two of my handwritten manuscripts with skill and love, plus being a loving and capable young lady.

ACKNOWLEDGEMENTS

I wish to thank Bruce and Diana Moroney for taking time out from their busy schedule to fly myself and Di Siebens, my American interpreter, over sights so breathtaking that they must have been brushed by angels' wings in passing.

Without flying over the almost two thousand northern and southern routes of the Iditarod trail I would have had to rely on videos and posters, which although good gave no idea of the immensity of the country.

I have to thank the Moroneys for allowing me to use their actual names and that of their kennels (I must accept responsibility for any errors).

In the almost two years it took me to research *A Far Distant Place*, I met so many helpful people that it's difficult to pinpoint and thank each one. Every Alaskan be assured it's easy to love Alaska, Alaskans and, of course, the four-footed ones, without whom their would be no Iditarod.

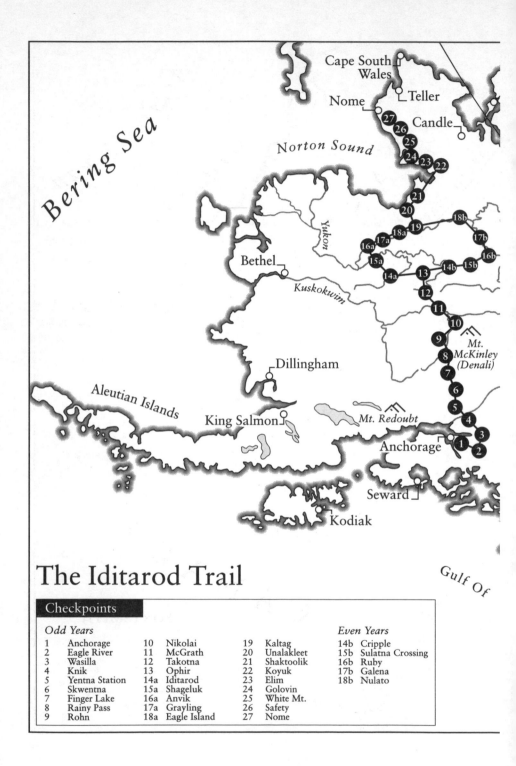

The Iditarod Trail

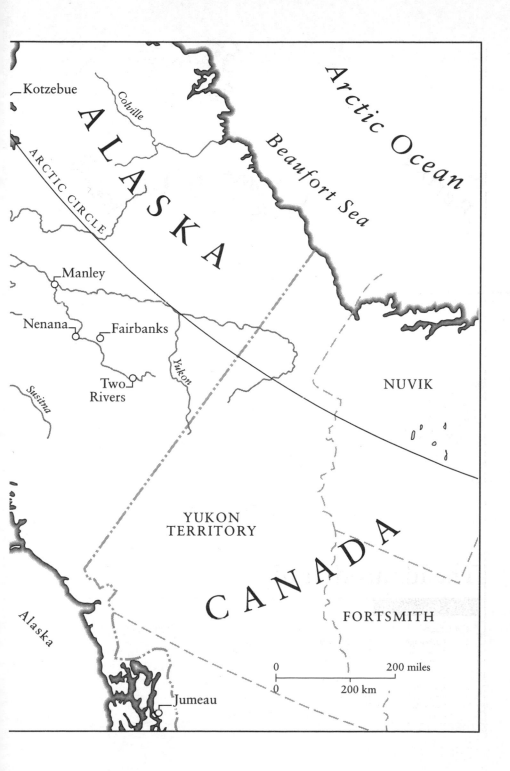

Prologue

IT WAS WINTER. In the North Slope, land of the Inupiat, the sun would not rise for sixty-six days.

It was early morning, though still as black as midnight. A group of Eskimos, bulky in their caribou parkas, formed a tight circle around a woman whose face was as seamed and weathered as the driftwood that washed onto the beaches in summer. The woman swayed slightly as the gale forced its way through gaps in the circle and buffeted her. The wolverine fur edging the Eskimos' hoods lay flat in the wind.

The group spoke little and in gruff, low voices. The men's eyes narrowed as they tried to pierce the darkness. They constantly searched the bleak, white plain which stretched from the mainland to the Beaufort Sea ice.

Beneath the suffocating white blanket they could visualize Pingkok Island, a barrier island sheltering Simpson Lagoon from the frozen sea. The lagoon stretched for four miles and lay in globs and streamers, like a careless squeeze of toothpaste.

They knew it well, as the ice usually broke a month earlier in the protected lagoon. This meant that the men could hunt the migratory geese and duck which rested on the open waters.

The Eskimos returned their gaze to the woman, as one of the men stepped out of the circle and stood beside her. The wind immediately funnelled through the opening, screeching as it tugged at parkas and threw back fur-lined hoods. The men shuffled together to close the opening and braced themselves against the gale.

'It is right,' said Trapper Jack, pulling the hood of the woman's parka well over her head.

His words put an end to the muttering. Trapper, a short, squat man, was a respected leader of the community and no one was prepared to gainsay him. Though he was still a subsistence hunter he was a learned man, both an author and a poet. The Inupiat were proud of him.

'It is her choice. The choice our old have always taken. It is part of our traditional culture.'

'A culture which to the world seems barbaric,' grumbled a youngster who now worked on the North Slope oilfields. He pulled his hood deeper over his head as if to hide his face from Trapper.

'People who are set on destroying the very planet which gives them life have no right to sit in judgement,' boomed Trapper Jack, suddenly angry.

He glanced to the east where, on a clear day, one could see faint black clouds, telling of flare-offs in the North Slope oilfields. Fancifully he thought of them as banners of mourning for Natû, his daughter, who had followed her lover to live and work in the Prudhoe Bay oilfield.

'I say Oline has the right to choose the manner of her death,' he repeated firmly. Trapper was protective of Oline, the woman who helped raise his daughter when his wife died giving birth to the girl.

The youngster looked away, embarrassed.

Trapper Jack put his arm gently around the old lady's shoulders. She trembled. He felt that he was holding a tiny gull in his hands and that, if he squeezed it, the frail bones would crumble.

'She does not have the strength to battle the wind across the lagoon to Pingkok,' said another. 'Why does she not stay here?'

'We Inupiat have hunted and lived on Pingkok for over five hundred years,' growled Trapper. 'Pingkok has been ours since the Inupiat first walked this land.' Trapper tightened his grip around Oline and she leaned against him.

Her father and husband were both great hunters, and she wishes to honour them by going to Pingkok. 'Enough of this. Let us go and respect her wishes.'

Instinctively the men edged nearer to her as if to protect her and stay the execution.

'It is time,' she agreed, her voice but a whisper above the roar of the wind. The men moved stiffly and slowly across the dark frozen lake to where they knew Pingkok Island lay.

It seemed an endless journey to 'the rising earth over the mound of ice', the name early Inupiat hunters gave the island.

At last they reached the long sand dune, now covered in snow, which gave the island rare protection from the Beaufort Sea storms.

The old woman's face was suddenly radiant as she instinctively recognized the land beneath its bleached sheet. She broke away from the circle of men and hobbled painfully towards the dune. She dropped onto the snow and her limbs folded beneath her like a dead bird plummeting to the ground.

'This is my place,' she said, looking up at Trapper Jack.

Her smile exposed teeth worn with softening animal skins. Trapper Jack brushed at his eyes harshly. There was a time when all the old Inupiat women had teeth like this, but new methods of preparing skins for clothes had replaced the old, and it was uncommon to find a traditionalist. He felt an overwhelming love for the elderly lady and what she was doing.

'It is time,' she said with another smile. She tugged at the fastenings of her parka. 'Take it for Natû. It is better than the one she bought from the store.'

Tenderly, Trapper eased the caribou-skin jacket from her shoulders. Immediately her thin body shook as the wind sliced into her. She hung her head and shivered, like an eider duck strung up on a line in a hunting camp.

Trapper Jack bent low and whispered into her ear, but she made no movement or sign of recognition.

The men turned and hurried away, short, powerfully built men. The younger ones climbed onto their snowmobiles and soon the air was filled with the stench of fumes. The roar of engines replaced the shrill scream of the wind.

Trapper Jack grimaced and watched as two of the machines

headed for the North Slope oilfields forty miles to the east. The tracks dug into and damaged the fragile tundra vegetation.

He turned his back to the wind and the old woman and walked to where he had left his dog sled. The huskies, more wolf than dog, greeted his arrival with howls and yelps. They, like wolves, were born to run, and tugged at the reins as he loosed the snowhook which kept them from bolting with the sled.

'Down, Sockeye,' he roared as the lead dog tried to reach him.

Trapper sighed as he untangled the reins and kicked the dogs into order.

He resisted the urge to look back. The old woman must be given her dignity. He knew she had *Quinuitug*, the deep patience practised by his people in the Arctic. She would wait.

Let the cold dull her feelings and freeze out the *kappia*, he thought. The apprehension of what she faces will not be as dark and dreadful if hypothermia claims her senses first.

The old woman heard the roar of the snowmobiles and the howl of the dogs. She closed her eyes. Once again she was young with two small sons, living on Pingkok Island while her husband and the men hunted geese and ducks on the lagoon, caught char and belukha whales. She remembered the joy in the camp when the men sighted the bowhead whales heading for the Bering Strait, or found one of the caribou herds.

She could smell the rank odour of whale meat drying on the racks. She could remember sitting on a log in the brief summer sunshine, skinning seals and cutting the meat into small pieces, proudly dismembering a carcass without breaking a bone.

The old woman was happy, she was young and strong, she was going back to the land of her ancestors. She had chosen the manner in which she was going to meet them. Around her, Pingkok Island was flushed with summer flowers and filled with birdsong and insect chatter. The summer swarms of biting mosquitoes and stinging gnats which settled on exposed flesh and drying meat were but a distant memory. Oline smiled inwardly.

*

Out on the polar ice, a male bear hunting the ice margins headed slowly towards the ridge on Pingkok island. Its front legs swung from side to side, its huge paws folding inward as if disjointed. The 'ice bear' moaned softly as it walked, a sad, lonesome song. This white desolation was its territory. It paused to inspect a crack in the ice, then yawned. In its gaping, violet mouth the grey tongue lay thick and flaccid. The long white canines and shearing molars proved the bear was a flesh eater.

In winter, while the grizzly hibernates, the polar bear hunts on the featureless ice.

Suddenly the thousand-pound animal lifted its Roman nose to the wind. He caught the slight and hated scent of a human, the only hunter he avoided. But this fear did not prevent him from hunting man if hunger gnawed at his insides. Angling slightly to the east, he lifted his long sinuous neck and probed the icy air.

Skilfully he followed the scent. He fed only lightly in winter, but he had not eaten for many days and was hungry.

He approached the ridge cautiously, stopping motionless for long moments, blending and disappearing into the austere landscape. His footprints, over a foot long, were obliterated by the wind almost as soon as he lifted his feet.

For an animal that can stun a belukha whale with a blow from a front leg, and toss a three-hundred-pound bearded seal high into the air, it moved with unusual grace. The polar bear seemed to glide effortlessly up the slope. He paused on the crest to survey the leeward side. The scent was strong. He flattened himself on the snow, becoming a mound of white in the gloom. He scrutinized the bottom of the slope.

A movement, as slight as the wind moving through the erect guard hairs of his coat, caught his attention.

He slid down the slope, keeping a wary watch for other two-legged animals, but there was only the small huddled figure in front of him.

The intense cold had quickly lowered the old woman's body temperature. Her metabolic rate had dropped to where she was scarcely breathing, but she was an Inupiat. She was attuned to extreme weather and a lifestyle that would daunt or kill a European. She and her people had learned to respect and live with the land. They feared the terrifying might of nature, but neither hated nor tried to fight it.

Sensing the presence of something nearby, the woman opened her eyes. The heavy epicanthic fold that covered her upper lid and came down over the inner corner of the eye gave her eyes a slanted appearance. She saw a mound of snow move slowly towards her.

'Nanuq,' she said silently. 'You have come.' She closed her eyes as *ilira*, the trepidation of what was to happen, swamped her.

Suddenly the bear's breath was hot and sour in her nostrils. She could sense his huge body looming over her. Oline waited to feel the teeth sink into her flesh.

'Grandfather Nanuq,' she whispered. Her cracked lips barely moved.

Chapter One

TRAPPER BOTH loved and feared this harsh land, but could not imagine living away from the northern coastline of Alaska.

Here, the wind whips down from the North Pole, relentlessly scouring the arctic tundra, and lowers the temperature to minus forty degrees. Add the force of the wind to this temperature, and you have a dangerous wind-chill factor that can drive the temperature down to minus a hundred and twenty.

The land becomes a dark, terrifying nightmare, as gigantic wedges of polar sea ice crack and climb over each other in the frozen ocean. The ice extends so far out to sea that only black frost mist on the horizon tells of open water.

Inupiats living on this coastline fronting the Beaufort and Chukchi Seas experience fear and *perlerorneg*, the deep depression that causes some to rip at their clothes and throats with knives. Death is often kinder than the seemingly never-ending blackness and numbing cold.

Yet to Trapper Jack it was home.

'Hike!' shouted Trapper.

The dogs seemed to fly over the snow as they sensed the village of Barrow ahead.

'Sockeye!' shouted Trapper Jack to his lead dog. The dog responded to his tone and slowed down. The dogs loped sedately through the outskirts of the village and Trapper pulled them to a stop at his home, which, like most of the houses in Barrow, leaned drunkenly on the permafrost.

It is not possible to dig foundations into frozen earth, so the buildings seemed to stand as haphazardly as a deck of hastily stacked cards.

Trapper gave each dog a piece of dried fish, but Sockeye received a wedge of dried beaver. Trapper favoured his lead dog, as Casey had named it Sockeye.

Casey was the girl whom Trapper looked upon as a daughter when Natû, his only child, left Barrow for the North Slope oilfields with her rigger. She loved dogs, and was a strong, excellent skier. She completed the short dog-sled races which enabled the racer to sign up for the gruelling one-thousand-and-forty-nine-mile Iditarod race, from Anchorage to Nome on the Bering Sea. Trapper had high hopes for her as an eventual champion.

But Casey, the British girl with a thin trace of Eskimo blood, married Hank, a fishing guide and Trapper's friend. They settled in Yorkshire, where she gave birth to twin boys. A few years later she had a girl. Until the birth of the babies, Trapper hoped that Casey would remain in Barrow with Hank, and become more Inupiat than English. She seemed to have an inherent understanding and love for the natives.

Hank and Casey still returned to Barrow every summer. But Casey was now more preoccupied with her children than with Inupiat culture and training sled dogs.

But her boys had quickly learned the ways of the tribe. Trapper delighted in telling them the legends of the ten-legged bear and the woman who fell in love with a bear. Though they were out of their teens and well past the age of listening to stories, the young men still sat and listened to him in fascination.

Trapper smiled to himself as he thought of his godchildren. How he loved them all. Soon it would be summer, and the boys would have a break from university. They could come to the hunting camp with him again. Scott and Patrick had already run their first short dog-sled races. As soon as they were old enough Casey taught them to ski. Trapper had allowed them to check his traplines when they had the strength to handle the dogs and sled. Both boys were adept mushers. They could handle dogs and dog sleds easily.

*

Patrick, the eldest of the Butler twins by an hour, was a well-built, strong boy who delighted in pitting himself against the elements. He was a favourite with the hunters, as he showed no fear. He seemed to have inherited the tireless patience of the Inupiat hunter. He serviced the trapline when he was able to spend winters with Trapper. He wore traditional Inupiat clothing and could run beside the dogs for hours.

Patrick seemed to have been cloned from his father Hank. Both were well over six foot in height. His hair was a richer red than Hank's, but he had the same green eyes flecked with brown.

His brother Scott was also lanky, but more finely boned than Patrick. He showed an astonishing love for the land and knowledge of its creatures. His eyes were the same dark brown as his mother's, though his light brown hair was shot with the deep amber of his father's beard. He was a gentle boy with an attractive, ready smile.

Savannah, their sister, was 'the baby'. The boys loved her but did not understand how anyone could prefer the pollution and noise of London to the peace and purity of the air in Alaska.

Savannah was an independent young girl, intent on doing graphic design, and spent as many summers in London as possible. She loved the bustle and noise of the great capital and disliked almost everything about Alaska, from the insects that searched out every inch of exposed flesh, to the dogs who howled and jumped on her with muddy paws.

The family could not even persuade her to visit Barrow in winter, so they left her in London with her grandparents. Occasionally Casey remained with her and the two women visited the opera and saw every play in the city.

Casey was delighted that her boys loved the wilderness and the freedom found in Alaska, and she allowed them to spend as much time as possible with Trapper.

It had not been difficult for the boys to persuade their parents to let them go to the University of Alaska in Fairbanks.

The Butler boys were completing their second year at the

university. Patrick was taking a degree in engineering, and Scott in geology.

They were now out on the ice hunting seals. Patrick sat motionless at a lead waiting for the sleek head of a seal to break through the black water, but Scott was restless.

'What are you planning to do when we finish our degrees at varsity?' he whispered.

'Probably work on one of the new oilfields,' answered Patrick, not taking his eyes from the lead.

'How can you say you want to work on an oilfield when you have your degree? You know that the big companies are trying to drill for oil in our Arctic Wildlife Refuge,' said Scott scornfully.

'I know, but we can still work to preserve the Arctic National Wildlife Refuge. Our work for ANWAR doesn't have to stop because one of the oil companies is paying our salary,' reasoned Patrick.

'Working for them also means having every second week off if we get in with one of the big boys like BP,' Patrick continued. 'We could run dogs, hunt . . .'

'Fish and camp out,' interjected Scott, suddenly interested in the idea.

'Right, kid,' agreed Patrick, still watching the lead.

Time passed quickly as the brothers planned their future, sitting at an ice crack waiting for the seal.

'Come on,' said Patrick eventually. He unfolded his long frame, stretched and threw back the hood of his parka. 'Have some gum.' He handed Scott a piece of Eskimo gum, made of solidified seal oil and willow catkins.

Both boys chewed happily as they trudged across the ice to where they had left the dogs. The dogs, bored with the inactivity, greeted them with a deafening cacophony of yelps and barks.

'Let's go, Sockeye,' shouted Patrick as he took up his place to run beside the lead dog. Scott stood on the runners of the sturdy sled. It was a heavy work sled that weighed almost three hundred pounds when empty. It was fashioned from driftwood and the runners were made of bone and ivory. Frozen mud and water gave the runners a layer of frictionless ice where it slid over the ground.

We'll need one of the lightweight racing sleds, Scott pondered as the sled bumped its way across the tundra to Trapper's house. This is great for hauling caribou carcasses and chunks of whale or foxes, wolverines and beavers from the traplines, but not for the Last Great Race, the Iditarod.

The Iditarod was a secret between the Butler brothers. They were both determined to run the race which their mother had given up when they were born. They had worked out the costs very carefully.

The boys were certain that Trapper would let them have Sockeye as lead dog. They knew that there were some good dogs in the native villages. Occasionally Iditarod racing dogs were left in the care of the natives to be collected after the race, and were mated with any village bitches who were in heat.

Good pups resulted from these matings. The boys were certain that with Trapper Jack's support, they could build up and train a strong team, perhaps even a winning team.

I'll talk to Patrick, then we'll tackle Trapper, thought Scott.

He concentrated on riding the sled, and dreamed of the day he would be standing on the runners at the start of the Iditarod Dog Sled Race in Anchorage.

The brothers had not yet decided who would have the first chance to run the race, but Scott was afraid that Patrick would use his position as eldest brother, to claim the right. The thought made him nauseous with envy.

They seldom fought. Scott usually made up for his lack of brawn by out-thinking and out-talking Patrick.

We'd better leave this one to Trapper, thought Scott, watching his brother keep up easily with Sockeye. He'll decide. 'Haw!' he shouted suddenly, as he saw Sockeye veering towards a rack of drying belukha muktuk and seal meat.

Patrick headed Sockeye away from the tempting Eskimo jerky. The dogs yelped and barked in anticipation of a snack, when they recognized their home.

Trapper heard the howling and smiled. The boys would be as hungry as the dogs. He stirred the pot on the stove and then walked to the door and waited.

Scott waved to Trapper and mushed the team round to the back of the house. Here, the brothers tied the dogs to pegs to prevent them from coming into contact with foxes or wolves, who often carried rabies. The boys fed each dog its portion of dried fish mixed with warm water, then, finally satisfied that the dogs were fed and secured safely, they went into the house.

'Moose stew.' Trapper greeted them.

'Great,' Patrick rubbed his hands together. 'I'm so hungry I could eat a raw moose.'

'With its rack?' scoffed Scott. 'Settle for stew instead, Pat. It'll be more digestible.'

Patrick glared at Scott. He hated his name being shortened to Pat, which he felt was a feminine name. He would have accepted Rick, but definitely not Pat.

Trapper glanced at the two young men as he dished great mounds of the glutinous stew into dishes.

Something must have happened out there today, he thought, Scott seldom taunts Patrick.

Scott was immediately contrite. It was not Patrick's fault that he was envious of his older brother, who might run the Iditarod first. He had not even discussed the subject with him.

'Here, Patrick,' he said. 'Have my sourdough roll. There's more of you to fill.'

'Thanks, kid,' answered Patrick with a grin.

They are like two young bull moose, thought Trapper, relieved that there was no serious dispute between the boys.

Perhaps they have both chosen the same girl at university, and now they are circling each other warily.

He joined them at the table, but his eyes constantly searched the desolate stretch of tundra, now white and featureless to all but an Inupiat, who felt and saw every inundation of the land.

'Tomorrow?' said Trapper in response to an invitation from

Patrick. 'I would love to join you boys and shoot ptarmigan, but I have to leave for Anchorage,' he explained, selecting a large piece of yellowish fat from the stew and swallowing it with relish.

'Anchorage?' echoed the boys in unison. 'Is this still to try to stop the US Congress granting the big companies the right to drill for oil on our tribal land?' asked Patrick. Trapper merely nodded. He knew that the boys were as opposed as he was to any exploration being carried out in the magnificent coastal plain and mountain range fifty miles west of Prudhoe Bay.

The Butler boys had backpacked across the almost nine-million-acre Arctic National Wildlife Refuge that swept from the Arctic Ocean across the coastal plain and into the Arctic Interior.

In 1960 this marvellous place, where animals and plants had adapted and survived for thousands of years, was declared a Wilderness, but when the Wilderness Act was passed a few years later, the Arctic Range was not included, as oil had been discovered at Prudhoe Bay.

One hundred miles of the coastal plain in the west of the Refuge was referred to as 10-0-2, and was the one and a half million acres currently under scrutiny for further oil exploration.

'Don't let them take it,' said Patrick. 'We may want to work on an oilfield after university, but to hell with them touching Ten-0-two.'

'Yeah,' agreed Scott. 'It's a calving ground for the Porcupine caribou herd.'

'And it's the main year-round musk ox range,' added Patrick. 'To say nothing of the hundreds of thousands of lesser snow geese who gather there in the fall.' Patrick sucked noisily on a piece of bone.

'And Nanuq,' said Trapper quietly. 'Our polar bears have maternity dens there.'

Both boys nodded, well aware of the respect due to bears in Inupiat culture.

'What have the geologists come up with?' scoffed Scott, disregarding the fact that he would soon be one himself. 'A nineteen per cent chance of finding economically recoverable deposits in Ten-0-two.' He answered his own question and snorted. 'Nineteen per cent!'

Trapper ran another piece of fat around his plate, mopping up the thick sauce, popped it into his mouth and pushed back his chair.

'I'll fight for our land if I'm the last Inupiat. My voice will be heard if it's the very last voice. I promise you that.'

Both boys stood up to clear the table and clean the dishes. Trapper looked at the two young men and smiled.

Yes, he would fight for the land to remain pristine. Youngsters like these had the right to enjoy a small part of the planet as yet untouched by man.

Alaskans should have some control over their magnificent country. If his was the last voice to be raised, it would be loud and strong. He felt his people had the first right to the North Slope resources. Trapper believed the Inupiat should decide the fate of 10-0-2.

The problem was that there were just over a dozen native corporations and as many opinions. Each seemed to have their own reasons for either protecting the Refuge or allowing further oil exploration, with the benefits of a larger revenue for the people.

Trapper waved goodbye to the boys at the small air terminal in Barrow, and boarded the plane for Anchorage via Deadhorse Airport at Prudhoe Bay oilfields. He pressed his face to the window as they approached the oilfield.

The Prudhoe Bay oilfield looks beautiful at night. The yellow glow of lights flicker and lie in pools of gold on the snow. The modular mustard-and-rust-coloured buildings are all a uniform black. The roads, pads and pipes disappear in the dark. The land seems to have swallowed the machinery which is pumping its stomach dry.

Outside, only men well padded against the weather, wearing hard hats on top of ice-encrusted wool balaclavas, pace between the buildings. They seem to be aliens as they move around silently, slowly, checking pipes and machines, alert for any oil spills on the ice-covered pads.

Trapper wondered whether Natû was one of the figures moving as steadily and purposefully as ants inside the large buildings.

At the thought of his only child, whom he believed was lost to him for ever, Trapper summoned the stewardess and asked for water.

These Eskimos never seem to stop drinking cold water, she thought as she poured out a glassful and handed it to Trapper.

The plane dipped in a wind pocket and water splashed over Trapper's hand and onto his seat.

As he flicked at the spots he noticed a narrow card wedged between the seat cushion and the armrest. Curious, he teased it out.

He smiled as he read the inscription. Alaska Airlines usually gave their passengers cards depicting Alaska's breathtaking scenery with a quote from the Bible.

This card was printed to honour the Iditarod dogs. 'The best long-distance runners in the world, eat raw meat, run naked and sleep in the snow.'

Trapper's smile faded as he fingered the card. He had hoped that one day he would play a part in helping someone run the Great Race. First he thought it would be Natû, then Casey. But both women had followed their hearts.

He felt strongly that the race, which now attracted worldwide publicity, should have native participants.

Our native people forget that the first race covered fifty miles of the present Iditarod trail, took two full days to complete and was won by Isaac Okleasik, an Eskimo from Teller, he thought.

'Natû and Casey could have run it,' he whispered, pulling at his ragged moustache.

The man seated beside Trapper edged as far away from him as his seat allowed.

One can never tell with natives, he thought. This one ordered water and seems sober, but now he starts talking to himself.

Trapper obliterated Natû and Casey from his thoughts, as quickly as a ground blizzard erases tracks from the snow.

He saw a tall, broad-shouldered young man with tousled dark red hair replace them.

'Patrick,' said Trapper, unaware that he was speaking aloud. 'He could run it. The boy has determination. He is as resourceful as a native, as powerful as a yearling polar bear, and I've given him the patience of an Arctic hunter.'

Trapper's neighbour nervously looked around for a vacant seat, but the plane was full.

'Yes,' said Trapper, 'I'll talk to him when I return.'

Trapper leaned his head back against the headrest and closed his eyes. He composed his speech to sway chairmen on the congressional committee.

The man seated next to Trapper watched him carefully for a few minutes, then satisfied that he was asleep and harmless, sighed and returned to study the anatomical details of the ladies in his magazine.

When Trapper Jack's daughter, Natû, first arrived at Prudhoe with her lover Bud Damas, she hated the machines that were despoiling her ancestral land.

After attending compulsory lectures on the oil industry and its concern for the environment, she was able to understand and marvel a little at the complexity of current technology, though she never entirely lost her dislike of the machines.

Masterminding this extraordinary operation on the oilfield was MOC, the Main Operations Control Centre. Natû felt she ought to tiptoe past the 'brain' of the oilfield, as inside MOC all was quiet, unnaturally quiet. The silent machines told tales of what nature buried beneath the permafrost, reminded her of the shamans with their knowledge of the secret world of her ancestors.

Natû found the lectures on the environment the most interesting. Like all natives, she had an innate knowledge of the land, snow ridges, mountain ranges and valleys. Maps were an enigma to her. She 'felt' the land.

The Trans-Alaska pipeline was a controversial subject to thousands of Alaskans, both native and European.

'The pipeline traverses some of the worst terrain in the world,' droned the lecturer. 'It runs from the Arctic where wind-chill factors cause temperatures to plummet to minus one hundred degrees and over mountains where between forty and fifty feet of snow can accumulate.'

Natû listened in silence. What does he know of wind-chill and snow? she thought. The lecturer glanced at the Inupiat woman apprehensively. She usually questioned his facts and was often correct.

'The migration of caribou herds, an important source of food and clothing for the native people, the Inupiat, will not be affected by the twisting pipeline and gravel haul road,' he continued.

'What facts support the theory that caribou, which have grazed on the North Slope for centuries, will now be channelled like cattle through the raised sections of the pipeline?' asked Natû.

The lecturer sighed and stroked his beard nervously. He had learned that Natû was knowledgeable, and not afraid to engage him in controversial issues.

She was fiercely protective of her ancestral land. 'You say this pipeline can withstand an earthquake up to eight point five on the Richter scale?' Natû paused and waited for his reply.

He merely nodded. 'We have also, at great cost, lifted the pipeline above ground to protect the land where heat from the oil in the buried pipe could melt the permafrost, causing the soil to become unstable,' he said triumphantly.

It was Natû's turn to nod.

Natû was in awe of what had been achieved at Prudhoe. She found it fascinating that scientists had discovered that Prudhoe oil does not lie in underground pools, but is trapped in tiny pores in the rock formations and flows up under its own pressure. Just as carbon dioxide escapes upward when a bottle of soda is opened, so oil and water fly up with the gas in Prudhoe.

She studied the diagrams showing how oil is brought at a hundred and sixty degrees Fahrenheit from beneath two thousand feet of permanently frozen ground to the surface, is routed to the oil station to start its eight-hundred-mile-long journey to the ice-free port of Valdez. Natû even understood that the water is re-injected into the formation to maintain reservoir pressure, and that the gas goes to the Gas Facility where natural-gas liquids are extracted and sent down the pipe with the crude oil. Some gas is used to supply fuel needs, and some re-injected into the gas cap of the oil reservoir to maintain the pressure.

She lost interest when the lecturer spoke of thirty trillion cubic feet of natural gas in the cap topping the twenty-four billion barrels of original oil. Numbers confused and bored her. But she well understood that the recovery of oil is a complex business, with the ever-present danger of fire.

When the short days of summer arrived, and she sat on the cotton-grass tussocks watching the small white heads bob and bend to the wind, holding seeds in their cotton wombs which are twenty degrees warmer than the outside air, she longed for the days when the North Slope was untouched and its treasure hidden deep in its belly.

At times like this she missed checking her father's traplines, the yelping dogs, the solitude, the intense cold and the dust-free air, clean and sharp as cut crystal.

Natû was a young woman torn between two cultures. Her love for Bud made her try to embrace the American way of life, but the non-rational, non-linear parts of our minds which emerge during sleep kept her chained to her ancient heritage.

Natû was sitting in a chrome and red chair in the multi-level dining room, rubbing her scuffed Nikes up and down the ruby carpet. The bright colours offended her; she preferred the bleak white winter landscapes softened by the gentle rose and misty greens of the aurora borealis.

She was waiting for Bud, who had been sent out to Pump Station One at the beginning of the Alaska pipeline.

'Yeah, she did, I tell you. I was there. I saw it.' Natû jerked upright. Two Inupiat men pulled out chairs at the table near her and put down trays filled with a three-course meal that would do justice to a top restaurant in Anchorage.

She recognized Nilak, one of the men. He was on her father's committee to keep native culture alive in the villages. The children attended school but were allowed a ten-day 'excused absence' to practise subsistence activities. Nilak reminded her of one of the modular buildings in Prudhoe, square and strong, built to withstand the harshness of the Arctic.

'Go and try that one on the ducks,' scoffed Edwin Kent, a lanky geophysicist, neat in a pale blue shirt and tie, who pulled out a chair at the same table.

His good friend Chuck Holden joined in the conversation.

'Superstition went out when they started schooling the natives in the villages.'

Nilak thumbed the thin black moustache under his nose and followed it down his cheeks to his chin.

'No,' he said, 'you are both wrong. We learn what the Europeans have to teach us, but we value and intend keeping our traditions.'

'Just like you keep the hunting rights on the North Slope lands. We can't even have a gun in Prudhoe and must have a licence to fish,' groused Edwin, fingering his striped tie.

'We need to fish and hunt to withstand the winters,' reasoned Nilak's friend with a small smile. 'Remember, we natives are subsistence hunters.'

'In the good old days, perhaps, but now you have the yearly pay-out from the oil revenue, supermarkets and heating for your homes. You are merely . . .'

Natû pushed back her chair and tightened the leather belt holding up her blue jeans. She walked to the table where the men were seated.

Nilak looked up in surprise. Natû usually kept company with Bud's friends from the Lower Forty-eight. She seemed to want to distance herself from the Eskimo workers on the field. They in turn could not understand how her love for Bud made her determined to become an American girl and renounce her heritage.

But the men greeted Natû with a smile. The olive-skinned girl with her coarse black hair was both liked and admired on the site. Everyone knew that she was always willing to do extra duties. Out in the field, she never complained about the weather and she worked as hard as any man.

'Hi, Natû,' greeted the physicist as she reached the table where Nilak was seated. 'Haven't seen you around for a long time.' He nursed an unrequited love for the girl and took every available opportunity to speak to her and be in her company.

'No. You have not. I don't understand those weird machines of yours, Edwin. It's like talking to the dead. Those quiet rooms are tombs. I prefer being with Bud out on the line.'

Edwin Kent, the acknowledged computer expert, shivered in mock terror.

'The computers are marvels of modern technology, Natû,' he said. 'Whereas the only marvel about winter up here is that anyone working outside survives it.'

They all laughed, and Natû accepted the chair they offered her.

'What was the superstition you were talking about?' she asked.

Nilak and his friend looked at each other and were silent for a few moments.

'Some nonsense about an old woman wanting to meet her ancestors. Her way of doing this was to be torn apart by a polar bear,' said Chuck. 'Imagine anyone sitting still on the ice and waiting for the bear to arrive. It's unbelievable.'

'Not to we Inupiat,' said Natû. She turned to Nilak and spoke in their native tongue. They sounded like fowls clucking to Edwin. He blew on his coffee to cool it.

Nilak's friend, big and swarthy with long black hair held back in a ponytail, rested his arms on the table top and spoke long and earnestly.

Natû paled. The woman who had gone to find death on the ice was Oline, the Inupiat, who, when Natû's mother died in child-birth, had made Natû a cap from the soft fur of the Arctic hare and underclothes of tiny birds' feathers to ensure that the baby grew up with a sensitivity for the land and the animals.

The Inupiat knew how important it was to establish an imme-diate relationship with the land.

'No,' Natû shook her head. 'Why was I not told? You were there. Why did you not tell me?'

'You wanted nothing to do with your background or your people, Natû,' answered Nilak, again smoothing his moustache against his skin. 'The old woman was a burden to herself and others. She went calmly and willingly to her death. That is our way.'

His friend nodded.

'Remember, you are now an American girl,' he said. 'When were you last in Barrow? When did you speak to Trapper, your father?'

'He misses his daughter,' said Nilak softly. 'Think about these things, Natû.' Natû stared at the two Inupiats. She pushed back her chair. Edwin stood up, but she ignored him and whirled from the room.

'What was that all about?' asked Edwin as she disappeared from view.

The Inupiats were silent. They shook their heads and started eating.

'You guys have obviously upset her. Bud's not going to be at all happy. You know he's hooked on that girl.'

Edwin Kent removed his glasses and rubbed the steam away with the cuff of his sleeve. 'Okay, guys, but don't say I didn't warn you, when Bud wants to know what happened here.'

He finished his coffee and stood up. 'I'd better go back to my "tomb" and talk to the "dead" again.'

Nilak smiled.

'Natû will always be an Inupiat. The love of the land and our customs are part of her life blood. She cannot renounce them.'

Nilak's swarthy friend nodded. 'She will eventually realize that this,' he gestured to the multi-tiered dining room, 'was merely a long vacation.'

'Better not tell Bud that,' warned Edwin, and with a wave of his hand he and Chuck Holden walked quickly from the room.

The two Inupiats were enjoying huge wedges of chocolate cake when a loud voice made them look up.

Bud started work on the oilfields as a driller, but had lost two fingers due to an accident he had when fixing a thirty-foot stand into place, pipes which penetrated the frozen ground beneath the pad.

His team had been persuaded to have a 'stranger' with them, as one of their mates was nursing a hangover in Anchorage and had missed the flight back to Deadhorse Airport. They worked in tightly knit groups of about seventy men, and fiercely resented newcomers foisted on them. Not accustomed to working with a stranger, one of the stands slipped, and attempting to prevent a major mishap Bud sacrificed his fingers.

He still missed the team spirit found in a drillers' camp, but he knew that with two fingers missing he was a danger to his mates. When he passed a pad with a drill rig, Bud longed to work with the Varco top-drive unit, a recent innovation that allowed drillers to use ninety-foot stands to accelerate the pace of the drilling.

Even though he could not be part of the 'high-tech' team, Bud often visited the camp where his crew explained the new method of directional drilling. The advances in rig design and drilling technology excited Bud. Once through the permafrost, they used directional drilling to tap a large area, which meant that wells could be as close as ten feet apart instead of the usual hundred and twenty feet. From a small well pad on the surface, they could target oil two miles from the location of the rig. Fewer roads and pipelines were needed, and less environmental damage was caused on the surface.

Bud tried to interest Natû in the new computer technology that was enabling the Prudhoe engineers to recover 'marginal' oils.

'If the oil is that difficult to recover then it should be left in the ground,' she reasoned. 'I'm sorry that geologists found oil seeps and knew it meant fossil wealth under the permafrost.'

Bud opened his mouth to protest, but Natû would not be silenced.

'My people have used oil from the seeps for thousands of years. We did not find it necessary to build roads, pipes and buildings and drain the oil from the ground. We took only what the land gave willingly.'

Bud did not attempt to reason with her. He had spent his childhood in Alaska, and had no desire to leave the marvellous country. He respected, though he did not always understand, Natû's childlike faith in nature and her love for the flora and fauna of the Arctic.

When the accident happened and Bud left his mates on the drilling team, he managed to obtain a position at Prudhoe oilfield doing inspection duty.

Working outdoors with Natû at his side, he began to enjoy the beauty of the tundra. He stood with his arm around Natû and for the first time enjoyed the majesty of a huge snowy owl sitting on a tussock. She showed him things his eyes had seen but not registered.

Life with his father, 'Cat' Damas, had been tough. He learned to enjoy the company of men who grasped life with both hands and throttled what they wanted from it. Now he had found a female mate. A woman who loved the rigours of the hard life he led.

'Have any of you jerks seen Natû?' Bud Damas stood in the middle of the floor. He could not find her, and so resorted to yelling at the diners in general.

A lanky youngster jerked a thumb in the direction of Nilak and his friend. 'She was over there about ten minutes ago,' he said.

'Thanks pal.' Bud walked across the rich red carpeting to where Nilak was licking chocolate icing from his fingers.

Bud Damas was both tall and muscular. His red and blue checked wool shirt strained at the seams across his shoulders. Black curls lay in his neck and across part of his forehead. His eyes were the clear aquamarine of ice mounds found in the middle of tundra melt ponds. In them was a gentleness which seemed at odds with his powerful frame.

He walked with a long, purposeful stride which made people give way to him.

'Hi,' he greeted the men, 'do you know where Natû is?'

'No,' answered Nilak, sucking his middle finger clean. 'She didn't say where she was making for.'

'But she was in a hurry,' added his friend, and received a glare from Nilak for his helpfulness.

Bud glanced round the room once again, then swung away from the table. He headed for the running track. On the rare occasions when he and Natû managed to sneak unseen into his small room, they lay in each other's arms listening to the thump of feet and heavy breathing of the runners on the circular track outside their cubicle. At times it seemed as if the runners were in the room with them.

There was little privacy in the centre, but after a week of working twelve hours a day, workers were given a week off.

Bud and Natû had found a place in which to spend their week away from Prudhoe. It was a small cabin in Chugiak, hidden deep in the woods. A long window set into the rounded logs allowed them a view of Mount Denali, magical in the silver moonlight and breathtaking when the cloud lifted from her peak and her snow-clad top shone as if fashioned in the sun from beaten gold. They both looked forward to the time spent there.

Bud's room was empty. He jogged past the other cubicles until he reached Natû's.

The sound of muffled sobbing greeted him. Bud stopped outside her door. He had never heard Natû cry. The sound worried him.

What has happened? he thought. I'll kill whoever has made my girl unhappy.

Carefully he opened the door. Natû was sitting cross-legged on her narrow bed, staring at a large poster stuck on the wall at the end of her room.

It was her favourite of all the Iditarod posters in her room. High on a snow-covered bluff, a pack of wolves watched a musher and a dog-sled team negotiate a bend in the valley far below.

The baleful yellow of the predators' eyes as they studied the lonely musher and dogs was chilling. The artist had captured the danger, loneliness and harsh environment perfectly.

Bud could not understand Natû's fascination with the subject. The poster, like the howling song of wolves, sent chills down his spine.

Natû did not turn her head. Tears streamed unchecked down her cheeks and blotched her cream t-shirt. Bud knew that this was not the time for words. He crossed to her bed and took her hands in his huge ones. Natû held onto his fingers as if hanging onto an umiak in a stormy ocean.

She cried for the time she had spent away from her father, for the pain she had caused him. Tears ran freely for the old woman who had been a mother to her, and whom she had not seen for so long. Oline, who had gone to Nanuq. Natû wept because she had not been one of those who escorted her to Pingkok Island.

Finally, she wept for her dream of running the harshest and most difficult race in the world, the Iditarod. She had chosen Prudhoe. Her dream now seemed dead and cold.

She turned to look around the room. Wherever she looked she saw dogs, snow, sleds and mushers, the men and women who ran the dogs. Bud, feeling that she had controlled her crying, put his arms around her. But through her blurred vision the posters accused her. She had allowed a dream to slip through her fingers. The wolves' amber eyes bored into her.

Coward, they howled silently. You are an Inupiat, you can run it. Why are you sitting in a heated place like a rare flower in a hothouse? Natû lifted her face, and even the mug filled with dry stalks of dwarf fireweed with Norman Vaughan's slogan on it, *Dare to Fail*, seemed to mock at her.

'Vaughan, not only did you go to the South Pole with Admiral Byrd, but you finished the Iditarod when you were eighty-four,' she sobbed.

'Go where you belong. Test yourself. Realize your dream,' taunted the wolves and huskies in the posters.

Natû sniffed into Bud's shoulder. He reached into his pocket and pulled out an oil-stained piece of cloth.

'Here, blow,' he said, 'you'll feel better.'

Natû blew her nose, leaving a smear of oil across the bridge. She looked at Bud, her face crumpled and she immediately burst into a fresh paroxysm of weeping.

'Hey, hey,' said Bud, holding her in his arms, 'nothing can be that bad.' He rocked her as if she was his child. 'Tell me,' he said tenderly. 'We will work it out together.'

Natû buried her face in his shirt. The wool prickled her skin, but she only pressed herself harder to him.

'No one can help.' Her voice was muffled, and Bud strained to hear. 'It's me, I'm an Inupiat.' She swallowed and was silent.

'Of course you are. You're my little Eskimo,' he soothed, stroking her hair, which followed his fingers as if it had a life of its own.

'You see, Oline died alone,' Natû hiccuped, trying to control the sobs. 'The old woman was a mother to me. I should have been with her before she made her last journey.'

'Oh, Natû,' whispered Bud, lowering his head onto hers.

The time he dreaded had arrived. Her native culture was pulling her away from him, as inexorably as the pumps drew oil from the sandstone in Prudhoe.

All he could do was kiss and comfort her with his body. But as he moved over her, and the bed squeaked to the rhythm of their loving, Natû still stared at the poster and saw only the gleam in the wolves' eyes.

'Natû,' said Bud, breathing raggedly as he lay wedged beside her on the single bed. 'What do you want to do? Let me help.'

Natû struggled up onto an elbow and ran her fingers gently across his lips. He closed his eyes and she kissed the lids softly.

How could she tell this man whom she loved so deeply that she had to leave him?

'I love you, but I must go back to my family,' she whispered. Hot tears braided her cheeks.

Bud heard the heartbreak in her voice. Rage, as strong and dangerous as an oil fire, threatened to engulf him. He was powerless to help the woman he loved.

'We leave for our week's break in Chugiak soon,' he said. 'Let's fly to Anchorage instead. We'll take a suite at the Captain Cook Hotel, and . . .'

Natû's face dropped and she knuckled the tears from her eyes.

He doesn't understand, she thought. Bud thinks that a glitzy stay in Anchorage will change things. Natû took a deep breath, ready to explain that the problem was serious. A change to Anchorage from their log cabin in Chugiak would solve nothing.

But Bud continued speaking before she could interject.

'We can find a priest, and you hopefully will agree to become Mrs Natû Damas.'

Natû gasped. Secretly she had hoped that one day Bud would want her to be his wife. Her dark eyes sparkled and her expression changed swiftly from sorrow to radiance.

Before she flung herself into Bud's arms, he spoke again.

'We can then buy or build a place of our own in Chugiak, or near Fairbanks if you would prefer to be near a large town.

'We both enjoy working on the pipeline, and until we start a family that won't have to change.'

Natû cuddled up to Bud. It would be so easy to let him plan their future.

Go on, a voice said silently, deep within her, you want to marry him, have his children and become a typical American. Say yes. Forget this Iditarod nonsense.

'What do you say, Natû,' whispered Bud, 'will you marry me?'

Natû placed her lips close to his ear and his curls tickled her nose.

As her lips formed the word 'Yes', her eyes once again strayed to the print of wolves studying the dog-sled racer with his huskies.

The dominant wolf's eyes held hers, and it seemed to be mocking her.

'Dare to live your dream.' The words rang in her head as loud as church bells.

Natû took a deep breath and closed her eyes, blocking out the wolves.

'I do want to marry you, Bud. I love you so much.'

'Wonderful. That's settled, then.' Bud hugged Natû to him, and she struggled to breathe.

'But I have to go back to Barrow.' Bud relaxed his hold slightly, and a frown marred his smooth forehead.

'Oh I see, you want to be married there with your family and friends.' He scratched his cheek.

'That's great. We'll have two weddings. One in Anchorage at the Cook, and one in Barrow.' He laughed and brushed the curls from his forehead.

'That way you will be doubly mine.' He kissed her in delight. He had made a major decision and felt good about it.

Suddenly Natû sat up on the bed. 'Bud,' she said, 'look at that poster with the wolves.'

Bud stared at the print that he had seen dozens of times. He could never remember whether it was a Jeff Schultz or a Lee Cable print. Natû collected the work of both artists. The artist had captured the menace and might of the tireless hunters.

At times, when he was out on inspection duty, the wailing howl of wolves would slice the night, their clear call riding on the icy wind. Bud hated the wolfsong. The hair rose on his forearms, and he hurried to get back to the iced road where he had parked his vehicle.

He preferred working the pipeline in summer. The long winter darkness played tricks with his eyes and his senses. He saw imaginary wolves in all the woods.

'Yes,' he said hesitantly, 'what about the print?'

'That's what I must do, Bud. That is all I lived for and trained for, before I met you and came to Prudhoe.'

Bud was puzzled. He stared at her and then back at the poster. 'Wolves?'

'No, Bud. The Iditarod. I want to run the Iditarod. It's like a burning fever. I have to run that race.'

Bud whistled, then was quiet, fingering the stubble on his chin. Natû watched him, afraid to say anything and break into his thoughts. Let him understand, she begged her ancestors. Oline, you loved me as a child. Please make the man I love understand that I have to live my dream. Please.

Bud suddenly shrugged as if he had reached a decision. He swung his long, muscular legs off the bed, tucked his shirt into his jeans, zipped up his pants and walked to the door.

'Bud?' said Natû tentatively.

'Let me live with it for a while, Natû,' he said. 'Come on, I'm hungry, and the food smelled good in the dining room.'

Natû ate nothing, anxiety gnawing like a beaver at her stomach. She felt ill. She sipped her coffee and watched as Bud swirled the last potato chip around his plate. He pushed his plate away.

At last he looked at her directly and intently. He spoke softly, and she leaned forward to hear him over the hum of the other diners.

'I don't like it, Natû. You're precious to me. It's the most formidable dog-sled race in the world. Edwin's brother, who has both the money and the experience, has had to scratch three times because he could not take the crap Mother Nature threw at him.'

Natû merely nodded. She knew that it was best to let men have their say. When their bile was at rest, a woman could continue with her plans.

'But I know you, my little Inupiat. You listen to me, nod, then do exactly what you originally planned. So . . .'

Bud paused and took a deep breath. 'I say what the hell, let's do it.'

Bud heard himself say the words that would change his life. For a moment he did not believe that he, Bud Damas, had said anything so rash. He wished he could swallow the words and pretend he had never uttered them.

'Let's do it,' echoed Natû. 'Do you mean let us do it, or do you mean you do it, Natû?'

'Us,' said Bud, now full of enthusiasm for what a moment before had seemed merely Natû's crazy dream. 'You don't think that I'm letting my wife run that hellish race on her own?'

Natû's emotions threatened to overwhelm her. She struggled to control them as each fought for supremacy.

Wife, she exulted silently. He still wants to marry me.

Run the Iditarod? a small voice whispered. He has never worked a trapline in winter. He has never mushed. He knows nothing about huskies. He could not survive if he got lost on the trail.

Teach him, said a stronger voice. You still have to raise the money and complete five hundred miles in Iditarod-sanctioned trail dog-sled races to prove that you can handle a dog sled. The Iditarod is in March, you have the time if you work hard. Trapper and every native village and corporation will help when they hear that an Inupiat will be running.

Suddenly Natû felt strong and confident. They could do it. They would do the seemingly impossible, they would run the Iditarod.

She turned her thought to the mug which always stood on the shelf above her bed. In summer it held tundra flowers. Now, with only a few stalks of dry fireweed in it, the words printed on the mug stood out in bold relief: *DARE TO FAIL*.

Natû smiled at Bud. The noise in the dining room seemed to fade as Natû said, 'Mr and Mrs Bud Damas will dare to fail. We'll run the Iditarod trail.'

Bud grinned, lifted her up and swung her around the tiny room.

'Bud, stop,' gasped Natû, as her feet hit the chair tucked beneath the built-in table top.

'I must talk to you seriously. Training for this race is not something one can do in a month or two. It is a lifestyle. For the rest of the year we will live dogs. I have read every book I can find on the trail and the handling of the dogs.'

Bud nodded, loving the way her mouth turned down when she was serious.

'Edwin's brother surfs the Net, and can keep us up to date with new rules or news.'

'Oh, Bud, this is going to be wonderful.'

Bud was not sure as to how wonderful the experience would be, but like every Alaskan and worker on the oilfields, he remained transfixed to either television or radio for two weeks in March as the media covered the 'Last Great Race'.

As a kid, Bud had a dog he loved dearly – they were inseparable. His father named the mongrel Heinz, because of its varied pedigree. Remembering the little mongrel, Bud felt the urge once again to experience the mystic bond between man and dog.

Bud sat at the table with Natû. He was silent, sifting through all the information he could remember about the race. His coffee cooled. Natû went to the counter and collected two fresh mugs of hot coffee.

Names of the top mushers and their lead dogs were familiar to him. He had read *The Father of the Iditarod*, Joe Redington Senior's account of how the race was started to commemorate the famous run by twenty drivers and a hundred dogs. They carried a twenty-pound package of diphtheria serum to Nome, where an outbreak of 'bubonic plague' threatened an entire region, as the natives had no immunity against this 'white man's' disease.

This epic 'mercy race' publicized the sled dogs and their value. Two-thirds of that early run was incorporated in the present-day Iditarod trail.

He knew that the Iditarod Dog Sled Race, which now attracted worldwide attention, had to a large extent ensured that the huskies were not edged out of existence by modern machinery and aircraft.

Facts flooded and jostled for space in Bud's memory as he thought of the race.

Natû was humming one of the popular Iditarod trail songs as she wound her way past the chairs and tables to where Bud waited.

'Thanks,' he said, pushing his hair away from his forehead. 'I sure need this. One poster and my life has changed.' He shook his head. Natû watched the curls dance on his neck. She wanted to reach out and wind them around her fingers, but she was conscious of the other diners and kept her hands clasped around her mug.

'You enjoy working outdoors,' she said.

'In summer, when I know where I am and can see things,' Bud qualified.

Natû smiled.

'I'll teach you to see in the dark, Bud,' she promised. 'You'll find that starlight can become sunlight. You only have to listen carefully and feel what is out there.'

'Yeah?' said Bud dubiously.

'We'll do it together. It'll be a . . .'

'I know. A kick,' Bud finished the sentence. 'I also know that what you consider "a kick" makes strong men wish they had stayed home with Ma.'

'Strong men,' echoed Natû. 'You say that riggers are the toughest of the tough. When you've run the Iditarod, you'll see that they don't come any tougher than mushers.'

Bud suddenly realized that the workers seated near them were silent, listening to their conversation.

'Mushers may be tough but they are also plumb crazy,' burped a burly man. His leather belt was on the last notch and barely holding. He licked the ketchup which stained his lips like badly applied lipstick.

'They mush one thousand miles, looking at the south end of dogs going north.'

His friends laughed uproariously and slapped him on the back until he held up his hands choking and coughing.

Natû waited until the hilarity died down. 'A clever quote by the race manager, Niggemyer,' she said.

The bulky man looked disgruntled.

'You have to be suicidal to run that race,' said one of the reservoir engineers. He glanced at his watch to check how long he had before he needed to return to his computers and create further high-resolution images to drag the secrets from the Prudhoe reservoir.

'Then Natû and I are suicidal,' declared Bud firmly. 'We have decided to run the toughest race in the world. We will be able to tell our children that we ran the Iditarod.'

Bud pushed back his chair and pulled Natû to her feet.

'If Joe Redington can run his eighteenth Iditarod at the age of seventy-four, then Bud and I can run our first,' said Natû firmly.

The reservoir engineer studied the two of them for a moment, then clapped his hands loudly.

Yes, he thought. It'll be damn good publicity for the oilfields. It may even cool the debate on 10-0-2. The Iditarod is the one event that brings all Alaskans together. It'll be great to show that we are participating.

Silence fell over the room as he climbed onto the table.

'Guys,' he yelled, his voice carrying up the tiered room. 'We have our very own Prudhoe team to run the next Iditarod: Bud and Natû.'

At the mention of the Iditarod there was a spontaneous cheer. Men and women scrambled over chairs and around tables to slap Bud on the back and hug Natû. Suddenly they were the most important and popular people on Prudhoe.

'Money,' said the engineer. 'They'll need big dollars to run.'

'How much?' called a voice from the crowd. 'Nowadays, thirty thousand dollars minimum. Fifty would be comfortable.'

Low whistles and a shuffling of feet greeted his announcement.

'Let BP sponsor them,' said the bulky man whose stomach rumbled with the assortment and amount of food he had loaded into it. 'It'll be good for their "oil baron" image.'

He belched, swallowed hard and continued: 'They can afford a hundred thousand big ones.'

'No,' said Natû. 'Only fifty for Bud. I'm running as an Inupiat. My people will raise the money.'

'Natû,' whispered Bud. 'Be sensible. Hardly any natives enter nowadays, they can't afford it.'

'I know, that's why I have to do it my way. I will run as an Inupiat with village dogs and Inupiat money.'

Bud hugged her to him and took the opportunity to whisper in her ear.

'Do it the easy way, Natû. Let BP sponsor both of us. I'm sure they will. It'll be great publicity for Prudhoe.'

'My people don't know the word "easy" Bud. For thousands of years they have lived with the terrifying might of nature, paralysed with fear in winter, hunting and fishing through summer, merely to sustain life. I'll run for them.'

Bud shook his head. At times like this her intransigence infuriated him, but secretly he admired her stance.

Conscious that they were the subject of intense scrutiny, Bud pulled away from Natû.

'I have another announcement,' he shouted. 'Natû and I are getting married at the Cook next week. Anyone who is in Anchorage is welcome.'

Another cheer resounded and echoed round the dining centre.

Natû tugged at Bud's hand. He looked down at his future wife and felt a deep tenderness for this girl who had left her family and her dreams to follow him to a strange environment.

Bud looked back at the crowd and recognized some of his friends who had joined the group encircling himself and Natû.

'One further announcement.' A teasing groan. 'This is the last,' he promised. 'I will be marrying this girl twice. Once in Barrow with her family, and again in Anchorage.'

He bent down and kissed Natû to the accompaniment of clapping, yelling and whistling.

'Just making doubly sure she's mine,' he explained as he buried his face in the soft skin at the side of Natû's neck.

Natû felt the need in his lips and the pressure of his body against hers.

'Come,' she said, taking his hand and pushing her way through the crowd.

'Hey, hey, you're not married yet,' shouted one of his friends.

'Are we invited to this as well?' teased another.

The group watched Bud and Natû walk away arm in arm.

Chapter Two

INSTEAD OF going to Chugiak for their week off duty, Bud arranged to fly to Barrow. The time had arrived to meet Trapper Jack.

Bud and Natû walked out of the air terminal in Barrow and immediately turned their backs to the wind. Hastily they closed their parkas and pulled the hoods over their heads.

The wind zigzagged between the houses, cold and strong. They bent their heads to the gale and walked slowly down the dark streets. Pale spills of light from the houses brought to their attention the snowmobiles, umiaks, aluminium boats, discarded stoves and machinery scattered around the homes.

Accustomed to the neat layout and cleanliness of Prudhoe, Bud felt that they were wandering through a dump, or a scrap-metal yard. Natû did not notice the detritus. This was her home. She knew that her people threw nothing away which they thought they could use in the future.

Their presence in the village was marked by the barking of chained dogs and the quick opening and closing of doors and windows.

'By tomorrow, every native in Barrow and beyond will know that I'm home,' said Natû, hugging Bud's arm.

'You, Bud Damas, will be the subject of native whispers,' she added, and giggled at his puzzled expression.

'Native whispers? I've heard of the game Chinese whispers.'

'Same thing. One of the villagers will have recognized me and caught a glimpse of you. My people love gossip; a little added malice is like ketchup on a burger to them. When the story reaches the last person in the village, you won't recognize yourself, or me.'

'It'll be interesting to hear what they think of me,' laughed Bud, hugging her to his side.

Natû was silent. She was not sure how the people would react to her return with her lover. She realized that she was nervous of seeing Trapper. Guilt weighed her footsteps, and she found herself slowing down.

In the distance, a wolf wailed in answer to the howling dogs.

The resonant call seemed to follow them to the door of her father's house. Natû raised her hand to knock on the bleached blue door, then turned to Bud and wound her arms around his neck as if she were drowning.

'Its okay,' said Bud, instinctively understanding her fear. 'He'll be happy to see you, Natû, you're his only child. He loves you.'

Natû turned back to the door, but before she could knock, it swung open. Filling the doorway was a tall, muscular young man. They could not see his features, but he exuded strength. He did not notice them standing to the side of the door in the dark.

'Sockeye,' he shouted, 'shut up.'

The husky gave one defiant bark and was silent.

'Don't know how long that'll last,' he said, slamming the door and turning to someone in the room.

'Until the next wolf sets them off again,' answered another male voice.

Natû was puzzled and a little nervous.

'This is my father's house, but strangers have moved in,' she whispered to Bud.

'Let me find out where he is,' said Bud. He hammered on the door and the dogs set up a deafening chorus.

'Damn.'

The same young man opened the door. 'Yes?' he queried, peering at Bud, and battling to keep the door from swinging wide in the wind.

'Is this Trapper Jack's house?' asked Bud, standing legs astride to brace himself against the gale.

'Yes, but who are you?' asked Patrick suspiciously. Trapper had not mentioned visitors when he left his house in the Butler boys' care.

Listening to the exchange, Natû was puzzled. The man had an English accent but with a slight American drawl. Who was he, and where was her father?

'I'm Trapper Jack's daughter, Natû,' she said, before Bud could answer.

Patrick was stunned. The whole family knew the story of Trapper's only child, who had left for the oilfields with an American rigger.

Their mother and father often spoke of the daughter Trapper had lost, and how deeply her defection had hurt him, though it was difficult to detect any emotion either in his face or voice when she was mentioned. Hank, their father, said that for years Trapper looked upon Casey as his daughter.

'Trapper obviously recognized more Eskimo traits in your mother than I do,' their father had laughed.

The wind whipped around the room, taking the warmth away with it as it swept through the open door.

'Shut the door, Patrick,' yelled Scott, clutching at the sheets of newspaper now carpeting the wooden floor.

Patrick glanced over his shoulder, then opened the door wide. He gestured for Bud and Natû to enter.

Scott was about to shout again, when from his position on the floor gathering the loose sheets of paper he saw two pairs of muddy boots. His eyes travelled up the smaller pair and he saw that they belonged to an Inupiat. The girl was sturdily built without being masculine. She gave an impression of strength while retaining her femininity. Scott studied her face. Apart from the coarse black hair and slight upward slant of her eyes, she could be American.

'Hi,' she said in a soft voice.

So she is American, he thought. Up here so many have Inupiat or Athabascan blood that it's difficult to tell. But it certainly makes for a strong breed.

Scott turned his attention to the man.

Wouldn't like to get into a fight with him, he mused. That guy has muscles he doesn't even know about.

'Scott,' said Patrick, 'meet Natû, Trapper's daughter, and Bud.'

'Her future husband,' Bud ended the sentence for him.

Scott jumped up, banging his head on the table. He left the last of the paper on the floor in his haste to meet and study the couple who had been the subject of so much family discussion.

'Hi,' he said, shaking Natû's hand. He watched as she took off her parka and shook out her hair.

Good-looking in a wild, Alaskan way, he thought.

Bud gripped his hand in a bone-crushing handshake.

It's no bull about riggers being tough, he mused, as he thrust his hand into the pocket of his jeans, resisting the temptation to massage his fingers.

'Have some coffee,' offered Patrick, placing four mugs on the table.

The four young people sat around the table sipping their sweet, strong coffee and studied each other curiously.

Like dogs circling and sniffing a newcomer to the pack, they questioned each other closely.

'In the sixties, when federal controls were relaxed, my pa was promised big dollars if he could deliver Cat and sleds to the North Slope by land,' Bud explained to Patrick. 'As you know, stuff can only be brought in by sea for three months of the year, and it was too expensive to fly in dismantled equipment. Pa made up a train of three D7 Caterpillars pulling a bunkhouse and sleds piled with equipment, fuel and food.'

Scott and Patrick listened to Bud in fascination.

'He and five guys set out to cut a road through the wilderness. The whole trip almost ended when one of the Cats broke through ice and settled deep into the mud of a pond. A sudden gale whipped up the snow. Cables snapped as the crew tried to winch the Cat out. Temperatures were about minus fifty degrees . . .'

'Where were you?' asked Natû suddenly.

'I was in the other Cat listening to voices cursing and men threatening to beat up my pa if he didn't turn back. I could see nothing in the white-out, but I bit my tongue till it bled to stop from calling for my pa. I had to be tough for him,' Bud answered.

'My pa was an ace Caterpillar skinner,' he continued. 'He blasted the pond apart with dynamite and did the impossible, handled a Cat train where no one had been.'

'You were one lucky kid,' said Scott.

'Yeah,' nodded Bud draining his coffee. He was not about to tell them of the nights he silently cried himself to sleep, terrified of the wolf wails which told of dark horrors, afraid that he would freeze to death during the night, scared that the Cat train would leave them behind as it pushed towards the North Slope.

'Now tell us about yourselves,' said Bud, eager to forget the terrors of childhood. 'How do you know Trapper? What do you guys do?'

Soon the questions changed to laughter. 'So you have Inupiat blood as well,' grinned Natû, gesturing at Scott and Patrick with her mug.

The boys looked nonplussed for a moment.

'I suppose we have,' said Patrick finally.

'That makes us almost family,' added Scott.

Natû was pensive, and stirred another spoonful of sugar into her already sweet coffee.

'If my father accepted your mother, Casey, as a daughter, then you are my family,' she said firmly.

'Great, that gives us two sisters, one in London and one out here. What could be better?' declared Scott.

'Once they're married, Bud will be our brother-in-law,' added Patrick. 'We can do with another man to deal with Savannah.'

'A strong man, to help beat off her constant stream of admirers,' laughed Scott.

The hours passed in animated conversation as the young people became friends.

Eventually seeing Natû yawn, Scott looked at his watch.

'We should catch some sleep. Trapper will be back in a few hours.'

Patrick stood up and stretched. His fingers brushed the ceiling.

'Right on, kid, and is he in for some surprise.' The air of gaiety was replaced with apprehension, as they each wondered what Trapper's reaction would be to the appearance of Bud and Natû.

'You use Trapper's bed, Natû,' suggested Patrick. 'Bud can bunk with Scott and I.'

Natû wanted to protest. She desperately needed the comfort of Bud's body that night. She wanted to cling to him and bury herself in his strength before meeting her father.

'Patrick is right, Natû,' said Bud, his words sealing her fear and anxiety.

'We'll work this out in the morning, when your father arrives.'

The small house was soon dark and quiet. Outside the dogs curled into tight balls. They tucked their noses beneath their tails, like children snuggling under duvets.

The ominous crack of sea ice and the unrelenting howl of the wind were the only sounds in the dark, sleeping village.

Chapter Three

THE AIRCRAFT bucketed in the wind as it hunted for Barrow Airport. Trapper held onto the armrests of his seat. He turned his face from the window. The glow from the Prudhoe pumping stations which lit much of the North Slope vanished long before they reached the small town of Barrow, where sea fog pulls its dirty grey sheet over the land and sea ice.

Trapper Jack closed his eyes and thought of the peace afforded by the barren expanses of sea ice. He imagined that he felt the cold searing his nostrils as he breathed in air so clean that it was like inhaling pure oxygen.

He forced his consciousness to drift away from the present. He needed to forget that he was in the plane.

Trapper let his mind hang suspended above a fish hole cut into the ice of a frozen river. He felt the thick caribou hide under his knees, and he imagined the curved hook carved from a dog's tooth jerking up and down in the black water.

The plane dipped. To calm himself, he pretended it was a fat grayling which was impaled on the metal barb set into the end of the hook. He pulled the fish up quickly from the hole and shook it loose, leaving it to die on the ice. Trapper's mind took him fishing in winter and calmed him. Resignation jostled out fear.

'This is not the way I choose to go to my ancestors.' His lips barely moved. 'But if it is planned then it will be my fate.'

The pilot cursed the long sunless winter, the gale and the ice fog which claimed this area, as she turned the plane onto finals in preparation to land in Barrow.

She fought to keep the wings level for touchdown, as the wind seemed to take a fiendish delight in testing her skills.

The wheels hit the runway and bounced up. The plane floated, then finally settled. Trapper kept his eyes closed with his hands on the armrests until the pilot announced that they were in Barrow and could disembark. It took a few moments for Trapper to register that the pilot was a woman. Like most men, he felt safer if a man was in control, though women proved themselves extremely competent and safe pilots.

'You can unfasten your seat belt now, sir,' said the air stewardess, bending low over Trapper. 'I'm sorry for the rather bumpy approach, but this weather is really awful. We were lucky Control allowed us to land.'

'Yes,' said Trapper weakly, suddenly feeling queasy.

'You need not worry when Anna McInnes is flying. She never "stretches the envelope". You're as safe as a baby in its ma's arms, with her in charge.' She was one pilot who took no unnecessary risks.

'Thanks,' said Trapper, squeezing out of the seat.

In his hand he clutched a plastic folder bulging with papers. No hint had been given about the final decision on the Refuge at the meeting, but Trapper gained an ovation for his eloquent and moving plea to leave 10-0-2 untouched for future generations to enjoy.

'In the cesspool we have made of our planet, we need one small corner to remain as the Great One created it. A place where we can allow our souls to sing. A place where, for a short while, we can be one with the land. As we care for our children, so we should care for the land. As we pass laws against the abuse of children, so we should have laws against the abuse of land refuges.

'Remember gentlemen:

> 'There is only one great thing,
> To live to see the great day that dawns
> And the light that fills the world.'

42

Trapper's voice sank to a whisper as he quoted the words of the poem he had written so long ago. There was silence in the room, and an involuntary shiver ran through the assembly.

'Gentlemen,' Trapper ended, 'let the Refuge and Ten-0-two be places where we and our children can see the light that fills the world.'

Trapper sighed as he felt his way down the steps from the aircraft.

He trudged past buildings that were now only dim outlines in the flying snow and the steam from vehicle exhausts left running by their owners, in case the trucks could not be restarted. He was so engrossed in his thoughts that he did not realize he was home until Sockeye uncurled himself and barked a welcome.

Natû put the pillow over her head as she heard the yelping, and cuddled into the warm bedclothes.

Let the guys check whether it's a prowling fox, she thought sleepily. I'm not getting up. I have only just fallen asleep. It feels like the middle of the night.

Suddenly a deep, familiar voice boomed out.

'Patrick. Scott. I expected coffee and breakfast, not two hibernating grizzlies.'

Natû threw the pillow from her face and sat up. The door swung open. The light blinded her, and she blinked owlishly at the bulky figure outlined in the doorway.

The silence between father and daughter seemed to stretch out and shame eternity.

'Father?' Natû broke the tension first. Her voice quavered. Trapper heard the tone his daughter used when she was small, and wanted something from him.

He saw his daughter chosen for the blanket-toss, and heard once again the cheers and laughter as she sighted the first whale for the village. He remembered how proud he was when she checked her first winter trapline, brought back the animals, skinned them and reset the traps.

He studied her face illuminated by the light pushing into the room, and tried to find the teenager he loved and thought was lost to him for ever.

But the figure huddled in the middle of his bed was not his young daughter. This was a woman, a strong, attractive woman. Her nose seemed more aquiline than he remembered it, and she did not have the heavy jaw so prevalent in the Inupiat.

The epicanthic fold did not cover most of the eye. Her large brown eyes tilted up a little, like those of an Arctic hare. They were filled with apprehension as she stared at him.

Trapper stood silent and still as Nanuq waiting at a lead in the ice.

'Father?' questioned Natû hesitantly. 'May I stay here?'

Trapper merely nodded his head. He closed the door quietly behind him and turned to face Scott, Patrick and a stranger grouped at the stove. Scott and Patrick were making a great deal of unnecessary clatter preparing coffee. The muscled stranger studied Trapper, then stepped forward.

'Should have come sooner, Sir,' he said.

Trapper nodded and smoothed his wet moustache.

'Sit down. Have some coffee and we can talk.'

Patrick and Scott were obviously relieved that the outburst they had feared had not occurred.

Silence, as oppressive as the sea fog choking Barrow, settled over the men.

Scott, always the lover of peace, broke the impasse.

'Trapper, this is Bud Damas.'

Trapper nodded, not taking his eyes from Bud's face.

So you are the young ram who cut my daughter from the family herd and took her away, he thought. I may not like you for what you did, but you seem strong enough to look after Natû.

He studied Bud's left hand with the missing fingers. He liked the fact that Damas did not try to hide his deformity, but kept his hands clasped around the mug.

This man is a worker, he decided.

'Why are you here?' asked Trapper gruffly, wiping the steam

from his moustache with his shirtsleeve. 'Why have you left the comforts of Prudhoe to come to this native village?'

Patrick and Scott sat as still and silent as if they were watching the down feather of an eider tied to a stick at a seal's aglu, his breathing hole. They waited for Bud to answer, with the intensity of waiting for the breath of a surfacing seal to move the feather.

'I want to marry Natû,' answered Bud. He hurried on before Trapper could object. 'We would like to have a wedding in the village with her family and friends, and later, one in Anchorage with our pals from the oilfield.'

Trapper nodded gravely. His face betrayed no emotion. Bud was uneasy and looked at Scott and Patrick hoping for help, but the Butler boys kept their eyes fixed on the coffee mugs.

'We natives do not hold formal weddings. Our women often go off with men they choose four or five times before settling down. That usually happens when they start a family,' said Trapper drily.

'Natû chose you, and it seems to me that you are married. But if Natû wishes it, we will hold a feast for friends to welcome you and wish you a future of good hunting.'

Bud's brow furrowed.

'But sir, I am not a hunter. I was a rigger, and a damn good one. Now I run inspections on the pipeline.'

'To us a good hunter is all-important. He supports his family, helps feed the old and shares the kill. Without good hunters we subsistence people would be extinct.'

Bud nodded, still not understanding.

'He's wishing you good luck for the future,' whispered Scott, turning his head away from the table as if wanting to cough.

'Where are you going to live once you have married Natû?' queried Trapper, holding out his empty mug to Scott for a refill.

Scott jumped up and knocked over the chair in his hurry to leave the table and fill Trapper's mug.

If only Trapper would yell at Bud, or say what he really feels about the marriage, he mused, as he filled the mug to the top and placed it carefully in front of Trapper.

'Here in Barrow, Father,' answered Natû, appearing from the bedroom. 'We will also have to spend time in Chugiak, as the dogs need to run through forests and become accustomed to trees.'

Trapper turned to face his daughter.

It is good that I listened to Oline and gave Natû her mother's name. My wife's soul did not have to wander around lost and lonely, seeking a home. Her soul did not have to live in the third world of the dead, where unskilled women and unsuccessful hunters snap listlessly at butterflies, their only food. Neither did it go to the underworld, even though that is comfortable and warm. It found a place immediately in her newborn child. I see my wife in Natû's eyes, he thought. Now she lives again in Natû.

The idea of his beloved wife being reincarnated in his child satisfied him. Trapper relaxed a little as Natû walked to the stove and poured herself coffee.

'What is this talk of dogs and trees?' he asked her as she seated herself. A gust of wind hurled snow at the windows and shook the blue wooden door.

Natû waited until there was a lull in the gale before answering her father.

'You know that I have always wanted to run the Iditarod. Run the Last Great Race, as a native, an Inupiat. Run it on native money and with native dogs. This was my dream before I left Barrow.' Natû watched Trapper closely, and skirted away from the subject of her leaving him and the village, as if avoiding open water on a dog-sled trail. 'It is still my dream, Father, and now I have Bud to share it with.'

'Bud wants to run the Iditarod?' said Scott in amazement. His astonishment made him enter the conversation.

Patrick felt as if he had been trampled by a moose.

The Iditarod, he thought. But that is my race. I need Sockeye and Trapper's help. Now he'll give it all to his daughter. For a moment he felt an unreasoning dislike for Natû.

She walks out of his life without a care. Now, when it suits her, the prodigal returns home to receive everything to help her run the race.

Trapper stared at Natû, then shifted his gaze to Patrick. He noticed that the young man's knuckles were white and the veins stood proud on his hands as he clenched the mug.

So, he thought. I do not need to talk to this one about running the Iditarod. It has been heating his blood all the time he has been checking the traplines with the dog team, and hunting seal and walrus with the hunters in the village. He has earned the right to experience the awesome forces of nature on the trail. He will make me proud. Together we can earn him a placing in the race.

Natû moved uneasily on her chair. Trapper turned to her.

But what of my only child? She is both my son and my daughter. She has no mother. She has come to me for help. It would be good to have a native, an Inupiat, run the Iditarod again, he mused.

Thoughts battered his brain like the wind-driven snow against the windows.

Two pairs of eyes were fixed on Trapper's face. Natû's dark brown ones begged him silently for forgiveness and his support, without which she could not even enter the event.

Trapper turned his gaze from Natû to Patrick. Fancifully he imagined the brown flecks in the boy's green eyes to be lichen painting the colours of fall on the tundra. The brown seemed to darken as Patrick looked steadily at Trapper.

If only I had spoken to you about the race before you left for that damn meeting in Anchorage, the boy thought. I know you would have given me your backing. Natû would have been too late.

Come on, Trapper, he willed the old man silently. Stay with me. I can and will do it. Together we can make the top twenty. Let Natû marry and have babies. It should be a man's race. Already there are too many women running it.

As if reading his thoughts, Trapper spoke. 'There was a time, Natû, when I believed that you could be an Inupiat, a native Beverly Jerue, a Dee Dee Jonrowe, Susan Butcher, Diana Moroney, or a Libby Riddles,' he said flatly, reeling off the names of women who successfully ran and often won the gruelling race.

'But you have lived away from the land too long. I fear you no longer hear its heartbeat. It will break you. Nature tolerates only those who live in harmony with her; eventually she will eat all others.'

Patrick felt a sudden surge of hope as he listened to Trapper.

Perhaps I still have a chance. I'll talk to him later, he decided silently.

Scott leaned back in his chair. He sensed what his brother was thinking.

Trapper will need the wisdom of Solomon to settle this one, he thought. But he has always been fair. He'll make the right decision.

He stood up quietly, trying not to attract attention to his movements. Before he could push his chair away from the table, Natû spoke.

'I know, Father. I too hoped to be first to cross the finish line in Nome. I am sure that I can. You taught me, when I was a little girl, that nothing is impossible if you want it badly enough and are willing to work and sacrifice to get it. I believed you then. I still believe you.'

She paused. Trapper gazed at the window as if the flying flakes of snow hitting the panes, like moths beating themselves against a lamp, could answer this dilemma.

'Remember, Father, that the Iditarod was founded not only to encourage people to breed and train sled dogs and use them in the villages, but also to honour the mushers of the famous serum run. More than half of those extraordinary men were native mushers. I am a native. Women have proved that they can win the Iditarod. I am a woman.'

Natû paused to draw a deep breath. Trapper tapped his spoon lightly against his mug.

'You should also be on our native corporation,' he smiled. 'We need people who can reason and speak well. Let me think about this, Natû. You have given me too many surprises before breakfast. No man should make decisions on an empty stomach, it muddles the brain.'

Scott and Patrick pushed back their chairs. The smell of sizzling fat and fresh tea soon filled the room, and the windows steamed up.

Trapper ran a piece of sourdough round his plate, cleaning up the last trace of fat. He leaned back in his chair and hooked his gnarled fingers over his belly.

'As you all probably know, and as Patrick and Scott certainly do,' Trapper paused, as Bud looked perplexed. 'I'm about to discuss the native corporations, and their lack of ready money, Bud,' he explained.

'Of the original thirteen native corporations, only six, led by the Cook Inlet Region Inc., CIRI, are fiscally sound. The CIRI is of course the star. I know the president very well. Our mothers were friends.'

Natû sat up straight and her eyes sparkled. Bud put his hand on her knee and squeezed hard. She rested her hand on his, and he could feel the excitement course through her fingers.

'I could approach him,' said Trapper. 'The Iditarod committee and the corporations are now realizing that it costs a native living in a remote area about ten thousand dollars extra to prepare for the race, as they have to pay to freight in dog food and other goods. Competitors living near towns can obtain what they need easily and usually at less cost. I think they may sponsor a woman native competitor.'

Shock stole the blood from Patrick's face. Trapper had decided in favour of his daughter.

Unfair, he wanted to shout.

She is his daughter, the small, often ignored, voice of reason whispered to him. She is his child. It's only right for Trapper to help her first. He likes you, but he loves her. They share the same blood.

Unfair, unfair. If you want it badly enough, go for it, said the voice that usually trampled on sense.

'Trapper, what about the other corporations?' Patrick heard himself say. 'Could you persuade them to sponsor a man with only a trickle of Inupiat blood in his veins, but a burning desire to hit the trail?'

Trapper pulled thoughtfully at the straggly ends of his moustache. He smiled, a puckish grin.

'Can you eat raw meat, run naked and sleep in the snow?' he asked, quoting the Alaska Airlines tribute to the dogs.

'No, but I can eat blubber, drink seal oil, run in traditional native gear and yes, I can sleep in the snow,' Patrick answered seriously.

'I'm sure you can do it, young man,' agreed Trapper, impressed with Patrick's fervour. He paused, deep in thought; only the constant fiddling with his moustache showed that he was still awake. Scott noted once again the native's amazing ability to sit motionless for hours.

'I could try the NANA corporation,' said Trapper finally. 'The Kotzebue Regional Corporation are doing well with the Red Dog zinc mine. They have a few native activists who are intent on preserving our culture. Perhaps I can persuade them to sponsor you and use the media coverage of the Iditarod to promote their cause.'

'Thanks, Trapper,' said Patrick, 'I appreciate your offer of help.'

'What about the other corporations?' asked Scott, thinking ahead to when it would be his turn to run the Iditarod. 'What happened to the nine hundred and sixty-odd million dollars they received for claims settlement?'

'It's estimated that over one million dollars were paid to lawyers. You boys know about the never-ending lawsuits. The natives fight each other over sharing revenues from the sale of natural resources; they make unwise investments and issue challenges over subsistence rights,' explained Trapper dispiritedly.

'The lawyers prosper and the corporations go bankrupt,' said Patrick, stacking the dirty plates beside the basin.

'May I say something?' said Bud.

Trapper nodded, and took the opportunity of studying Natû's future husband as he spoke. He decided that she had chosen well. The man seemed strong and healthy.

When Bud saw Trapper studying him he did not drop his gaze, but kept his eyes on Trapper's, as if trying to gauge what his future father-in-law would think of his suggestion. He did not want to antagonize Natû's father, as it was obvious that Natû both loved and respected the older man.

Bud placed both of his large hands flat on the table and leaned towards Trapper.

'There is one thing we have not told you,' he said.

'I, too, am going to run as a rookie.'

Trapper's expression did not change. He merely tugged more vigorously at the trailing ends of his moustache.

'What?' said Patrick and Scott in unison. 'But you . . .'

'I know,' said Bud. 'I know nothing, and will probably be awarded the Red Lantern for being the last one under the burled wood arch in Nome.

'I may not have even one drop of native blood, but I sure have the love of Alaska running hard and fast in my veins. One good legacy from my pa.

'As a kid, I knew this was my land. I remember camping out under the stars with my pa, certain that the wolves would get me but too scared to confess, in case he sent me back to the Lower Forty-eight to stay with my aunt. Living on the oilfield wrapped in American comfort is not living in Alaska.'

Bud cracked the knuckles of one hand. The sound was loud in the room. Natû recognized it as a sign of nervousness, even though Bud's demeanour was calm and his voice held steady.

'I was raised hard by a tough wildcatter, the best wildcatter in the state. As a kid, fear and hunger were my mates. Alaska was and is my love. I'll train with Natû. I've saved enough not to have to return to Prudhoe for a year or two.'

'And after the race?' said Trapper quietly.

'There's always work on one of the fields for experienced men. I'll have a job. I'll support Natû.'

Trapper sat silent and brooding, like a snowy owl on its hummock.

Now I have three people who need sponsorship, he thought. At thirty thousand dollars each, it'll be impossible.

Trapper shook his head slowly. The long, wispy ends of his moustache brushed his neck.

'I know what you're thinking,' said Bud quietly. 'You may find sponsorship for two, but not three.'

Trapper nodded. Patrick and Scott took their seats at the table and listened intently.

'Before we left Prudhoe, whispers were circulating that BP would sponsor me for the full fifty thousand dollars. Perhaps Natû as well.'

Scott gave a low whistle. 'Right on,' he shouted, and pumped his arm in a gesture of success.

'If Trapper can't swing the Kotzebue crowd, I'll split the fifty with you, Patrick. I'm sure we can scrape something together with twenty-five thousand each. They say thirty is the minimum, but with hard work and Trapper to train us, we'll make Nome.'

She has chosen a man, thought Trapper, listening to Bud.

'I'll be happy just to complete the race,' continued Bud. 'So young dogs, oldest sled, borrowed native winter gear will do me fine. It'll be like camping in winter,' he laughed. It was an infectious laugh, and the young people joined in. Only Trapper sat with his head bowed.

'Father?' said Natû, concerned at his silence. 'Father?'

Trapper stood up and stretched. It had been a long and arduous two days away from his beloved home and Barrow.

'No, Bud,' he said gruffly, 'not a camping trip. When you pit yourself against the power and majesty of winter in the Arctic, you will realize how insignificant and weak you are. At times you will pray just to survive. That is what we will have to teach you, to survive.'

Trapper turned towards his bedroom. He stopped with his hand on the door.

'Remember that although they now have "checkpoints", radios and aircraft to drop dog food and take out injured dogs and mushers, you are alone at the mercy of the elements between the safety points. A camping trip, no, Bud.'

Trapper pushed open the door and yawned. 'But you will experience the thrill of fear,' he said over his shoulder.

'Now I have to sleep. Ptarmigan or hare would be good for supper, Patrick. Take Bud and begin his training,' he ordered.

The door slammed behind him. Trapper smiled as he pulled

the blanket up under his chin. The yapping and barking of dogs told him that the youngsters were giving Bud his first lesson in hitching up dogs.

There would be fresh meat for supper.

Chapter Four

A GROUP OF tourists bundled up in down parkas with mukluks warming their feet, pushed open the heavy glass doors of the Captain Cook Hotel. They stamped the slush from their snow boots before stepping onto the tiles. They pushed into the heated foyer, thankful to be out of the wind, which gave the lie to the designers' claims of windproof parkas.

They were attracted to Alaska in winter by the new drive to sell winter sports. The travel brochures painted enticing pictures of youngsters snowshoeing, skiing and racing over sparkling snow in a dog sled.

The brochures did not warn them that winter sports were not suited to overweight, out of condition people, who did little if any exercise during the year.

They were puffing and grumbling as they tumbled into the foyer. They hurried past the brightly lit hotel shops, offering toy bears and Eskimo artefacts, drawn by the strong aroma of fresh coffee and spare ribs, to the Pantry.

As they trooped past one of the function rooms, the door flew open and a sudden burst of music and laughter poured out and flooded the passage.

'Its a wedding,' said one of the tourists, unzipping her dark green parka. The women in the group paused and peered into the room hoping to see the bride. The men milled around uncertainly, hoping the women would lose interest and continue to the Pantry.

The young man who flung open the door stood framed in the doorway. The lights reflected the deep auburn in his hair. His brown eyes studied the group of tourists for a moment.

'Come in,' he invited. 'There's a spare table here near the door. Come and join in the fun.'

'But we don't even know the couple,' said one of the women, edging into the room.

'It's a wedding,' said Scott, 'you don't have to know them. Come in and enjoy yourselves.'

The women accepted the invitation promptly, but the men looked uneasy.

'Excuse me, guys,' a woman in her early twenties with blonde hair knotted behind her head tried to ease past Scott and the tourists without spilling the champagne she was sipping.

Talking stopped. There was silence as Scott and the men followed the bounce of her buttocks, firm and round beneath the skin-tight red Lycra dress. Her high-heeled sandals accentuated the thrust of her hips and drew all eyes to her long, shapely legs.

'Whew,' whistled one of the tourists softly. 'Are all the wedding guests built like that?'

'Don't know,' answered Scott, still watching the girl disappear in the direction of the ladies' cloakroom.

The men hurriedly streamed past him and joined their spouses at the table Scott had showed them. He remained at the door. He had to speak to the girl in red. The speeches started, and still she did not reappear.

I'll walk to the ladies' pretending I'm looking for the gents', he thought; perhaps I'll find her. Once she's back in that wedding crush I'll never see her again.

Scott ran his fingers through his hair and strolled nonchalantly down the passage studying his shoes. He did not want any of the Cook's security staff asking why he was walking to the ladies' toilet.

The sharp click of heels on tiles alerted him, and he looked up just as the young woman rounded the corner.

She's stunning, he thought, trying to memorize every detail of her face and body in the few moments he had before she walked past him.

Hanna McInnes, known as Anna to her friends, was almost as tall as Scott. She was so slender that it seemed to him as if the wide black belt nipping in her waist would snap her in half. But unlike the catwalk models in London, she did not look wasted and starved. Her blue eyes were as dark and mysterious as his were guileless.

Suddenly aware that he was staring unashamedly at her décolletage, Scott looked away and hurried past. But he could not resist the temptation to turn round and watch her body move under the dress as she returned to the function room.

A clear peal of laughter confused him. She, too, had looked back at him. She came towards him with her hand out. 'Anna,' she said. 'Hi!'

Scott wiped his sweaty hand down the leg of his trousers.

'Scott Butler,' he answered.

They smiled at each other, still slightly embarrassed to have been caught turning round, showing interest, but pleased to have met.

Scott looked into the crowded function room.

'No one will miss us in this noise,' he said. 'Let me find my champagne, if it hasn't been taken. We can sit in the reception area, and talk without suffering permanent damage to our vocal cords.'

'Great. I'll wait out here.'

It took Scott a few minutes to battle his way through the throng of well-wishers. He topped up his glass and was preparing to force his way to the door when Patrick barred the way.

'No sneaking out of weddings, kid. Natû and Bud will think you're not enjoying yourself.'

'Have to go,' said Scott, attempting to bypass Patrick.

'No way. I've found someone I want you to meet. She's hot. You'll love her.'

Patrick nudged Scott, but to his surprise his sibling pressed towards the door.

'What's wrong, bro?' Patrick could not believe that Scott was passing up the opportunity of a woman for the night. He had discovered that women found his sibling very attractive. When they were younger it had annoyed him. Now he accepted it, and referred to Scott as 'my brother the lover'.

'Thanks, Patrick, but I've found the woman I'm going to marry,' Scott said firmly.

'I thought only women were sentimental at weddings,' Patrick called sarcastically, but Scott did not even turn his head. He glimpsed a bright red dress at the door and like a rigger forcing a 'stand' through the permafrost, he parted the crowd and reached Anna.

Patrick shook his head in mock amazement, and returned to claim the woman he had offered Scott for himself.

Anna grinned at Scott, and he felt as if they were old friends. He felt no shyness in the company of strange women. He took her glass and steered her to a corner set with comfortable sofas where they could talk.

A middle-aged couple waiting for the reservation clerk to check them in came and sat opposite Scott and Anna.

The youngsters neither paused in their conversation nor looked up. They were totally engrossed in each other.

'I thought all the kids up here were roughnecks and wore dirty jeans and mukluks,' said the woman, eyeing the lace tops of Anna's stockings as she unselfconsciously crossed her legs.

Anna turned to face Scott, and her dress rode up even higher on her thighs. The woman twisted to look at the reservation desk, then shook her husband's arm.

'Go see if our room is ready yet,' she said, but her husband sat transfixed, his eyes not moving from Anna's legs.

The woman shook him more vigorously.

'Now,' she commanded. 'Now, before another queue forms.'

He started and stared at her as if awakening from a dream.

'Now!'

She watched in satisfaction as he was beaten to the desk by an elderly couple. He took up his place behind them and turned to look at his wife. She shook her head, and gestured for him to remain there.

Men, she thought, even when they are too old to catch the rabbit, they still give chase.

Anna tucked her legs under her on the couch, seemingly unaware that this move now exposed her thigh, allowing the edge of her black panties to show. She was in animated conversation with Scott, and didn't notice the middle-aged woman opposite them heave herself from the comfortable leather chair and join her husband. She was not allowing him to return to see this new display of flesh.

Like most young people, Scott and Anna questioned each other, trying to complete the jigsaw of each other's lives. But within an hour Scott knew little more than that Anna was a pilot with Alaska Airlines. She knew all about his university and Iditarod ambitions.

'Why don't you join the Iditarod volunteers?' asked Anna intently. 'For the first few weeks of March it's a madhouse, we need every pair of hands available. They have estimated that we, the Iditarod Air Force, fly more than one hundred thousand pounds of freight during each year's race. To say nothing of leapfrogging officials and veterinarians from one checkpoint to the other.'

Scott, who had almost completed his private pilot's licence at Tri Star Flying School at Birchwood in Chugiak, was impressed.

His instructor also did volunteer flying for the race. A week before the start of the race, he had to juggle his pupil's lessons with flying the mushers' food drops to the checkpoints. As he taught Scott the finer points of landing in crosswinds, he told him nerve-prickling stories of landing on river ice in severe crosswinds in winter. The lessons were engraved on Scott's mind, as if in copper plate. He stopped fearing these fierce winds and learned to handle them.

'You don't look like a pilot,' Scott said, and Anna laughed.

'Wait until you see me when I'm flying.'

'I'd love to. Could I at least help you load and unload the plane during the race?' asked Scott seriously.

Anna thought for a moment. 'Let me contact the Iditarod Trail Headquarters in Wasilla,' she said. 'Who's your flying instructor?'

'One helluva guy, Bruce Moroney,' answered Scott.

'Bruce! I know him well. That guy was born with wings. The best pilot here. You're lucky to have him. You'll be a top-drawer pilot when he's done with you,' said Anna.

'Scott!' Patrick's voice boomed down the passage. Scott looked up in annoyance.

The wedding party jostled past the long wooden reception desk. Bud and Natû were lost to view in the centre of the laughing crowd. Natû flipped the train of her long white satin dress over her arm to avoid the guests stepping on it and tearing the material.

'Come on,' shouted Patrick, extricating himself and crossing to where Scott and Anna were seated. 'Come and see the newlyweds leave.'

'Let's,' said Anna, grasping Scott's hand and pulling him to his feet. Like all women, she was easy prey to the emotion of weddings and christenings.

The doorman, smart in grey and burgundy, opened the doors wide and waited to see the reaction when the lightly clothed guests felt the wind. To his surprise, the shouting and hilarity merely rose in volume.

Bud and Natû were tucked under a fox kaross in the dog sled waiting on the road. Trapper stood on the runners of the sled controlling the excited, barking huskies. Friends of Trapper's from Tri Star Kennels in Chugiak had let him use one of their sleds and a team of huskies to take Bud and Natû to the cottage in Chugiak. Natû had chosen to spend their honeymoon in their rented cabin.

Unbeknown to Natû, the Butler boys had booked a suite for Bud and Natû at the hotel. They persuaded Trapper to drive the bridal couple towards Chugiak, then make an excuse to return to the hotel. There, the guests would be waiting to escort them up to their suite.

At first Trapper was hesitant.

'Natû wants to go to the cabin. She may hate the idea of staying at the Cook for the night.'

'She's a fun girl, she'll love it,' the boys assured him.

'Even Bud thinks she'll love the idea.'

Trapper remained uncertain, but hoped that the new Mrs Damas would see the humorous side of the situation.

Natû snuggled up to Bud as Trapper called, 'Let's go.' His voice was lost in the hubbub.

Vega danced on her hind legs to the music of the excitement around her. She looked over her shoulder at Trapper, waiting to hear the command to go. He nodded and made a sharp forward gesture with his right hand. Vega was at least forty feet ahead of him and would never hear his voice. The lead dog understood immediately. She pulled the gangline straight and strained forward. The others followed as smoothly as a well-trained chorus line.

Trapper eyed the tight tuglines with approval. Well-trained dogs, he thought. They must sense that this is a special event: no tangled lines, no fighting and jumping over the gangline to get at each other. He shook his head. I hope Bud does not think that this is dogs' usual behaviour.

Bud covered his nose with the neck warmer Patrick had pulled over his head as he and Natû ran for the sled. The icy air seemed to scrape his nostrils raw, and made every breath agony.

Bud turned to look at Natû. He pulled the wide wolverine ruff of her parka aside and saw to his astonishment that her neck warmer was still crumpled under her chin. She was smiling and breathing easily.

'You have a lot to teach me, little Natû,' he whispered.

Natû laid her head on his shoulder and the fur of her hood tickled his face. Bud closed his eyes.

'Easy,' shouted Trapper. Vega slowed to a gentle trot. 'Whoa!' Vega stopped and the team came to a halt.

'Come, gee,' yelled Trapper. The lead dog followed the confusing commands perfectly. She pulled to the right, moving the sled around one hundred and eighty degrees. Trapper Jack nodded his approval. The dogs had followed the manoeuvre perfectly.

'What's wrong?' said Natû, as the sled returned the way it had come.

'Left something important at the Cook,' shouted Trapper. Natû nodded and closed her eyes, enjoying the bumping of the sled and the feel of Bud's padded jacket beneath her cheek.

The dogs' feet did not seem to touch the snow. They were doing the thing they loved best – running.

Holding Natû tightly, Bud felt disloyal about fooling his new wife. He struggled with his feelings silently, then lifted Natû's head from his shoulder and put his lips to her ear.

'Natû,' he said, 'I have something to tell you. Trapper has not forgotten anything at the Cook. The boys thought that you would enjoy one night of luxury and pampering in a suite, instead of cooking and making the bed at the cabin. They were so excited about their plan, I could not stop them.'

Natû stiffened and Bud realized that he should not have been swayed by the Butler boys.

'I love you, Bud Damas,' said Natû, 'but . . .'

Bud did the only thing he could think of to defuse the situation: he kissed her until her tightly compressed lips softened and parted beneath his. Their faces were hidden in the large hood of Natû's parka and their breath was hot. Bud no longer noticed the icy wind; the air around him was warm and perfumed with the smell of Natû.

Natû broke away from the embrace. 'Bud, I would love to lie in your arms as your wife in our cabin, please. Not the hotel. The cabin has always been such a special, private place for us. Let's go there tonight. Please.'

Bud nodded. He pulled his arm from under the kaross and signalled for Trapper to stop.

'Whoa!' This time, with the wind behind them, Trapper's voice carried clearly to his lead dog.

Vega ignored it. The snow beneath her feet and the cold air on her flopping tongue excited her – she wanted to run.

'Whoa, Vega!' At the second command she stopped reluctantly and looked back at Trapper reproachfully.

You're a great dog, Vega, thought Trapper, but as a lead dog you're headstrong.

Bud and Natû both turned and spoke to Trapper simultaneously,

Bud in English and Natû in their native tongue. Trapper held up his hand and Bud let Natû do the explaining.

Vega seemed to shake her head as Trapper called out the command to turn round again. The large, strong wheel dogs running just in front of the sled swung the sled around to follow Vega.

'Thank you, Bud,' whispered Natû as she cuddled into his side.

Bud smiled at her, then suddenly he jerked upright. 'The guests, Natû,' he said. 'They are all waiting to escort us up to our suite.'

'They'll go back inside to where it's warm and there's food, drink and music,' she answered calmly. 'We'll phone when we reach the cabin.'

Bud sank back into the fur covering. Natû pulled the caribou hide over the top.

Trapper and Natû are right, thought Bud as the sled slewed and bumped along the road. I have a lot to learn before I can even contemplate running the race. The toughest part will be handling these wolves.

Bud wondered whether he would ever love the dogs that looked so much like the wolves he feared. An involuntary shiver ran down his spine. He knew that he must overcome this childish, irrational fear of wolves.

Bud watched the huskies' muscles bunch and stretch beneath their thick fur. Their flying feet and waving tails were mesmeric. The caribou cover allowed no needle of wind to creep in beneath the fur kaross.

He tightened his grasp on Natû's hand. His eyes closed and he slept.

Natû watched her new husband for a few moments, then turned her attention to the dogs, judging their potential as Iditarod runners.

She lost herself in dreams of the day when she would stand on the sled runners and realize her childhood desire.

Chapter Five

ONCE THE sled carrying the bridal couple was just a black speck in the distance, the guests pushed their way back into the warm womb of the hotel. The music in the function room housing the wedding guests changed from a frantic, pulsating beat to a slow, mellow rhythm.

'Come,' said Scott, and held out his hand to Anna. She followed him onto the packed dance floor.

Scott was a good dancer, and Anna found it easy to follow his lead.

'It seems as if I've known you for ever,' said Scott softly.

Anna rested her head on his shoulder in reply. Across the floor, Patrick studied the woman in his brother's arms.

Not bad, he thought. But he's too young even to think of marriage. He's had too much champagne and his hormones have replaced his brain.

Anna and Scott swayed past Patrick and he turned his head to watch Anna.

'Your tongue's hanging out,' said his dance partner, flicking her long hair over her shoulder in annoyance.

The words jerked him out of his reverie and back to the woman in his arms.

'Just checking on my little brother,' he explained.

'Yeah, so I noticed. It was his red dress that worried you.'

Patrick laughed, then, as he saw he was being paged, turned and walked to the main table. His dance partner watched his expression change as he read the note handed to him. He picked up the microphone and his voice boomed out across the room.

'Quiet please! I have something to tell you. Bud and Natû are not returning to the Cook. They are staying at Chugiak.'

Groans greeted his announcement.

'But they want you to party all night.'

Cheers replaced the groans. The band broke into 'Purple Rain'. The room vibrated to the beat, along with the thumping of feet on the wooden floor.

Anna moved out of Scott's arms and broke into an abandoned orgy of movement. Scott stared at her for a moment, then laughed and matched her steps.

Soon they where dancing in the centre of a ring of admirers. Patrick tried to force his way past the throng to claim the girl he had left on the floor, but no one would give way. The guests were clapping and singing the chorus to Prince's song, as Scott and Anna writhed and shook.

Eventually Patrick gave up the attempt and stood on the edge of the circle. His height allowed him glimpses of Anna and Scott. To his surprise, he found himself clapping and shouting the words to 'Purple Rain'.

Abruptly the music stopped and changed tempo.

Scott claimed Anna. She was breathing rapidly, and her breasts rose and fell against his chest. He tightened his arms around her and his mouth found hers. Scott was oblivious to the people around them. The softness of Anna's lips, her warm, questing tongue were all that existed.

They did not feel the soft bumping of dancers moving slowly round them. They were lost in the world known only to lovers.

'Anna,' Scott whispered huskily. 'Anna.'

She leaned away slightly from Scott and moved her hips as if to the swing of a pendulum against him. There was a small smile on her moist lips as she studied his face.

Scott groaned and dug his fingers into her buttocks, pulling her hard to him.

He found her mouth again. This time there was a urgency to his kissing which excited Anna.

'Scott, let's leave,' she whispered.

They walked out of the room with their arms around each other's waist.

Patrick resisted the urge to call out to his brother.

Not at all Scott's type, he thought as he watched his brother bend his head to hear something the girl in red was saying.

He always goes for the sweet, shy, English rose. This one is an exotic scarlet orchid. I should warn him to go easy. He'll fall hard and she'll break his heart. My kid brother has a lot to learn about women.

Patrick wrestled with his feelings of protectiveness for his brother. He watched him kiss the top of Anna's head tenderly as they passed through the doorway. Patrick shook his head. This was not the time to lecture his sibling.

Let him have one night with her, he thought. That's about all she'll give him. A girl like that is sure to have a boyfriend somewhere; she's too good-looking to be alone.

Patrick refilled his glass and sauntered across to a table where two pretty blondes were whispering and giggling.

'Dance?' he queried, putting his arm under the elbow of the prettier girl.

The streets in downtown Anchorage were quiet after the gaiety of the wedding.

Anna steered Scott towards Fourth Avenue, which seemed deserted in the early hours of the morning.

The wind whistled down the wide street. Anna shivered. She removed her arm from Scott's waist and thrust her hands deep into the pockets of her long down coat. She stepped out purposefully, walking fast in the mukluks which she had put on before leaving the Cook Hotel.

'The starting point for the Iditarod,' said Scott, recognizing the huge yellow neon M above a McDonald outlet.

'It stretches for five blocks along Fourth Avenue,' said Anna. 'Its great fun, the best.'

'Where are we going?' asked Scott, looking dubiously at the empty road.

'We're here,' replied Anna, stopping beside a sleek Mercedes sports car. She unzipped a small purse and pulled out a bunch of keys.

'Yours?' asked Scott, puzzled as to how a pilot could afford a Mercedes 500.

'Yes, all mine,' said Anna shortly, as if reading his mind. 'Jump in.'

Scott sank back into the leather seat and sighed.

'I could become hooked on this sort of thing,' he said, leaning forward to study the dashboard.

'I have.'

Scott looked up quickly at Anna but she had her head down, fiddling with the ignition key.

The motor started, a deep, rich roar. Anna laughed and pressed a few buttons. The haunting strains of one of the *Solitude* tapes filled the car. The mournful howl of wolves rose, blended with the music and died away.

'Wolfsong,' said Anna, answering Scott's unasked question.

Scott edged the flap of Anna's down coat aside and put his hand on her thigh. It was warm in the car. He rested his head on the back of the seat and closed his eyes. Softly his fingers caressed the flesh above her stocking.

Anna examined his face in the flickering street lights.

He really is a hunk, she thought, but I'll have to be careful with him. Inside that sexy body there is a lot of gentleness. He'll react like a puppy kicked in the guts. A smile danced over Scott's mouth.

Abruptly Anna swung the car round a corner. Scott opened his eyes and sat up straight.

'What's wrong?'

'Nothing. Wrong turn.'

No, thought Anna, I can't hurt him tonight. He can find out about my ever-loving 'Double Dick' husband later. Much later.

The drive seemed to last for ever. Scott realized that they had left Anchorage and were heading for the Chugach mountains. Eventually Anna braked hard and switched off the ignition. Scott looked around, but could see only the outline of a small cabin.

'I'll go first,' said Anna, swinging open her door, letting in a blast of cold air. She lifted Scott's hand from her thigh and put it on the seat.

'Come when I call.'

Scott sat in the car, perplexed and bemused. Suddenly lights beamed from the windows of the cabin and seemed to warm the snow.

'Okay Scott,' called Anna as the front door swung open.

Scott climbed out of the car and picked his way across snow-covered rocks to where Anna stood.

'There's a path that goes round the back. Its easier walking,' she laughed as he finally stepped up onto the wooden deck.

'What's this?' said Scott, gesturing at the living room with its comfortable wooden sofas and chairs piled high with plump cushions and the open fireplace stacked with split logs.

'My place. My secret,' replied Anna, scrabbling in the top drawer of a cupboard painted with tundra flowers.

'Here it is.' Triumphantly she held up a box of matches. She squatted in front of the stone fireplace, her coat spreading around her on the floor.

Scott shrugged off his parka and threw it over the back of one of the chairs. He moved across to help her, but before he could take the matches, small gold flames tasted the paper, then devoured it ravenously.

'That's it,' said Anna, rubbing her hands together. She watched in satisfaction as the flames gnawed at the wood. Anna turned from the fire and bumped into Scott, who still hovered over her.

'Sorry. Didn't see you.'

Scott did not answer. Gently he eased the long cream coat from her shoulders. The padded coat filled his arms, as thick and white as tumbling cumulus clouds. He laid it on the mat in front of the fire where the flames streaked it orange and gold. Anna

67

watched him in silence. She reached up behind her back and unzipped the skin-tight red dress. It fell to the floor around her knees.

Scott gasped. She was magnificent. Her body was as slim and creamy as the stamen rising from the curved red petals of an anthurium. Her breasts, released from the constraints of the dress, were full and heavy. Scott choked back a cry of desire and reached out for her. Anna shook her head and gestured for him to undress.

Scott tore off his clothes, hurling them on top of his parka. When he was naked he knelt in front of Anna on the cream coat. They studied each other for long moments without moving.

Finally, Anna seemed to reach a decision. She spread herself on the coat and the down filling welled up around her. Scott knelt between her legs as if afraid to touch her. Anna reached up and ran her fingers through the auburn hair on his hard chest and let her long fingernails flick lightly over his manhood. She stared at him as if amazed at the reaction.

Scott caught her hands and held them outstretched on either side of her. He lowered himself over her. Anna's breath came in short, eager gasps as Scott's mouth sought for and found her proud nipples.

She fought to free her hands and hold his head, but Scott easily kept her arms pinned down.

Only when Scott had traced a path of gentle bites down to her shaved, plump pudenda, did he release his hold on her arms.

Anna immediately grasped his head as if wanting to draw his mouth into herself. Scott tried to raise his head and move back to the firm, round breasts, but Anna held him in place, moaning softly.

Scott was amazed at her strength.

No, Anna, he thought. You've made all the moves tonight. Now you'll do it my way.

He kept his mouth in Anna's warm flesh and quickly forced her hands up and out of his hair.

He leaned forward and once again found her rigid nipples.

'Don't stop, Scott,' she pleaded, as he once again forced her hands back. 'Please.'

'I won't,' his breath was ragged and heavy with the musk of arousal. 'But we are playing this my way.'

Later, satiated, Anna and Scott lay beside each other, letting the fire dry the sweat on their bodies.

The pale light of day was creeping beneath the door of the cabin as Anna straddled Scott. Her breasts swung heavily above him, but Anna leaned back, keeping them just out of reach of his grasping hands.

'This one we'll play *my* way,' she whispered.

Scott smiled happily and let Anna use him.

The grandfather clock chimed in the corner of the room, waking Anna, who had fallen into a doze beside Scott. She slid away from him and placed some logs carefully on the dying fire. Scott was curled up, fast asleep. Anna tiptoed to her bathroom, changed, showered and flung a blue parka over her flying jacket.

The wooden door squealed as Anna eased it open. Scott moved in his sleep and felt for her at his side.

Suddenly he opened his eyes and sat upright.

'I'll be back later this afternoon,' said Anna, crossing to where he sat on the down coat. She bent down and kissed him, probing his mouth with her tongue. Scott reached out for her, but Anna moved away quickly.

'Do that and I'll never get to work,' she smiled. 'It's lucky I've only one flight today. I don't have the energy for any more.'

'Don't go, Anna.'

'You have a shower. There's food in the kitchen. You'll need your strength, big boy. Build it up while I'm away. How does Chinese sound for dinner?'

'Great.'

'Good. We'll eat here. That way we don't have to get dressed. Bye, lover boy.' And with a wave she was gone.

Chapter Six

THE BRITISH PETROLEUM tower block stood high and proud in midtown Anchorage, defying either seismic or volcanic activity to disturb its clean lines. In summer, bright yellow marigolds outlined the geometric gardens around BP Exploration headquarters. BP Explorations owned fifty per cent of the oil and gas reserves in the Prudhoe field, providing forty per cent of the state's revenue. Ted Dawson was well aware of the importance of the company, and he basked in the reflected glory of the corporate giant.

'Gentlemen,' he said, 'that wraps it for the day.'

The eight men seated at the table shuffled papers in front of them, and clicked open briefcases.

'Just one further thing,' said Chuck Holden, an official from the fields who had flown to Anchorage for the meeting. 'There's a rumour on Prudhoe that you have agreed to sponsor Bud Damas for the Iditarod.'

Ted Dawson smoothed back his fair hair, which hung straight and lank to the collar of his jacket. Money and heavy drinking had taken their toll of his once athletic frame. His stomach now waged a daily battle with the leather belt holding it in. Good food had softened his once rugged features.

Dawson pushed back his chair, crossed his feet on the table and laced his fingers over his stomach, hoping to hide the bulge.

'Rumours,' he said. 'The subject has been discussed. In principle it's a good idea. One of our employees at Prudhoe marries a native, that's good public relations on its own. Then he wants to run the Iditarod and BP Explorations, one of the top five private employers in the state, sponsors him.'

Dawson groped in his pocket and flapped out a large blue and green handkerchief. He blew his nose, carefully wiped around the large nostrils, cleared his throat and fixed his pale eyes on the Prudhoe executive.

'You may tell them that BP Explorations is prepared to sponsor one of our men from Prudhoe.'

Ted Dawson lifted his legs from the table and eased himself upright in his chair.

'See that we get maximum media coverage,' he ordered another neatly attired man at the table.

'Sir.'

But Chuck Holden spoke quickly before Ted could leave the room. He had promised Edwin, his closest friend at Prudhoe, that he would try for a double sponsorship. Now, seeing Dawson's mouth set in a tight irritable line, he regretted his promise.

'Mr Dawson, this is another small point. The Inupiat that this rigger Damas has married is also determined to run the race.'

'Yes?'

'Could BP not sponsor both of them? They are excellent workers, and popular on the oilfield.'

Silence, as thick and deep as snowdrifts, settled over the room. Dawson steepled his fingers and rested his lips on them. Chuck stared at the manicured fingernails pressing into the soft flesh and hoped that he had not jeopardized Bud's chance of sponsorship. He knew Natû wanted to run under native sponsorship, but he also knew that the native corporations were fiscally unsound. The Prudhoe staff did not believe that Natû would find the sponsorship she needed.

Even though Natû was now married to Bud, Edwin's secret love for the girl remained warm and alive. He wanted to see her run the race, and was prepared to coerce everyone to help her attain her dream. He had cornered Chuck before he left and extracted a promise of help.

Damn Edwin, thought Chuck Holden, as the men at the table began to fidget. Why was I suckered into this? I should have let 'Double Dick' Dawson leave.

It's a great name for a guy who has a classy wife like Anna, yet keeps two broads in a cabin in Anchorage and screws both of them. Jerk, thought Chuck Holden. Wonder what he would do if he knew what he was called? Probably lose one of his dicks. The thought made him smile.

Ted Dawson looked at him sourly. 'Is the idea of taking one hundred thousand dollars from the company amusing?' he said, his voice clipped and short.

'No, sir. My apologies, I was thinking of the money I'll take from bets when the new well we are drilling on Prudhoe comes in tops,' said Chuck, thinking quickly.

Double Dick Dawson sat up straight. 'You guys are betting on it?'

'On this one, yes, Mr Dawson. They are through the permafrost and have almost reached the two-mile mark with directional drilling. I should be back in time to rake in the dollars.'

'Good,' said Dawson, a small smile forcing his lips up. 'In exchange for the dollars, you can tell them the good news that the company they work for will do a double sponsorship for the Iditarod.'

'Thank you, sir. I know it will mean a lot to them. Thank you.'

Chuck could not believe that his desperate excuse for smiling had gained the sponsorship of both Bud and Natû.

Dawson swung his chair away from the table. 'That will be all for today. I have another appointment.' He drew back his cuff and looked at his watch, fashioned from raw gold Alaskan nuggets. Chuck thought it ostentatious and in poor taste. 'I'm late.'

Dawson hurriedly left the room. The door banged behind him and the men relaxed.

'Double Dick is off to make sure his reputation remains high,' laughed one of the men.

'Not only his reputation,' added another, and they all laughed uproariously.

'I have enough problems managing one woman. How he keeps the peace between two of them in the same house . . .?'

'If I had a wife like Anna I'd make damn sure that I stayed close to her,' said another.

'Neglect a woman like that, and some other stud will move in.'

'I'm surprised one of the pilots hasn't made a move. She works with those guys in uniforms every day. They say women can't resist a man in uniform.'

'Anna McInnes Dawson is special,' said Chuck. 'Why does she stay with Double Dick?' he asked, not expecting an answer.

Anna was a favourite with the men at Prudhoe. She enjoyed flying to Dead Horse Airport and chatting to the staff who, over the years, had become friends. She was also friendly with the workers at BP headquarters.

'Who knows anything about women, except that they are totally illogical, their behaviour is usually irrational and we cannot live with, or without them,' pontificated one of the executives.

The men chuckled, united in their constant battle with the female sex. Chairs were pushed away from the table and soon the room was quiet and empty.

Chapter Seven

TRAPPER AND Natû decided to start Bud's training in Barrow.

'Let him use my team with the heavy sled,' said Trapper. 'Once he can handle that team in the dark on the flat tundra, he can move up to the treeline.'

They decided that while Bud and Natû ran the dogs along the coastline and over the tundra. Trapper would canvas the native villages that had dog teams, and would try to obtain sixteen good, fast dogs who had heart and loved to run.

Bud and Natû moved into Trapper's home, and their life became a routine of feeding, cleaning and running the dogs.

Sockeye seemed to sense that something important was in the offing. He now strutted stiff-legged to his place at the head of the gangline and snarled at any dog who was fighting or tangling lines.

'Sockeye is now as virtuous as a reformed prostitute,' said Natû. 'He used to be in the front if there was a fight. He usually started them and he was a master chewer of lines.'

Bud nodded a little doubtfully. He was still not certain of the husky who looked so much like a wolf. He kept a wary eye on the dog during training runs, and was happy to let Natû hug and kiss the big husky. He contented himself with a pat on its head.

'I think that in Sockeye we have found the brain for the team,' said Natû, after returning to Barrow from a harsh training run along the coast.

Bud nodded. The winds slanting in from the sea swung the sled and dogs across the tundra as if they were goose feathers blowing in a summer breeze.

Sockeye battled against the gale without hesitation, forcing the other huskies to follow his lead.

'He has the brawn to be a wheel dog,' she continued, 'but we've found a leader.'

'Your leader,' said Bud, folding her in his arms. 'Mine we'll find later. You and Sockeye speak dog talk. I think that wolf understands the wildness in you. He thinks you're also a wolf.'

'Sockeye is not all wolf,' said Natû, defending the lead dog she loved. 'I'm sure that at least his nose and ears are husky.'

Bud laughed and turned to the pails lined up beside the door, to stir what he called slops.

'Whew,' he groaned, 'this stuff stinks.'

'The dogs couldn't run the way they do without it.'

Bud zipped up his parka, lifted a pail and walked outside. The wind punched him in the ribs and he staggered. He recovered his balance and moved behind the house to where the dogs were staked.

The old wooden building broke the force of the wind and he was able to give each dog its allotted amount of food.

He dug into a bag in his pocket and pulled out thin strips of dried beaver. Sockeye was the first to receive a titbit. He gulped it down and looked up eagerly for more.

'That didn't even touch the sides, you glutton,' chided Bud as he moved on to reward the rest of the team for their hard work.

Natû sat and listened to the hysterical barking and yelping of the native huskies as they strained at their chains to reach Bud and the dried beaver.

At the thought of the beaver her stomach churned. She held her hand over her mouth and ran to the bathroom.

As she knelt over the bowl, sickened by the warm, sweet smell of vomit, she railed against being a woman.

'No, Oline,' she pleaded, 'don't let this happen to me now. I must run the race.'

A fresh spasm racked her body, and once again she hung her face into the bowl of the toilet.

Suddenly she was aware that the dogs were silent. An occasional bark told her that Bud had fed them and left. Hurriedly Natû stood up, flushed the toilet and quickly doused her face in cold water in the basin. She gargled with the water, unable to find any mouth-wash. She slapped her cheeks hard, as the face reflected in the mirror was wan and miserable.

Natû pasted on a smile and walked into the central room as Bud rushed in from outside.

'Damn wind,' he groused. 'I'm so hungry I almost ate the dog slop. Is there any stew from last night?'

Natû gagged silently, turned her back to Bud and ladled out a plateful of fish stew. Carefully she selected a small piece of fish, scraped off all the sauce and put it on her plate.

No, she thought, he'll want to know why I'm not eating. Taking a fork, Natû flaked the fish and spread it over her plate.

Bud attacked his food, hardly noticing that Natû was toying with the fish.

'Eat up,' he said finally. 'You'll need your strength, come March.'

Natû thought quickly. 'I'm training myself not to need a lot of food after exercise,' she said. 'That way seal oil, blubber and chocolate will do me on the trail.'

'Oh,' Bud pushed his plate away. 'In that case . . .'

'No. You're a man. You need more than me. Remember that I come from generations of subsistence hunters. We're accustomed to long periods of eating nothing or very little.'

Bud pulled back his plate with relief. He had a large frame to fill, and running with the dogs seemed to burn up all the calories he stuffed into himself.

Natû sighed silently.

He's bought it. He believes me, she thought. The strident call of the phone brought Bud to his feet.

'Probably Trapper,' he said.

He lifted the phone and as he listened, his hand tightened on the receiver. Natû studied the dark hair running down to his wrist. At times Natû fancifully imagined Bud to be Nanuq, the bear who married a woman, denned with her during the black of winter and fathered children on her. It was one of the many Inupiat stories of bears and people that Natû loved.

Bud slammed down the phone, strode across the room, swung Natû out of the chair and engulfed her in a smothering hug. Natû felt her gorge rise. The fish tasted old and oily in her mouth. She could not let Bud know that she was vomiting. He would insist that she go to a doctor and stop training.

He would then know what she was determined to keep secret until after the race.

Doggedly she swallowed back the bile and fish.

'Natû, Natû. We've got it,' he exulted, swinging her round until her head spun. 'That was Chuck Holden. It's official. Edwin persuaded Chuck to ask for sponsorship for both of us. Dawson said okay. Double Dick came up for us.'

Natû caught her breath and swallowed hard as Bud put her down.

'Great stuff, Bud. Now we can buy you really good dogs and gear. You're going to be the best rookie of all time.'

Bud smiled at his wife. 'I certainly have the best teachers of all time in you and Trapper,' he answered seriously. 'This will be some news to tell Trapper tomorrow when he comes home. He won't have to bust a gut for sponsorship. The big boys are dropping popcorn.'

Trapper arrived in Barrow two days later than expected. Persuading the native corporations to part with money was more difficult than he had envisaged.

He was hopeful that CIRI would sponsor Natû for thirty-five thousand dollars, but they were definitely not prepared to find money for Patrick.

The NANA council said that they would give him an answer the following Monday.

There was no barking welcome from the huskies. The house was quiet and empty. Nothing was simmering on the stove.

Trapper slumped into his chair and stared out of the window

as if his eyes were able to pierce the darkness. He felt tired and despondent, and for the first time age reared its hoary head and mocked him.

He sat stroking his moustache until his hand dropped and his eyes closed. Trapper Jack had no idea as to what time it was when the door flew open and in tumbled Bud and Natû. They were laughing and breathless. Neither noticed Trapper sitting quietly in the dark room.

'Come here, my little Inupiat wife,' said Bud, pulling Natû into his arms. Trapper's face was without expression as he watched Bud embrace his daughter. Natû stood on tiptoe and wound her fingers into the dark wet curls on Bud's neck.

'Love you, my musher husband,' she answered.

'So, is Bud now a musher?' queried Trapper softly.

They spun round to face where his voice came from.

'If so, congratulations. You have both worked well. Tomorrow I'll come out and you can show me your mushing skills, Bud.'

Natû heard the weariness in her father's voice, and it made her uneasy. Trapper seemed ageless and indestructible to her. Now he sounded like a vulnerable old man.

She put the lights on and studied her father, but his face showed no sign of weariness or weakness.

'Dinner,' she said. 'It'll be ready soon.'

Natû bustled round the room, setting the table and clanging pots while Bud sat beside Trapper to tell him of the BP sponsorship.

Trapper's face remained solemn, but he listened intently to Bud. Bud ended his story, then threw up his hands in a gesture of disbelief when Trapper was silent.

Trapper's mind twisted like the braided rivers on the tundra, making and discarding permutations about the BP sponsorship.

He knew that Bud's offer to split his sponsorship with Patrick was not feasible. Large corporate bodies required an account of exactly how their money was spent. Giving twenty-five thousand dollars to a friend would not be acceptable.

He would have to persuade CIRI to help Patrick, with his slight claim to native blood, instead of Natû.

Trapper seemed to emerge from his trance as Natû placed a huge bowl of pasta in front of him. She had topped her father's plate with chunks of caribou instead of the bottled salsa, tomato and chilli mixture from the store.

Trapper smiled his thanks and bent low over the plate as he spooned the pasta into his mouth.

Bud blew Natû a kiss and gave her the 'O' sign of appreciation. When in Barrow he ate moose and caribou, but after a few days his stomach rumbled for the taste of hamburgers, french fries, pasta and ice cream.

'Father,' said Natû, when Trapper pushed his plate away and lifted his mug of tea, 'I think Bud and I are ready to run the dogs in Chugiak. It's time to train them on hills and in trees.'

Trapper nodded, blew the steam from his cup and sipped the strong brew.

'I'd like to use the team you've built up here that we've trained with. That way I'll be a native running with native dogs and wearing native gear,' said Natû persuasively.

'But we now have money for both of us, Natû,' said Bud.

Natû shook her head.

Bud looked at Trapper beseechingly.

'If BP sponsor you, Natû, they'll want coverage and their logo on your clothes and equipment,' said Trapper firmly.

Natû tightened her lips, frowned and remained silent.

'It is only right. Fifty thousand dollars is a lot of money. Take it. Use the best equipment. Finish the race, and the following year the native corporations will line up to help you run in traditional clothes using native gear,' he argued.

'Don't let your dream of running the Iditarod fall away because of pride,' said Bud. 'I think Trapper is right.'

Natû was about to answer when she tasted the pasta and salsa in the back of her throat.

'Excuse me,' she said, and disappeared into the bathroom.

Trapper studied the closed bathroom door. There was something different about Natû, but what it was eluded him. He shook his head and turned to listen to Bud.

'Natû suggests that we buy or "rent" about twenty to thirty dogs in Chugiak. We'll train those as my team.'

Trapper nodded and stared out of the window. Bud no longer found this behaviour strange. The Inupiat seemed always to be looking for something in the distance.

'We'd like you to come to the kennels with us to choose the dogs and help train them,' continued Bud. 'There is room for you in the cabin.'

'Thank you. There are good kennels in the Chugiak and Knik area. We'll find strong, fast dogs for you to run,' said Trapper, looking up quickly as Natû entered the room.

She seemed pale and tired.

Probably training too hard, he thought.

'I'd like to watch Bud work the dogs on his own tomorrow, Natû,' he said. 'I want to be sure that he's ready for trees and hills.'

Trapper caught the flash of relief which crossed Natû's eyes, quick as the swipe of a polar bear's paw.

I'll have to watch her, he thought. Perhaps the years she's spent on the oilfield have softened her. The Iditarod does not tolerate weakness. She may have to wait another year before she runs. I should be able to decide when we run the dogs in Chugiak.

It was dark and all was quiet in the cabin in Chugiak. Natû wriggled deeper under the bedclothes. Her toes were cold. Bud turned over, humping the blankets across his wide shoulders, exposing more of Natû's bare feet to the night air.

She sighed and rolled closer to Bud. She nestled her toes between his calves and was rewarded with a startled moan.

'No, Natû,' he said, trying to dislodge her feet from their place between his warm legs. 'No. Not fair.'

'Neither is taking all the blankets.'

Bud was too sleepy to argue. Instead he turned to face Natû, took her in his arms, pressing her face into his chest, and covered her with the heavy blue blanket.

Natû lay quietly until she could no longer breathe, then she pushed herself away from the warm mat of hair covering his chest and gulped in a lungful of air.

She fashioned a cone in the blanket which allowed her to breathe easily, then snuggled up against Bud again.

'Are you awake?' she whispered.

'No, I'm asleep,' answered Bud, knowing from weeks of experience that once he admitted to wakefulness the daily routine of running the dogs would start.

He had read that Buser, an Iditarod champion, said, 'Iditarod racers keep a schedule of Olympic athletes to train their animals, then add on the schedule of a farmer to take care of them.' At the time Bud thought it was merely a clever saying. He now realized that it was true.

Natû was ruthless in her determination to teach him to survive in the Arctic, and meticulous in her attention to every minute detail concerning the training and running of the dogs.

Bud found himself hard pressed to keep pace with her.

But there was one area where he was top dog. He prepared to delay the day's training by exercising this authority. He lifted the blanket and found Natû's ears. He started kissing each ear softly. Natû squirmed into him.

She did not notice the blanket falling away from her shoulders. She buried herself in the warmth of Bud's body, and for a time forgot about dogs and training.

Much later, Natû curled herself into the foetal position. Bud wrapped his arms around her and rested his chin on the soft cushion of her thick hair.

The long, lone call of a wolf punctuated by the yapping of foxes eventually roused Bud, but Natû continued to doze contentedly, unaware of the call which raised a primeval fear in her husband.

The luckiest thing you ever did in your life, Bud Damas, was to marry this little Inupiat, Bud mused, as he eased himself out of bed without waking Natû. He tucked the blanket around her, making sure that her feet were covered.

He moved round the room quietly, careful not to wake Natû, who slept with a small smile of satisfaction on her lips.

Bud closed the door of the bathroom, delighted that Natû had not wakened.

'Bud?' she called, as the door whispered in closing.

'Damn you, door,' he said, kicking the offending wooden planks. 'Coming,' he called, and walked back into the bedroom.

He sat on the side of the bed and pressed Natû back into the pillows.

'Sleep,' he said. 'I'll feed the dogs and clean the lot this morning.' He grinned and placed his finger across her lips as she was about to protest.

'You have done your early-morning duty.'

Natû smiled back.

'I thought you were doing all the work. I was merely enjoying it.'

Bud bent down and kissed her. 'Then enjoy your sleep. I want you to be lazy.'

Duty fought with satiation. Eventually Natû nodded and closed her eyes.

Bud stood over her for a few minutes as if trying to memorize her features. 'I love you so much,' he whispered, and turned away.

Natû made slits of her eyes and watched Bud as he dressed.

You are becoming a good musher so much quicker than I dared hope, she thought drowsily.

Since Bud had completed the five hundred miles of dog-sled racing which was an obligatory requirement before racing in the Iditarod, his confidence and expertise were impressive.

Before Natû allowed sleep to claim her, she made one last effort to join him.

'Bud, it'll take you all morning without me to help clean the lot and feed the dogs. I also have to return the truck to the kennels.

I told them I only needed it to bring the new dogs over, and I'm feeling bad about still having it here. I'll be ready in a few minutes.'

'Want to bet on that?' Bud waved his hand as he left the room. 'Pancakes and blueberries for breakfast. I'm cooking today.'

'But it's not Sunday, your day to make breakfast,' Natû called.

Natû was now able to enjoy food; the nausea and vomiting were nightmares past. She felt well and strong again, and knew that Oline had heard her plea.

'Pretend it is. Love you.' Bud's voice was lost in the slamming of the heavy front door.

Bud stood outside on the decking and looked over the dog lot. It was still dark. The sun would barely breast the horizon by noon. Bud stretched his arms above his head and breathed in great, deep lungfuls of the cold air. The trees which towered over the dog boxes were bare; their leafless branches seemed to hang like bared fangs over the kennels.

The lights at the front door threw a soft glow over the nearest dog kennels, where the huskies were either curled up in their plywood, straw-filled boxes or standing on top of the flat roofs, watching what was happening around them.

The huskies on top of the boxes saw Bud and immediately bedlam broke out. The dogs pulled at their five-foot-long chains in an effort to reach him, and/or their neighbours. Others raced round the axle wheels fixed upright into the ground. The noise was deafening. Bud relished it. He strapped his headlamp onto his knitted cap, dragged out one of the sleds stacked beneath the decking, picked up a shovel and started cleaning up the dog mess.

As he passed each kennel he called the dog's name, and buried his face in its hair as he hugged it. Bud now enjoyed the warm smell of the huskies' thick coats. He and Natû believed that love and praise were the key to success with the dogs. He had learned to hug and pat them without fear. With the knowledge that BP were prepared to sponsor them, Bud, Natû and Trapper had obtained the best dogs available from nearby kennels. They would choose sixteen from the twenty-two dogs in their lot for the race.

'Damn lucky that they came up with the money,' he said, as he methodically shovelled up the faeces and dropped the spadefuls into the sled.

A white-faced husky with pale turquoise eyes nuzzled his arm as he shovelled the ground around its kennel.

'White-out,' he said as he stroked the dog. White-out yapped at its name and tried to leap into his arms. The chain brought it up short. They bought White-out as a lead dog, and paid ten thousand dollars for the well-bred, highly trained husky. Bud loved the dog and the lead dog responded to him. Man and dog seemed to be in telepathic communication with each other. Bud dug into his pocket and pulled out a piece of dried fish for his favourite dog. White-out gulped it down and looked around eagerly for more. 'No more,' said Bud firmly, leaving the second piece in his pocket. 'I'm going to feed you all. Wait.'

Eventually the dog lot was clean. Straw bedding was changed, the faeces buried and each dog received a hug or a pat. Bud looked up at the sky. A thin line of grey, as pale as a sickly child, lay on the horizon.

'Time to feed you.' He turned from the dogs and was about to climb the five broad wooden steps leading up to the decking when a creature the size of a small dog with a bushy tail crept out from beneath the steps.

Bud paused and stared at the creature in amazement. It had lost half of its right ear and the tip of its white tail. Instead of running away, the fox showed no fear of Bud and stood quietly watching him.

Bud crouched down on the step. He studied the red fox carefully. This was the first opportunity he had been given to observe one of these intelligent creatures closely.

'You've been beaten up, little guy,' said Bud, noting that the outsides of its ears were heavily suffused with black. 'Next time, pick on someone your own size.'

The fox fixed its bright eyes on Bud and studied him intently. Bud scrabbled in his pocket for the piece of dried fish he had denied White-out. He took off his glove and stuffed it in his inner pocket to make extracting the fish easier.

'Here boy,' said Bud soothingly. 'You don't look hungry, your coat is thick, but that's probably only winter fur.' The fox edged closer, its tail held low. 'I'm sure you'll go for this. Poor little guy.'

Bud crooned calming words to the fox. He held the piece of fish in his fingers and slowly extended his hand towards the fox, afraid that an abrupt movement would frighten the wild creature away.

Bud held his breath as the fox came to within stroking distance. Its nose seemed to lengthen as it inhaled the strong odour of dried fish.

Bud looked into its eyes and suddenly shuddered as if he had seen a ghost. The mammal's intelligent eyes now had the flat, dead stare of the insane. Before Bud could withdraw his hand the fox flew towards him. He felt a sharp burning pain in his hand as the fox's teeth ripped open his flesh.

Bud sat on the step and stared at his hand in disbelief. Blood, rich and red as the flesh of a freshly flensed whale, dripped onto his faded jeans leaving a dark spreading stain.

The fox streaked past the dog lot and the huskies jerked at their chains in an effort to catch it. They yelped and howled in frustration as the creature nimbly evaded them.

Hearing the dogs, Natû sat up and reached for her jeans and parka. 'I knew I should have helped him,' she muttered. 'He can't manage the lot on his own.' She stuffed her feet into thick socks and wedged them into high duck boots.

The dogs were now in full wolfsong as the red fox vanished between the dark tree trunks and tangle of fallen branches.

Natû flung open the door and looked for Bud among the dogs.

'Quiet!' she yelled. A few of the huskies stopped howling, but the rest kept their heads lifted to the pale arc above them and sang the song which for centuries, terrified man.

A slight movement below the decking attracted Natû.

'Bud?' she queried. 'Bud, are you okay?' Why are you sitting there? Bud!'

Receiving no answer, Natû clattered down the steps and crouched beside Bud. They both stared at the globs of blood soaking into his pants.

'What did you do? How did you cut your hand?' she asked.

'A fox,' said Bud quietly. 'It was a red fox.'

Natû stared at her husband in horror. She put her arms around him and rocked him, so that he could not read the probable sentence of death in her eyes.

Oline, she wailed silently, help me. Don't let one of the other worlds take my husband from me.

As if in answer to her silent prayer to her ancestor, Trapper slammed the front door of the cabin. The hysterical note in the dogs' howls had alerted him.

'What happened?' He moved across the decking surprisingly quickly for a man of his age, to where they sat. Trapper listened to Bud's story in silence.

'Inside,' he ordered. 'We must wash out as much of the saliva as we can while it is still fresh.'

He turned to Natû. 'Do you still have the truck from the kennels?'

She nodded, unable to speak.

'Good. We'll need medical help.'

'But it's only a bite. I've had worse,' said Bud, holding up the hand with two fingers missing.

Trapper and Natû exchanged glances.

'A small bite, Bud, but it's from a fox.'

'Yes?'

'Any wild carnivorous animal which comes to humans or homes and shows no fear must be suspect,' continued Trapper.

Bud dropped his head onto his knees, as if onto an executioner's block. He thrust his arm as far away from his body as he could and watched the blood as if it was a snake writhing in the misty light.

'Rabies,' he croaked. He lifted his head and stared unseeingly at Trapper. Saying the word was the ringing of a death knell to the small group.

Natû's heart constricted as she saw fear replace the horror of realization in Bud's eyes.

'There's a chance,' said Trapper. 'Quickly, into the house. We're wasting time. It should have been washed out with soap and water already. If the fox is rabid the virus is transmitted in the saliva.'

Bud staggered to his feet and leaned on Trapper, as unsteady as a man affected with palsy.

'How much time do I have?' asked Bud, watching Trapper hold the lips of the wound open as he cleaned it.

'I'm not certain, but if the animal has rabies, I think the disease usually develops in four to six weeks.'

Trapper paused and poured fresh water into the wound. 'It can be as short as ten days, or long as eight months.'

'And I felt sorry for the little guy. He looked as if he had been beaten up,' said Bud, holding Natû close to his side as Trapper held his hand in a grip as unyielding as a wolf trap. Bud bore the pain stoically as Trapper probed and scrubbed the raw flesh.

'Perhaps it ran into a fox or wolf in the vicious and aggressive stage of rabies,' said Trapper, wiping his forehead with the back of his hand.

'Natû, did you bring the truck round to the cabin?'

Natû merely nodded, unable to take her eyes off Bud's face.

'Phone the doctor. He should be at Chugiak Medical Centre. Try there. Explain what's happened. Say we'll be leaving here in ten minutes.'

Trapper left Bud for a moment, spun Natû round and pointed her towards the phone. Natû moved to the phone as if walking in her sleep.

'Hurry,' shouted Trapper.

He returned to Bud and poured fresh warm water into the wound. Only when he heard Natû speaking to the local doctor did he relax.

Rabies was a daily threat to Trapper's people as they were in contact with the carnivores which carried the disease.

Trapper had seen the effects of the virus when carried by the central nervous system to the human brain. Pictures of the rabid man, his muscles and face contorting as seizures racked his body, haunted Trapper each time he inspected his trapline.

Trapper tried not to think of the scene that had happened so long ago, but concentrated on Bud's wound.

He shook himself back to the present as Natû replaced the phone.

'Start up the truck,' he said. 'Find Bud's cap. It's cold and he's had a shock. He needs to be kept warm.'

Natû picked up the keys from the kitchen counter and ran outside.

'Watch out for that fox! It may come back.'

Natû stopped in the doorway.

'We'll have to leave a note for Patrick. He said he'd be here for breakfast.'

'Tell him to take the two four three and check the dog lot while we're away. I don't want that fox running amok. He's to shoot it.'

Trapper pulled the navy balaclava down over Bud's ears.

'Leave the doctor's number with him as well.'

Natû nodded. Her hand raced over a piece of paper which she tacked to the outside of the door.

The drive to the medical centre seemed to take for ever, though it was only minutes.

Natû held Bud to her as if she would never feel his body again. She forced her sobs of fear to remain unshed. She had to be strong for the man she adored.

The trees were a blur as the truck raced to the doctor and help. Natû fancied the stiff spruce spines were fingers pointed accusingly at her. You haven't told him about his child. What will you do if he dies raving, and unable to understand what you are saying?

Natû shuddered and closed her eyes, blotting out the trees. Bud felt her shiver and he pressed her head onto his shoulder. Together they waited.

The doctor saw them as soon as they arrived. Trapper waited in the truck and let the two walk into the hospital. Hospitals reminded him of the time he had spent at his wife's bedside, watching her slip away to join her ancestors. Medicine had been unable to save his wife. He now prayed that it could help his daughter's husband.

Bud and Natû followed the doctor into a small, well-lit room. Bud wrinkled his nose at the sharp smell of disinfectant and ether and tried not to look at the tray of instruments and syringes beside the examination couch.

Like most men, he was uncomfortable in the confines of a hospital.

'Tell me what happened,' said the doctor, lifting Bud's hand and examining the torn flesh.

Bud recounted the story, and sat in silence waiting for the doctor to say something. When the doctor kept his head down over the pad and continued writing, Bud spoke again. 'Will this mean that I have to be tied to a bed to keep those around me safe when the virus reaches my brain?' He struggled to keep the tremor from his voice.

'You have been watching too many television shows,' he answered, attempting to dispel Bud's fear.

'But humans do die of rabies,' insisted Bud. 'One of our conservation lectures on the oilfields was about rabies. Now I wish I'd paid more attention.'

Realizing that Bud needed to know more about the virus, the doctor started explaining the nature of the disease, diagnosis and treatment.

Like most patients in shock, Bud heard only parts of the talk.

'Death usually occurs within three to five days after symptoms appear.'

'Abnormal sensations near the wound are an early symptom of rabies.'

Bud felt the flesh immediately tingle around the bite.

'The fear of water is due to very painful contractions of the throat muscles when swallowing.'

Bud swallowed his saliva twice, and was relieved to find it painless.

'You have received treatment well within twenty-four hours after exposure to the virus. Humans are lucky. They have a long incubation period before the virus reaches the brain.'

The doctor pulled his glasses onto the end of his nose and studied Bud over the top of the frames. The movement reminded Bud of his wildcatter father. Suddenly he was back in camp with him reading a five-day-old newspaper. He fought back tears which would shame him.

The doctor pretended not to notice the moistness in Bud's eyes.

Probably shock, he thought. It usually hits the tough ones worst.

'As I explained when you arrived, Mr Damas, rabies is often a fatal disease. We look upon all suspect cases as potentially danger-ous. But, as a human, you have between a one- to three-month incubation period before the virus can multiply and overwhelm the body.'

Natû leaned across and held Bud's hand, which was trembling. He tightened his fingers around hers and visibly relaxed.

If only more people realized the importance of the human touch, thought the doctor. It is one of the great miracles in medicine.

'So you see, we have time to immunize you,' he said, selecting vials and breaking the seal on a needle for the hypodermic syringe lying in a tray on his treatment table. 'I'm giving you a dose of globulin, half of which I'll inject around the bite site.' Bud winced as he looked at the torn flesh on the top of his hand. 'The other half will go into the muscle on your buttock.'

'And as you have never been vaccinated for rabies, you'll also have a dose of human diploid-cell rabies vaccine.'

'I don't understand what that means,' said Bud, gripping the edge of the examination couch on which he was now lying.

'The globulin around the bite will give you some protection immediately. The vaccine will stimulate your body's immune sys-tem to make its own anti-rabies antibodies,' explained the doctor patiently.

'In other words, the vaccine will kick-start his body into

90

fighting any virus which may have remained in the saliva in the bite,' said Natû calmly.

'Exactly. We do have a few things in our favour. The wound was cleaned, or should I say scrubbed, immediately. I think very little saliva remains. Mr Damas has received treatment within twenty-four hours of the fox bite.'

The doctor was silent as he concentrated on inserting and extracting the needle into the flesh around the wound.

'Important to get this in as close to the tear as possible,' he grunted, not lifting his eyes from Bud's hand.

Bud gritted his teeth and closed his eyes. The injections were painful.

'Right. Now, let's have you on your stomach. Jeans down.'

The doctor felt for and found the muscle he needed in Bud's left buttock.

Bud tightened his buttocks in anticipation of the jab.

'Relax, Mr Damas. It's easier if the muscle is not tensed up.'

Bud gasped as the needle stabbed into the muscle. He was pleased that he was lying face down on the examination couch. His buttocks tightened until the muscles would have shamed a bodybuilder.

'Shout if you like. I know it's painful, Mr Damas.'

But Bud kept his lips compressed, though he could taste blood where he had bitten the inside of his cheek.

'That's the globulin; now for the vaccine.' Bud tensed his buttocks again.

'No. You can turn over, Mr Damas. The vaccine is injected into your shoulder.'

Natû hurried forward to help Bud pull up his jeans and strip off his shirt.

The Doctor studied Bud's powerful chest and arms.

The guy is all muscle. He's not going to enjoy this.

Skilfully the doctor felt Bud's shoulder, selected a spot and inserted the needle. He saw the black hair on Bud's chest stick to his skin with beads of perspiration.

The doctor watched as the vaccine emptied into the shoulder.

'Mr Damas, that's the first of the vaccines. We do them on the first, third, seventh, fourteenth and twenty-eighth day after the bite. Take it easy. I'll see you the day after tomorrow.'

Bud paled.

'But I have to run the dogs, clean the lot, train for the race. I can't take it easy.'

'Oh, yes you can,' said Natû. 'And Patrick can take over your dogs until you're fit.'

The doctor nodded and Natû continued: 'Your body needs rest. It has to fight the rabies virus. You now want to exhaust yourself running dogs. No.'

Chapter Eight

SCOTT SAT in front of the fireplace in Anna's cabin, watching the flames twirl around the logs. He was trying to remember how many days he had spent with her. Time was unimportant. He had contacted neither Patrick nor Trapper. He wanted nothing to interfere with his love. Days passed in a haze of longing for the nights, when the rich roar of the Mercedes would announce Anna's arrival.

There seemed to be no end to the inventiveness and depth of their loving. Scott had enjoyed numerous liaisons with women, but he was entranced with Anna, and for the first time he knew the richness of love.

That's what Anna does, he thought, watching the flames touch the wood and retreat. Every time I talk of our future or marriage she retreats. He threw more wood on the fire.

It worried him that Anna refused to commit herself. She would not even discuss it; instead she kissed him and changed the subject.

Tonight, he promised himself, tonight I'll make her give me an answer.

The loud slam of a heavy car door put a stop to his reverie. He jumped up and moved to the front door of the cabin. But before he could open it, Anna rushed into the room.

'Come,' she said. 'Come quickly. I've just heard from the guys at Dead Horse. Bud was bitten by a rabid fox. He may have rabies.'

Scott was dumb with shock. His mouth opened but no words formed.

'Jump into the car. Natû and Bud are with Trapper at their cabin. It's not too far from mine.'

Scott spoke only once during the drive.

'How did the news get to the oilfields?'

'Native whispers,' answered Anna shortly. She was concentrating on holding the powerful car into the corners without losing speed.

'Nothing is secret up here for long.'

Not even us, she added silently.

Suddenly she tapped the brakes and swung the sports car onto a rutted road which seemed to be little more than a footpath in the birch and spruce forest.

The headlights pinpointed dozens of red and green eyes in the darkness. A challenging chorus of barks broke out, which brought a tall bearded man to the door of the cabin.

'Patrick,' said Scott softly. He had not seen his brother since the night of the wedding. He now realized how much he missed him. Scott shook his head as if awakening from a dream. Anna touched him lightly on the arm.

'Go on in to them. Don't worry, I'll be in touch. I know where to find you.'

Sensing that he was about to protest she added, 'I have a very full flying schedule for the next week or so.'

Scott was torn between his desire to remain with Anna, his concern for Bud and the need to discuss his new-found love with his brother.

He took Anna in his arms, and as he kissed her it seemed that he had never known a time without her.

'I love you so much,' he whispered.

Anna was saved from replying by Patrick, who bounded down the steps and flung open the car door.

'Come back soon,' said Scott. 'Promise me that you will. Promise?' he repeated softly.

Anna looked up at Patrick leaning into the car, and she saw only dislike in his eyes. He resented the woman who was the first to come between him and his sibling. Patrick sensed that Anna had taken a part of Scott which she would keep for ever. A part he could not share.

Anna ignored Patrick. She knew who he was, but was not prepared to exchange pleasantries with someone who resented her relationship with his brother.

'Promise,' she answered, not knowing if she could keep it.

Scott enfolded her in his arms, and Anna could not resist a small glance of triumph at Patrick as she curled her arms around Scott's neck.

Patrick, his nerves shredded by Bud's fear and the tension in the cabin, grabbed Scott's arm and hauled him out of the sports car.

'Hey, hold on Patrick,' protested Scott.

'Time for that crap later,' snapped Patrick. 'The family need our support. Bud, Natû and Trapper need us.'

Scott turned to wave, but Patrick tightened his grip, almost lifting his brother off his feet as he hustled him to the steps.

The screech of tyres wrenched into a tight turn at speed greeted Scott as they reached the front door. He turned his head and watched the gloom swallow the red brake lights. It seemed to him that it was Anna's red dress fading and leaving him. An unreasonable sense of loss chilled him.

Trapper was seated in an old armchair facing the window which usually framed Mount Denali. Now her splendour was shrouded in cloud. The sun was still skulking near the horizon and had no strength to brighten the sky.

Scott glanced round the room quickly, searching for Bud and Natû.

'It's day seven,' said Trapper. 'They are at the medical centre, where Bud is having his shots.'

'How is he?'

'Doing well,' answered Patrick. 'They'll be pleased to see you. Finally,' he added pointedly.

'I only heard a short while ago,' Scott defended himself. 'We came immediately.'

'We?' queried Trapper. 'Who's with you?'

'No one. A friend brought me, but she's left. She has to fly today.'

Trapper turned to face Scott. He had noticed the trace of bitterness in Patrick's voice, but had ignored it. Now he thought he understood the reason for the older brother's antagonism.

'Is she leaving on holiday?' asked Trapper.

'No. She is a pilot. She flies for Alaska Airlines. Anna McInnes.'

The name seemed familiar to Trapper.

'She heard about Bud when she flew into Dead Horse late yesterday. It was Anna who drove me here. She's a great girl.'

'Yes,' said Patrick sarcastically. 'Instead of brains, your skull is full of hormones. You know nothing about this woman.'

Trapper looked up sharply. First he studied Patrick's set expression, then he looked at Scott, as if trying to read his innermost thoughts.

A confident man stood before him, a man willing to defend his right to love the woman of his choice, even if it meant alienating the brother he admired.

'There comes a time in a young man's life when the wish for a mate, the need to have his own woman, overwhelms him. It seems that Scott burns with that fever, Patrick,' said Trapper quietly.

'He's too young and is certainly not thinking straight. He disappears for over three weeks and no one knows where he is. He doesn't care if Mother is crazy with worry about him. He does not even contact us.'

Suddenly Scott realized that his sojourn at Anna's cabin had caused distress to those he loved. 'Sorry Trapper. Sorry Patrick,' he said. 'I really did not think. You're right, bro, I must have exchanged brains for hormones. But . . .' he added, 'Anna is marvellous and I'm going to marry her.'

Patrick stared at Scott, his face pale and expressionless.

'Not now I hope,' said Trapper lightly, hoping to break the tension. 'We need you to help with the dogs. Bud has to rest for the next two to three weeks.'

'Sure,' answered Scott with a smile. 'Did you get the fox?'

'No. It's probably dead by now.'

Scott spun round as icy air gusted into the room.

'Scott, it's great to see you.' Natû stood on tiptoe to kiss him. Bud closed the door and stamped his feet.

'Damn cold out there today. Good to have you here, Scott.'

Scott scanned Bud's face, but could find nothing unusual in his demeanour or his clear, steady gaze.

'Great to see you. Sorry it took me so long to come, but I've just heard the news.'

'I should have known better,' said Bud. 'Lived in Alaska almost all my life, tied up the dogs in Barrow every day. I come here and feed a wild fox. I suppose I asked for this.'

He looked down at his hand as he gingerly pulled off the thick glove. Scott pointed to the bandage.

'Still painful?'

'No. This is only to stop my glove rubbing the scar. It's still a bit tender.'

'The injections?' queried Scott, having heard horrendous stories of the pain associated with anti-rabies injections.

Bud glanced at Natû.

'That's another story. They seem to be really bad,' she said. 'But Bud's taking them well.'

For the next hour the cabin resounded with loud voices as the four young people exchanged news. Once they had eaten, Trapper stood up. They listened as he outlined the training schedule.

'Father?' said Natû when the old man sat down. 'Patrick and Scott can work Bud's team for him and do the dog lot. You don't need me here. My team are ready for a good run.'

'Yes?' said Trapper warily, as if sensing what Natû was about to say.

'I know that Bud is out of danger,' Natû squeezed his arm.

'Yes?'

'I want to do the run to Rohn, stay overnight in the Rohn hut and start back the day after.'

'You're talking about a hundred to two hundred miles,' said Scott.

Trapper smoothed down his moustache and ran his fingers through the thinning fringe hanging over his forehead.

'Rainy Pass can be hell in the high heavens in March. You'll be on your own now, with no back-up. I'm not even sure that the dogs are ready.'

Bud saw Natû's face set and her lips compress.

Let Trapper fight this one, he thought.

'I'll run with her,' said Patrick quickly.

'I can give Bud's team a taste of what real running is about.'

'Don't break their hearts,' warned Trapper.

Natû let out her breath. She was not aware that she had been holding it.

'Remember, the dogs must want to run. It has to be enjoyable. If not, you'll have a lie-down strike on your hands, and unless you are ready to carry each dog home, you'll stay out there with them.'

Patrick laughed.

'We'll treat it as a fun run,' he said. 'I'd love to do it.'

'Some fun!' said Bud. He had read every book available on the Iditarod, and was worried now that Natû wanted to climb the three-thousand-foot Rainy Pass through the Alaska Range. She seemed tired lately, and he noticed that she was not eating well. He thought it was due to the fright she had had when she believed he would die of rabies. But if she wanted to spend a few days trying out the dogs on the trail, she was less worried about him.

I wonder what has happened to her? he thought. She'll probably tell me when she's ready.

Bud knew that Natû could not be pressed into disclosing her feelings. He would have to wait until she confided in him.

Chapter Nine

THE TANTALIZING aroma of salami, sun-dried tomatoes, olives and cheese pressed into pizza dough baking in the oven filled Anna McInnes's nostrils. Anna was hungry and was waiting impatiently for the pizza she had ordered to be packed into a box.

She was tired and irritable as she drummed her fingers on the counter top. She had flown from Seattle to Anchorage, picked up her car and was on her way to the Iditarod Trail Committee's permanent headquarters in Wasilla.

The girl behind the counter at the local Pizza Hut in Eagle River studied Anna. Envy and dislike clouded her expression.

Bet she eats the whole damn pizza and it doesn't make any difference to her figure. But let me have a slice and my scale adds on the pounds, she thought. It's not fair.

Anna glanced at her watch. She did not notice the diamonds twinkling in the bezel. She was concerned only with reaching Wasilla before Claire left her office in the log cabin.

'Hurry it up, please,' said Anna, leaning over the counter. The move outlined her firm buttocks and long, strong thighs, to the delight of a group of local males waiting for their fast-food orders. One of the men whistled softly and appreciatively.

The girl serving Anna dumped the pizza into the box, crumpling up one side.

Good, she thought, hope she has indigestion. She and the men watched as Anna walked to her car.

Anna dropped the box onto the passenger seat. She would break off pieces and eat as she drove.

Twenty-nine miles, she thought. That won't take long. I'll catch Claire.

The curved Iditarod headquarters sign spanning the road and held high by two sturdy wooden poles told Anna she had reached her destination.

Anna licked her fingers clean and brushed the crumbs from her lips as she spun the red Mercedes into the parking lot and zipped up her parka before she stepped out. The tall spruce trees were bending to the wind. She flipped the fur-lined hood over her head and drew the drawstrings tight beneath her chin.

Anna breathed in great lungfuls of the oxygen-rich air. She felt good. The pizza was tasty. The lights were still on in the cabin, which meant Claire would be there. She was certain that she could persuade her college friend to let Scott help in the Iditarod.

Anna pushed open the heavy log door and walked into the cabin. The door to Claire's office was closed, a sign that she was busy. Anna wandered over to where the packed Iditarod sled rested. It still amazed her that people relied on that relatively small sled to hold all they needed to survive for two weeks in one of the most hostile yet beautiful areas of the world.

For years she had flown small aircraft along the winding one-thousand-mile trail. Looking down on the tracks winding like snail slime over a frozen ocean, she wondered if the mushers would run the race if they could see the terrifying immensity of the wilderness beforehand.

'Anna?'

Claire came out of her office and walked to where Anna was admiring the Perpetual Victors Iditarod Trophy. The large silver cup stood high on its two-tiered base, engraved with names of the winners of the race. Anna was never certain as to whether the winged figure on the top with her hands clasped high above her head was a symbol of victory or an angel.

'Hi, Claire, good to see you,' said Anna, studying the huskies on the four corners of the base of the trophy, guarding the cup.

'In my book it's probably the best trophy in the world,' said Claire. 'The mushers and dogs bust their guts to win it. Hold that victor's trophy and you hold a piece of heaven in your hands.'

'Probably the closest most of the guys will ever get to heaven,' laughed Anna. 'Claire, I need to talk to you. Do you have time?'

Claire nodded. She was pleased to see Anna, but unhappy about the news she had to give her friend. Claire closed the door of her office and motioned for Anna to be seated.

'Claire. I know you're always short of volunteers for the Iditarod.'

Claire nodded and waited for Anna to continue.

'I have a friend. A guy I've met. He's a mad-keen Iditarod fan and wants to help me with the food drops and picking up dogs. I could do with some muscle.'

Claire said nothing, merely fiddled with a pile of brightly coloured paper clips. It was not the reaction Anna had expected. She faltered a little as she continued.

'It'll speed up my time. He's also one of Bruce's pupils at Birchwood. He will probably run as a rookie next year. You would be doing me a real favour if you let him sign on as a volunteer, Claire.'

Anna stopped talking and waited for her friend to reply.

Claire looked ill at ease, and shifted uncomfortably in her chair.

'I'm going to do you a favour by what I'm about to tell you, Anna.'

She picked up a pink paper clip and pulled at the loops until it was a straight piece of pointed metal.

'I was in Anchorage a few days ago. We're trying to work out a new system to make it easier to control the ten to fifteen thousand fans who cram into the city for the start of the race.'

'Yes?' said Anna quietly.

'There's a rumour that Ted is reconsidering the sponsorship of Bud and Natû Damas.'

Anna listened without paying attention. In Anchorage stories spread like spilled oil.

'Probably native whispers,' she replied carelessly. 'I'm sure Bud will have recovered from the bite and be fit for the race.'

Claire twirled the clip unhappily between her fingers. She did not want to be the one to destroy her friend's new-found happiness, but she had to protect Anna.

'No Anna. It's more serious. Ted knows about you and the Butler boy.'

Anna stared at the pink clip in her friend's fingers.

'How could he?' she said, so softly that her full lips hardly parted.

Anna's mind raced. She numbered and discarded friends and acquaintances who could have told Ted of her and Scott's involvement.

'Probably those whispers again,' said Claire sympathetically.

She did not like Double Dick Dawson, and felt that Anna deserved to find love elsewhere. But Ted Dawson was a powerful man, and their committee was obliged to court sponsors.

'No one knows about my cabin. Ted was not at the wedding. We left the Cook unnoticed. Fourth Avenue was empty when we climbed into my car. No, Claire, he cannot possibly have found out about Scott.'

Claire shook her head and her long grey plait swung over her shoulder.

'Even if he does know about Scott, why should it bother him? It never has before. He knows that I see other men occasionally. It seems to please him. Gives him an excuse for his two bedmates,' said Anna, the first trace of bitterness edging her voice.

'Oh, he knows all about the cabin and Scott. There are no secrets up here in the Forty-ninth, Anna. This is Alaska, remember? The Forty-ninth state may be large but it is sparsely populated.'

Anna shook her head as if denying Claire's news.

Anna slumped back in her chair. Her husband must have paid to have her followed. But why? He was happy with his menage in Anchorage.

They met only when he needed her as a decoration, a prize to be flaunted.

He showed Anna off in public, as proudly as hunters pose beside trophy animals they have shot.

Claire leaned across the desk and placed her work-hardened hand over Anna's slender fingers. The touch seemed to jerk Anna from her confusion and shock.

'Why Bud and Natû?' she said, sitting up straight. 'What do they have to do with Scott? And why is he anti-Scott?'

'Probably feeling the effects of middle age. People no longer think that he's a bull with two cows to service. They now see him as a guy trying to hang on to his youth and virility. He's become a figure of fun. It's the sort of thing Ted cannot accept. You and Scott have pricked his pride. No pun intended,' Claire said with a smile.

Anna thought about Claire's explanation; it made sense.

'But Claire, why punish Bud because he thinks I am serious about someone else?'

'Some men are vain and stuffed with pride. When you deflate either the pride or the vanity they become irrational. Ted knows that Patrick and Scott Butler spend most of their time with Trapper Jack. They are his godchildren. Trapper is a powerful native voice and an eloquent speaker. He is openly opposed to exploration for oil in the Refuge and has recently addressed the Republican chairmen on the subject. Ten-0-two is his baby. Needless to say, he is not one of Ted's favourite people.

'Trapper's daughter Natû is married to Bud, as you know – you met Scott at their wedding.' Claire watched Anna closely as she continued. 'Your husband has been doing his homework and does not like the answers. Suddenly he realizes there is a strong link between Scott, the couple he is sponsoring and Trapper Jack.'

'Right. I understand Ted's dislike of Bud and Natû, but their link with Scott is tenuous, and as I've said, he has ignored other guys I've met.'

Claire straightened a yellow clip and laid it beside the pink one on her desk.

'How many guys have you taken to you cabin, Anna? None.'

Claire answered her own question. 'If the whispers are true, you have been tucked up with Scott for over three weeks.'

Anna rubbed the back of her neck. Time had escaped, while she spent every spare moment with Scott, secure in the knowledge that none knew of their relationship and she could indulge in her passion.

Her friend's words had numbed her with the sharp, painful shock of breaking through thin ice and dropping deep into black water. Anna felt as if her lungs were constricting and she gasped for air. She missed the first words Claire said.

'Ted probably feels threatened. He calls Scott your toyboy.'

The words infuriated Anna. She could imagine the mocking sneer on Ted's face as he sullied her relationship with Scott.

'He's only two years younger,' said Anna defensively. 'And in many ways he is a lot older.' A shiver tickled the base of her spine as she thought of their lovemaking.

'Two years is a lifetime when your husband is looking back on his youth and feeling the first aches of middle age,' said Claire. 'Anna, you have to stop seeing Scott. Break it off publicly. That will satisfy Ted, and I know he will not withdraw the sponsorship. His pride will be restored.'

'No. Definitely not.'

Claire lifted the heavy plait from her shoulder and threw it over her back.

'Anna, please be sensible. Do this, help your friends. Help Scott. If he means anything to you, stop seeing him.'

The look on Anna's face made Claire long to enfold her friend in her arms and rock away her anguish.

Anna stared out of the window where soft, fat snowflakes were patting the panes. Now that she was faced with the necessity of leaving Scott, she realized that he had become a major part of her existence in a very short time. The thought of Scott not being in the cabin every evening was unbearable.

Think, Anna, she urged herself silently. Think. Don't let Ted manipulate you again.

As slowly as the sun clawing its way above the horizon

to mark the end of winter, a solution dawned. Anna smiled inwardly.

'Claire,' she said. 'Forget that I asked you to let Scott act as an Iditarod volunteer. I know that you'll see Ted before I do. Tell him of our conversation and say that I've already found someone else. Scott is not for me. My affair is over. He can relax.'

Claire's forehead furrowed like deep snow ridges. She kept her hand on Anna's and searched her eyes, but found nothing except innocence. Claire sighed. She had succeeded. She could tell Ted that Anna was reasonable, and that Scott was merely a passing fancy.

She had helped avoid the embarrassment which the committee would suffer if sponsorship was withdrawn after all the publicity it had received.

Anna pushed back her chair and embraced Claire as they walked to the door.

'You're a pal,' she said. 'Thanks for telling me about Ted.'

'Anna,' said Claire as her friend pushed open the heavy wooden door. 'Is your fling with Scott really over?'

'Scott who?' laughed Anna as she bent her head, keeping the puffs of snow from her eyes.

'Scott who, indeed,' she muttered angrily as she ran across the snow to the car park.

Anna was about to swing the car in a tight squealing circle when she became conscious of Claire watching her through the window. She reversed slowly, blew a kiss to Claire and drove sedately away from the Iditarod Trail Committee Headquarters.

As Anna passed beneath the headquarters' sign spanning the road, she slammed her fist onto the steering wheel until the pain in her knuckles forced her to stop.

'Damn him, damn him,' she shouted to the birch trees, which linked bare branches as they lined the road. The dark trees swayed and nodded as if in agreement. 'Damn Ted to hell.'

Chapter Ten

TRAPPER CHECKED the two heavy-duty sleds. He could not shake off the sense of unease that chilled him like a ground blizzard.

He kept glancing around the lot, trying to rationalize his fear. It was the same feeling he experienced as a hunter when he sensed, but could not see, the animal. It was an innate knowledge of danger. Trapper was too old and wise in the ways of the wilderness to dismiss what his subconscious was trying to tell him. Yet he could not stop Patrick and Natû from starting the run to Rohn cabin by telling them that he was disturbed.

Instead, he drew out his inspection of the packed sleds.

'Dog food?' he shouted at Natû, who was putting Sockeye into his bright red harness.

'Patrick's sled,' she yelled, as she finally secured both tuglines to Sockeye's straps.

Trapper looked on with satisfaction. Natû worked quickly and professionally.

She will be all right, he thought. Patrick is with her. I'm just getting old and nervous because she is mine, and I have experienced again the joy of having my child with me.

Trapper walked over to where Patrick was strapping Bud's team into their blue and yellow harnesses. White-out stood quietly looking back over his shoulder at the rest of the dogs jumping and barking as Patrick connected their necklines to the gangline. Quickly Patrick clicked the heavy brass snaps on the tuglines into the loops at the back of the harnesses.

'Not using toggles?' asked Trapper, thinking of the traditional

106

ivory toggles the natives used which were cheap, did not freeze and could be used without removing one's gloves.

'No. Only the best high-tech stuff for Bud. So it's brass snaps,' laughed Patrick.

The huskies who had not been chosen to run watched the proceedings with dismay. They lifted their heads and wailed in unison. Their song of woe seemed to excite the huskies already connected to the two ganglines. They added their hysterical yapping and barking to the wailing of the dogs in the lot.

'Father,' said Natû. 'If we don't leave now they'll hear this noise in Anchorage. Please don't let Bud work the dog lot until the doctor says he's okay. Scott has agreed to take over.'

Trapper walked past his daughter and put his hand on Patrick's arm.

'Look after her,' he said quietly.

Patrick nodded. He was too amazed to answer. Trapper never showed emotion.

'You'll be okay here?' he said, afraid that something was wrong with Trapper.

Trapper gave the young man he loved a rare smile.

'Yes. May the trail be good.'

'Line out,' shouted Natû.

Sockeye immediately pulled the gangline tight.

'Good,' she applauded the husky.

Natû had arranged for Scott to take Bud to the medical centre, then to collect food and veterinary supplies for the dogs so that he would not see them leave. She knew how hurt he was that Patrick would be running the dogs with her.

'Tell Bud I love him. See you in a day or two.'

Trapper lifted his hand and nodded.

'Let's hike,' she shouted to Sockeye.

Natû's team leaped forward and she hung onto the handlebar as the sled lurched and bumped up the hill.

She glanced back to see White-out bounding forward as if he could pull the sled alone. The large dog's hind legs seemed to overtake his front ones as he raced to catch up with her team.

'You're not going to trash-talk my team, then do a dog gloat as you pass them and take the lead, White-out,' she shouted.

As if he heard her, Sockeye strained forward in his harness and Natû's team felt the surge down the gangline. They responded to their leader. The gap between the two teams widened.

'So, it's a competition, is it?' muttered Patrick keeping his team to the side of the road. 'Okay. Wait until we hit the hills.'

The dog teams raced along, happy to be running, excited because they were not on their usual route. Natû laughed out loud. Life was good. She was doing what she loved best. She felt well and strong. She was now certain that her pregnancy would not interfere with her running the race.

My ancestors stopped working and rowing umiaks only when birth pangs forced them to rest. Why should I be different? It's a normal thing that my body is designed to accept. No one has guessed my secret, so I'm safe. I'll be the first pregnant woman to run under the burled arch in Nome.

Bud will be there to meet me, and I'll tell him that there are now two of us for him to love.

Trapper waited outside until the whisper of sled runners on snow and the soft footfalls of the huskies were no longer audible. He then climbed up the steps and lowered himself carefully on the top one. He stared out over the dog lot, trying to dispel the sense of loss which threatened to overwhelm him.

The huskies stopped howling. Some crept inside their huts to curl up in the straw, others stayed on top of the boxes staring in the direction taken by the two teams. The occasional moan marked their anguish at being left in the lot.

Long hours passed. Trapper leaned his head against the wooden rail, his wrinkled eyelids closed and he slept.

A flash of strong headlights raked the lot, arousing the almost quiescent dogs to a further hysterical pitch of excitement.

Trapper looked up as a metallic silver Dodge truck swung into the level area which was used as a parking bay beside the cabin.

Scott swung out of the driver's seat and ran round to help Bud, but Bud had slammed the door and was on his way to the house. He was growing weary of being treated like an invalid.

The thought of Patrick running his dogs while he stayed home, shovelled faeces and waited for his final anti-rabies shots, galled him. He longed to be away from roads, cars, fast foods and people. He wanted to be alone with Natû where the snow-covered mountains rose so high that they tore the dark cloth over them. Where one heard only the wonderful sound of silence.

Bud sank down on the step beside Trapper with a sigh.

'Natû and Patrick have any problems with the dogs?' he asked Trapper, hating to have to ask, but needing to know the details.

'No.'

'Who left first?'

'Natû, with White-out trying to catch her,' smiled Trapper.

'He won't. That girl drives the dogs with her mind. It's weird.'

'No, Bud. Natû uses the power of her subconscious, primeval mind. It's something you cannot rationalize. Like the dogs, she senses the land.'

Bud nodded. 'She's a special girl, Trapper, and I'm one lucky guy.'

'You will be if you stop feeding foxes,' said Trapper drily.

Bud grinned and they watched Scott walk round the truck, inspecting it closely.

Hank had given it to the two boys on their eighteenth birthday, and years later it still looked new. The Butler boys knew how Hank had saved to buy the expensive Dodge, and they were very proud to own a truck which most mushers valued as much, if not more, than the cash prize of fifty thousand dollars that went with a new Dodge to the winner of the Iditarod.

'How Scott loves that truck. He treats it like a baby,' said Bud. 'A baby!'

Suddenly everything was sickeningly clear to Trapper.

I've been a blind fool, he chided himself silently. I should have known. Her mother was the same. Pale, listless. Running to the bathroom. Not eating. Then all at once, everything was normal.

No, he thought. I have allowed my daughter to do the run to Rohn and she bears a child.

'No! No! No!' he groaned aloud.

Bud looked away from Scott and the truck and stared at Trapper.

'What's happened?' he said, alarmed by the note of desperation in Trapper's voice.

'Did you know?' whispered Trapper. 'Did she tell you?'

'What? Who?' said Bud, now truly worried about his father-in-law.

'Natû,' said Trapper.

'What's happened to her? Where is she?' shouted Bud. 'I knew we should not have gone to Anchorage after the doctor, but Scott wanted to leave a letter for this Anna McInnes at the airport. Then we picked up the stuff Natû wanted for the dogs. It took almost the whole day. Damn. I should have been here.'

'Perhaps yes. Perhaps no,' replied Trapper enigmatically. 'Natû listens to her own silence. It is not easy to change her.'

'But you've just said everything went well,' said Bud, staring at Trapper as if trying to read his mind.

Hearing the rising hysteria in Bud's voice, Trapper decided not to tell him of his suspicions. It could do no good. It was a task Natû would have to perform. Now he must think of something to calm Bud.

'I promised that I would let friends in Skwentna know that Patrick and Natû are coming through. There's nothing at Yentna Station. They have the check-in tent there for the race, but it's deserted now.'

Bud still looked unconvinced.

'It's the first time that they are on the actual route and they'll need a hot meal with friends. Patrick says it is a fun run, so time is unimportant.'

Trapper climbed heavily to his feet. 'Would you and Scott do the dog lot? I started, but did not finish.'

'Sure.'

Remembering Natû's words, Trapper added, 'Only if the doc has given you the okay.'

'He has,' lied Bud, eager to do some physical work.

'Come on, Scott,' he called. 'Leave your baby. Let's shovel shit.'

Scott grinned.

'My favourite job.'

As he swung the shovel, sweat broke out beneath Bud's woollen cap and he whistled softly. It was good to be out in the cold working around the dogs.

Bud had become used to the huskies since he had acquired White-out and Clarke. They no longer reminded him of wolves. Clarke's unconditional love made him realize why some people loved dogs above humans.

Trapper hurried inside to contact his friends in Skwentna. Patrick and Natû should be nearing Yentna Station. It is only fifty-two miles to Skwentna. He would ensure that they had a good meal and a rest with Kiluk and Herbie Owens before criss-crossing the infamous Happy River Canyon, followed by the steep, narrow ascent to Rainy Pass.

Now that he was certain his daughter was pregnant, Trapper feared the trail to Rohn.

Chapter Eleven

NATÛ'S HUSKIES broke out of the forest. Natû was relieved to see an open stretch of frozen marshes. Small ice ponds nestled in them like diamonds on a gemologist's velvet tray.

Her eyes followed the trail to where it dropped down to the Susitna River.

From media coverage of the race, Natû knew that until they reached Skwentna they would be winding up and down hills, through dark spruce forests and following sections of the Yentna River.

She looked behind her to check on Patrick. He surprised her with his expertise at handling Bud's team. He was strong, confident and the dogs responded to his commands.

As White-out came into view Natû mushed her huskies onto the open land. She laughed with delight as she heard Patrick urging his team to greater efforts.

'My team has more heart,' she said. 'That's one thing money cannot buy. Bud's dogs are perfectly bred, but mine are born to run and they want to please me.'

The wind shredded her words before they reached Patrick. He saw only her sturdy body handling the heavy sled with the ease of a strong man.

Natû was drunk with happiness. Her dream of running the Iditarod would become a reality within a couple of months.

'We're going to make it, baby,' she sang to her unborn child. 'You and I are going to look up at the widow's lantern swinging beneath the burled arch in Nome. We are going to run the race together.'

Natû stopped crooning to the child cushioned in her womb and guided her team up a hill cloaked in spruce trees.

'Trapper and Bud will be so proud of us.' She stopped talking as the gangline ran slack and she sensed fear run down its length. Her dogs were telling her something. But what?

Natû strained her eyes trying to penetrate the gloom which closed in and around the yellow beam of the headlamp strapped to her forehead. She struggled not to panic as she moved her head from left to right. Her headlamp cut the darkness like a laser. The fear she sensed in her dogs now transmitted itself to her.

Although she was wearing the caribou parka that Oline had left for her, Natû felt the cold fingers of dread that herald the unknown creep between the insulating hairs on animal-skin clothing. She shivered.

Patrick's headlamp was but a small, bobbing firefly a long way behind her. Thoughts of demons, controlled only by shamans, blackened her mind and threatened to take away her reason.

'Sockeye,' she screamed. 'Sockeye, talk to me. Tell me what you see.'

As if in answer to her call, the lead dog veered from the trail and raced blindly into the thicket of trees to the left, pulling the rest of the team behind him.

Natû hung onto the handlebar and tried to drop the snow-hook to stop the team. The giant barbless fish-hooks did not hold fast.

Natû had no time to stamp them in. She quickly swung them out of her way on the bungee rope. She had seen what damage they caused when embedded in flesh instead of snow.

'Whoa,' screamed Natû. 'Whoa, Sockeye, whoa!'

The wind played with her frantic commands. It lifted the words and twined them in the dark branches of the pines where they could not be heard by Sockeye.

As her strong wheel dogs running closest to the heavy sled swung round it to follow Sockeye, Natû's headlamp caught and for a few seconds held a pair of eyes, as cold and bright as glare ice.

She had to look up at the eyes, which were at least two feet above her.

'No,' she breathed as she discerned the fleshy, yard-long dewlap hanging from the animal's throat. She turned her head sharply and the yellow beam touched the pointed tines of the ruminant's enormous palmate antlers. 'Moose!' Natû's throat contracted and terror overrode common sense. The fear evident in her huskies transmitted itself to her.

She clung desperately to the curved handlebar of the sled, trying to guide it around the trees, as Sockeye raced along wildly, straining to pull the team away from the moose who stood unmoving, contesting the right of way to the trail.

Natû remembered stories of one of the contestants who had to scratch from the race because a moose rushed into the team, killing and injuring the dogs, and was only stopped when a fellow musher arrived and shot it.

She had not brought a gun, and Patrick was behind her with his gun in Bud's sled.

Natû was afraid. She was scared and vulnerable. She could no longer see the comforting glow of Patrick's headlamp. She could not rely on him for help.

'We must get back onto the trail,' she spoke out loud to reassure herself. 'Patrick will not know where we are.'

Nervously she looked behind her, hoping that the two-thousand-pound animal was not following. It could move surprisingly quickly with its stiff-legged, shuffling gait.

'Sockeye,' screamed Natû. 'Please get out of here. You'll have us killed in this place.'

She choked back a sob. This was not the time to give way to fear and panic. 'Please, Sockeye, please.'

Again Natû shivered. She felt impending danger. The black branches hit her as she used the handlebar to tilt the sled on the edge of its runners and swerve round obstacles. She knew that unless they left the forest and found the trail, she would not be able to handle the sled. It seemed to become heavier each time she edged the runners.

Natû tightened her grip on the rawhide which both bound and strengthened the handlebar. She tilted the sled automatically as her huskies ran round and over obstacles she could not see.

The team followed Sockeye as if they were running on fresh hard snow on the open trail.

'Gee!' screamed Natû in desperation. 'Gee!' Sockeye heard the single command. As if weary of playing hide-and-seek in the spruce forest, he turned right immediately. The team followed him.

Because Natû had shouted to him so often and he had not heard her commands, she was unprepared for the sudden sharp change.

Trees and branches flashed by, black skeletons in the beam of her headlamp. The huskies hurtled beneath the low branches of a birch. Natû ducked to avoid being hit by a heavy branch. As she did so there was a sickening crash. The arrow-shaped brush bow protecting the front of the sled crashed into a huge fallen spruce. Natû was thrown from the sled runners and the heavily laden sled slammed into her stomach.

As she fought for breath, Natû thought she was dying. Pain as sharp and deep as a steel snowhook embedded in flesh, tore into her ribs and stomach.

Her back burned with the ferocity of a runaway oilfire.

She was unable to move a limb. Natû lay in a crumpled heap in the snow, listening to the faint barks of her dogs as they dragged the damaged sled away from her. She was certain that she had cracked her spine and was paralysed.

Blood pounded in Natû's ears. Her head drummed. She thought it would explode. Gingerly she tried to draw a deep breath. Her lungs craved oxygen, but the pain in her ribs prevented her from breathing normally.

Natû remained curled up in the snow. Her arms were crossed protectively over her stomach as if they could reverse the damage done by the collision with the fallen tree trunk.

She lay still, trying to sense the baby in her womb. After the initial smash she felt no further pain: perhaps the soft watery bed had protected it from the violent impact. Natû forced herself to believe that she would not feel stomach pain again. The foetus would survive. It must. She could not lose Bud's child.

As her breathing eased and her head cleared, Natû assessed her situation. The dogs would keep running, pulling the laden sled behind them. Hopefully it would tilt onto its side and slow them down. Sockeye would almost certainly head back for the trail once the rank odour of moose no longer forced him to run in panic. Perhaps Patrick would find her team and come to look for her. The thought of seeing Patrick filled Natû with hope, until reason told her that it was unlikely he could find the place where her team had bolted into the woods.

It would have to be midday before the weak light thrown by the sun still hanging onto the rim of the horizon helped him.

Time seemed to have stopped with her fall. All was silent. She was alone. Her headlamp slipped down and hung around her neck. It was her lifeline to sanity. Gradually she found that she could breathe in short shallow gasps.

'Oline,' she whispered, 'be with me. You were the only mother I knew. You waited for death on the ice with strength and dignity. Give me your strength. Share it with your daughter.'

A cold silence answered her plea.

'I'll have to spend the night here,' she said loudly, as if the sound of her voice would dispel wolves, moose and the demons of the dark.

Natû tried to lift her arms and snap the headlamp around her forehead, but pain gnawed like ravenous wolves at her ribs.

She dropped her arms and waited for her breathing to slow again, before gingerly and slowly lifting her hand to where the lamp rested in the hollow of her throat.

Her fingers were clumsy in the thick gloves, but she managed to hold the light and swing it from side to side. It formed a golden crescent in the dark.

She shook her head when she saw the fallen spruce.

'Sockeye, how did you and the team bypass that with a smashed sled?' she said.

The sound of her voice comforted her. She trained the light

onto the snow, looking for a place which offered protection from the wind and a snowdrift into which she could burrow.

'You're lucky, Natû,' she told herself. 'It's only a three-dog, not a twelve-dog night,' referring to the number of dogs she would need to sleep under to keep warm. 'That looks good,' she said.

Snow lay piled against the dark bole of the fallen tree. Natû tried to lift herself onto her hands and knees and crawl to the trunk, but pain pinned her down. The headlamp dropped onto her chest and shone through the orange neck warmer, which drooped loosely around her neck.

She managed to inch her body around until she was curled up with her back to the wind. Painfully she tugged her fur-lined hood over her head, knowing that she would conserve fifty per cent of her body heat if her head was covered and warm. Then, like her ancestors, she hunched her head into her shoulders, closed her eyes and let sleep slow down her respiratory system.

A faint howl brought Natû back to reality.

'Sockeye,' she breathed, 'you've come back.'

But it was not Sockeye.

The bare twigs of the branches concealing where she lay seemed to splinter the approaching yellow glow into a dozen eyes.

Wolves? Natû closed her eyes. The lights seemed to surround her. Natû did not want to see them.

The moose, satisfied that the dog team had given way, moved off the trail searching in the snow for Alaska willow, its favourite food.

White-out arrived at the spot where the moose had forced Natû's team from the trail. He stiffened and his pace slowed. The other huskies felt his unease and stopped pulling. Tuglines went slack. Patrick dropped the snowhook and tramped the great curved hooks into the snow. He walked down his team, talking to the dogs and patting them. He reached White-out, but could see no reason for the lead dog's sudden refusal to run.

'Come on, boy,' he cajoled, 'Natû will be in Skwentna by now. Sockeye will trash-talk you, when you jog in hours after him.'

Patrick gave White-out a final pat, fondled the husky's ears and went back to the sled.

'Hike,' he roared as he released the snowhook. White-out listened but followed a scent only he could trace. He led the team into the spruce forest away from the moose.

'Trust your lead dog,' Trapper had said. 'It could save your life.' The old man's advice rang in Patrick's ears and he contained his anger at being led into the dark spruce forest. It was both difficult and dangerous running at random through the trees.

'You'd better have a good reason for this, White-out,' he muttered, 'or you'll be just one of the team. I'll find another lead dog for Bud.'

Patrick cursed as he tried to anticipate and negotiate the sled around the black pines, fallen branches and tree trunks. It was a nerve-racking ride.

He turned the sled sideways to miss a tree trunk which loomed up in the darkness.

'White-out!' he yelled, with little hope of the dog hearing him. 'Get out of these damn trees. This is moose country. I don't want to tangle with one of those bad-tempered beasts in here. Listen to me. Trail. Back on the trail!'

A faint bark answered him; but it came from the left side of the sled, not the front, where White-out was running.

Hearing sounds far beyond the capacity of the human ear, White-out slowed down. Sockeye barked again. The cold air ran the bark to where Patrick's team heard and understood it. Though they still had the smell of moose strong in their nostrils and needed to run from it, they answered Sockeye immediately. Within minutes the forest reverberated with the excited yelping, barking and howling of the two teams.

Patrick was stunned. What were Natû's huskies doing in the forest? He let White-out lead him to where her carefully packed sled had finally wedged itself in a tangle of rotten branches, helping to stop the bolting dogs.

The huskies were snapping at each other and biting the gang-line in a futile attempt to free themselves.

Before he could stop them, Bud's dogs rushed into the mêlée. Within seconds Patrick was faced with a musher's nightmare.

He had to separate two teams of fighting dogs. He put down the long prongs of the brake behind his sled and dug the snowhook well into the snow before throwing his sled over on its side.

'That should hold mine,' he said as he strode down the gang-line, wrestling his dogs back into place. He could feel the sweat soaking his underwear. Quickly he unzipped and dropped the top half of his sled suit. Patrick knew that damp skin loses heat about twenty-five times faster than dry skin, and he still had a lot of hard work ahead to untangle and quieten Natû's team, who were spinning round and dancing on their hind legs as if rabid.

'Come on, damn you,' he snapped as he manhandled her heavy wheel dogs back into their places on the gangline. Sweat dripped into his eyes and he quickly brushed it away with the back of his glove.

'I don't need hypothermia because you jerks won't behave.'

Trapper had drummed the 50.50.50 law of survival into Scott and himself when they were youngsters.

He remembered it now: if water is at fifty degrees, a person has a fifty per cent chance of living for fifty minutes.

'Damn,' he muttered as his heavy glove caught while trying to untangle one of the tuglines from around a dog.

'How did you manage this?' he groused at the husky, who still strained to reach the dog behind.

Patrick was about to pull off his glove when he remembered that flesh freezes solid in thirty seconds with thirty-mile-per-hour winds and a temperature of minus thirty degrees.

'The old thirty-thirty-thirty rule. Thanks, Trapper,' he said.

Patrick took a deep breath.

'You're not going to beat me,' he muttered. 'Not you dogs, or you, Mother Nature. I can take all the crap you have and more.'

Eventually the excited and frightened huskies settled down. Patrick was so preoccupied with the dogs that he had pushed the sickening realization that Natû was missing to the darkest recesses of his mind. But now he had to allow the knowledge to flood his brain.

'Natû,' he screamed, cupping his hands to his mouth. 'Natû!'

Only the heavy silence answered him. He pulled up his sled suit and zipped it closed.

'She must be nearby,' he muttered.

Making certain that the two teams were well separated and unable to free themselves, he unclipped Sockeye from the gangline.

'Let's see if you can track Natû,' he said. But as they moved away, the harnessed huskies howled and tugged at the sleds and snowhooks with such ferocity that Patrick turned back.

He knew that if both teams bolted, he and Natû would have to answer to an unforgiving master, the wilderness. It did not tolerate fools.

He led Sockeye to the top of the gangline and clipped him back into position. Patrick did not want to believe that Natû was hurt or in danger, but as he studied her sled with the shattered brush bow, fear as cold as the snow at his feet froze his stomach.

'Behave in the line, Sockeye,' he said. 'We may need the sled to carry Natû.'

Patrick walked back to the sled and manoeuvred it away from the branches. He examined the runners and breathed out heavily when he realized that it would still run.

'I'll replace the runners in Skwentna,' he said. 'Now let's find Natû.'

Sockeye waved his husky tail, and his lips seemed to lift in a grin as Patrick gave the command to move on.

The dogs moved more slowly now as Patrick kept the brake down. It caught on hidden branches and rocks, breaking their stride. Each time they paused, Sockeye looked back at Patrick reproachfully.

'You lost Natû,' shouted Patrick. 'Now find her.'

Patrick swung his head from side to side as he ran beside the sled, praying to find Natû. He had stopped calling as he needed his breath to run. They seemed to have run in circles for hours. Patrick was composing what to say to Trapper when a patch of light snow caught his attention. It seemed to be something gleaming under a large birch.

Probably an old trail marker that somehow ended up in this dump, he thought.

Sockeye was now pulling so hard that the team seemed to be falling over their paws to keep up with him.

Patrick negotiated the broken sled around a large fallen spruce which blocked their way.

'Sockeye, are you crazy or something?' he shouted. 'We need the stuff on this sled. Slow down. Whoa!' he bellowed.

But Sockeye was deaf to commands, pleas and entreaties. He scented Natû and was determined to reach her.

Suddenly the gangline went slack and the team stopped running. The huskies sat down and stared around them as if amazed to be off the trail and resting in the forest. But Sockeye jumped and pulled at his necklines as if desperate to run.

Patrick braked the sled.

'No more bolting,' he warned the dogs as he walked towards the patch of orange-tinted snow. Patrick squinted as he tried to see what was causing the faint orange glow ahead of him. It was not bright enough to be a trail marker.

His headlamp caught the bare, hag's-hair branches of the birch. The steady beam splintered like wolves' eyes as it filtered through the twigs, making it difficult to see whether the dark mass on the ground beneath the branches was an animal or a tree stump.

Suddenly Patrick realized that the orange glow came from a headlamp shining through cloth.

'Natû,' he said tentatively. 'Natû?'

The huddled figure sat as unmoving as a grizzly on its daybed.

Patrick moved forward slowly, folding his long frame beneath the low branches. Blobs of snow fell and melted on the shoulders of his purple sled suit.

Patrick bent down and played the beam of his headlamp over the dark mass, wary in case it was a sleeping animal.

The steady light now held the wolverine fur of Natû's hood.

Patrick felt bile bitter and strong rise and threaten to flood his mouth. He was sick with relief. He did not have to tell Trapper that his daughter was lost or dead.

Patrick put a gloved hand on Natû's bowed shoulders. He started as she shrank away and kept her head bowed.

'Natû. It's me. Patrick,' he said loudly.

Sockeye, tired of sitting still while in harness, barked at Patrick, inciting the rest of the team to join in the chorus.

The barking of the dogs lifted Natû's head from her knees. She looked up at Patrick and her shoulders shook with silent sobs.

Patrick knelt beside her in the snow and rocked her until she was still.

'Tell me about it,' he said, holding her close to him.

Words poured out as Natû relived the terror. She did not mention the pain, afraid that Patrick would not let her continue with him.

Patrick listened in silence. He admired Natû's courage. It had taxed his strength to manage a pelting dog team in the forest, yet when her team bolted, taking with them everything she needed to survive, she had not given way to panic but huddled up, conserving her energy.

This was the sort of woman he would find when he was ready to settle down and have a family.

Natû's voice grew louder as she spoke and Patrick's fear abated. Natû was well and strong. At last she was silent.

'Are you hurt?' he asked, realizing that she had not mentioned any injury to herself.

Natû shook her head. Patrick held out his hands to help her stand. Natû gritted her teeth, determined to run her dogs to Rohn.

But will-power was not enough to keep her standing. She sagged against Patrick as pain tied knots around her stomach and back.

'Into the sled bag,' he said.

'No,' whispered Natû, trying again to stand upright. Patrick caught her as she tottered.

'You are not acting like Trapper's daughter,' he said sternly.

'You'll be all right after a rest and we can go on. But you'll ride in the sled bag to Skwentna.'

The idea of riding in the sled instead of handling it suddenly seemed attractive to Natû.

'Okay, Patrick, you win,' she said, though she dreaded the thought of walking to where he had left the sled.

Before leaving her side to open the sled bag, Patrick pulled a piece of muktuk from his pocket.

'Eat this. It'll warm you,' he said.

Natû chewed the dried chunk of whale fat and skin with relish. It would give her extra energy and keep her body temperature up.

Patrick watched Natû chew the muktuk, then, satisfied that she was eating food that would help her, he walked to the sled to prepare it to carry her to Skwentna.

He zipped open the heavy nylon bag which rested in the framework of the sled. He checked that the Velcro fasteners and tab buckles were holding it securely to the sled. Working quickly, he repacked the gear and patted his pocket to make sure that the revolver was tucked into his sled suit. He wanted to be prepared if they encountered Natû's moose again.

He unrolled the warm sleeping bag and laid it in the sled bag.

'Shut up, Sockeye,' he shouted as Natû's lead dog lifted his long throat to the treetops and howled. He knew that the teams were ready to move.

Sockeye needed to run. Sitting in the forest with his senses alert to strange sounds and smells made him nervous. He sensed Patrick's unease and Natû's pain, and he wanted to do something he understood. He wanted to lead his team out on the trail.

'Shut up!' Patrick did not usually snap at the dogs, but he was more worried about Natû than he allowed her to realize. He stood still for a moment, debating whether he should try to take his team across to Natû, or carry her to the sled with the possibility of causing some serious injury.

One glance at Sockeye decided him. If Sockeye saw him release Bud's team, he would go frantic to join them.

'I don't need another knock-down, drag-out fight with you dogs,' he said.

Patrick trudged back to Natû. Her face was drawn and ashen.

'Where is the pain?' he said in a hard voice. He now realized that she had lied when she denied being injured.

'My stomach,' she whispered.

'I'm going to lift you and carry you to the sled, Natû. Moving you will be easier than controlling two teams of crazy dogs, who think they can hurtle through this forest as fast as they do on the trail. Okay?'

Natû breathed in deeply and nodded. Patrick lifted Natû. She remained in the foetal position, holding her knees. Patrick staggered and stumbled back to the sled. It was difficult to hold Natû against his chest and not squeeze her ribs. At last his boot bumped the sled runner. He handled Natû as if delivering a newborn baby.

Yet she could not control a gasp as he held her over the sled bag.

'There,' he said, as he pulled up the double zips of the sleeping bag. 'Comfortable?'

Natû nodded. She could not trust herself to speak.

Patrick zipped the large nylon sled bag shut. Only Natû's fur hood showed.

'You look like a husky,' he said, hoping to hear her laugh.

But a grimace was all Natû could manage.

'We'll try to get out of here in stages,' he said. 'Your team can't move. I've seen to that.' As Patrick said it, he glanced at Sockeye. 'One twitch from you and you're no longer a lead dog.'

Sockeye seemed to understand him. He curled up and tucked his nose under his thick tail. The others followed suit.

'We'll go towards the trail with Bud's team, letting White-out find the way. I'll stake the team, leave my gun with you and come back for your team. Hopefully the dogs will find the trail. I'm damned if I know where we are.'

Natû nodded. She could think of no better solution.

'We'll do a "follow-my-leader" till we hit the trail,' said Patrick with more conviction than he felt.

Chapter Twelve

KILUK OWENS put down the phone. The line was bad. It crackled, and Trapper's voice kept breaking off, but she heard enough to know that his daughter and Patrick should have been in Skwentna hours ago.

'Rookies,' she said. 'Rookies doing a run to Rohn. Trail not prepared. No officials on duty. They could be anywhere or dead,' she added sombrely as she let the door slam behind her and walked to the barn to find her husband.

'Who's dead?' asked Herbie, looking up as his wife waddled into the small barn beside their old log cabin.

Herbie had been born in the cabin, which stood where the Skwentna and Yentna rivers converged. The check-in point for the Iditarod race was now below their cabin. Before 'coralling' was the rule, all mushers had to stay in one place. Mushers looked forward to a warm welcome and a hot meal in the Owens's cabin.

'Who has died?' repeated Herbie, bending over the sled he was crafting. Herbie was a purist. He used no nuts, screws or nails when he crafted a racing sled.

Kiluk pulled up a small wooden chair and sat close to Herbie. She enjoyed watching him lash the babiche, steam-bent birch, into place with rawhide strips.

'This one is special,' said Kiluk admiringly.

Herbie grunted.

'You haven't answered my question,' he said, bending over to check that the babiche lashing the upright supports to the runners was holding them firmly in place.

'Rawhide is best. Allows the sled to give on bad trails instead of smashing up.'

Kiluk nodded. Herbie Owens had a waiting list for his Eskimo-style handcrafted sleds, and she was proud of him.

'Trapper phoned.'

Herbie looked up sharply. 'About the Ten-0-two and the Refuge?' he asked.

His wife was a relative of Trapper's, and was as firmly opposed to the controversial bill as was Trapper himself.

Herbie was inclined to view the subject more leniently. He felt that, provided the oil companies' activities were closely monitored by the Wildlife Agency, and they took every care to replant damaged tundra flora and respected the fauna, then they should be allowed to take oil from the rich oilfields. But Herbie did not dare say this in front of Kiluk.

She was an Inupiat, and a member of one of the famous mushing families in Ruby where she was born. She sided with Trapper, as did most of the 'sourdoughs' and natives.

People born in the marvellous wilderness of Alaska are allowed a taste of heaven on earth. They are very protective of their earthly paradise.

'Trapper phoned about his daughter Natû,' said Kiluk, and waited for her husband's reaction.

As Natû predicted, news of her return with Bud had reached all the outlying villages.

Herbie's sharp blue eyes studied his wife, but her face was expressionless. He knew that he would have to prise the information out of her. It was a game she enjoyed playing.

'What did Trapper say? And who has died?'

'He must be losing his senses,' answered Kiluk, regaining some of the indignation she felt earlier about Trapper allowing two rookies to run to Rohn.

Herbie nodded as Kiluk gave him the story. His strong, stubby fingers continued twisting and tightening the rawhide strips.

'They have both completed the shorter races, which enable then to enter for the Iditarod,' he reasoned. 'And Natû was brought up in Barrow – trapping, fishing and mushing are all in her blood. They may be rookies to the Iditarod veterans, but they are hardly newcomers to mushing. Though,' he paused, 'I can't say the same for that rigger of Natû's. Surprised Trapper is allowing him to enter. He is a real rookie.'

'I promised Trapper that we would arrange for our dog team and perhaps a snowmobile to go towards Yentna Station and see if they need help,' said Kiluk.

'Snowmobiles,' snorted Herbie, running his hand over the curved handlebar of the sled. 'Machines can't smell the trail. Dogs will sense and find Natû's team. If they are not here by lunchtime we'll hit the trail. We'll have the best light of the day, and may pick up tracks.'

Kiluk smiled. She was satisfied.

'I'll phone Muktuk,' she said. 'He's always ready to run dogs. If anyone can find them, he will.'

'Good.'

Herbie was pleased the matter was settled. He would have the sled completed by lunch, and could devote his attention to the rescue.

'The dogs are probably having a sit-down strike,' he said. 'It's not their usual run. Muktuk Peters will find them lying in the middle of the trail. He'll get them running. Dogs may not love him, but they sure respect him. When he says "Hike" they move.'

Chapter Thirteen

TED DAWSON stared at the whisky. It rolled smooth and amber over the ice cubes in his glass. He crossed his feet on the desk and settled comfortably into the leather chair. He smacked his fleshy lips in satisfaction as the alcohol warmed his throat and stomach.

Things were progressing well. Plans were advancing for the large charity ball and banquet he was arranging. His team ensured that there would be extensive media coverage, with emphasis on the fact that all proceeds were to go to Fish and Wildlife Management.

That will help sweeten the pill with 10-0-2, he thought. If I can swing the Refuge decision, then my future with BP is red carpet all the way to the top.

The thought brought a smile to his face and his secretary, still seated to one side of the boardroom table, shuddered involuntarily.

Whenever he felt the urge to humiliate her, Double Dick Dawson used his position of authority to run his stubby fingers up her skirt and around the edge of her panties. He knew that she disliked him, but as a single mother she could not afford to lose her job. Dawson knew this. It excited him to have his secretary at his mercy. He enjoyed watching her cringe as his broad fingers explored her intimate parts.

Anchorage was no longer a boom town. Since the Exon-Valdez oil spill had been cleaned up, thousands of workers had returned to the Lower Forty-eight, as Alaskans referred to the rest of America.

'Ms Robbins,' he said, taking a large swallow of whisky.

His secretary froze, steeling herself for what was to come.

'Come here. Stand beside me. I wish you to take notes.'

'Sir.'

She moved across and stood away from his chair.

'Put the pad on the table where you can write properly.'

'Sir.'

She bent low over him to place her notepad on the table.

'Good,' he crooned, as her blouse fell open at the neck exposing cheap, plain underwear. 'Good. Very good.'

His hand shot into her blouse and his thumb and forefinger closed around her nipple. The woman gasped as pain spread through her breast. She stood still, gritting her teeth, hating the man.

'Take this down,' he ordered, still pinching and kneading her soft flesh.

Her hand trembled as she wrote the words.

'Contact my wife. Tell her to meet me at our home at eight p.m. tomorrow night.' Dawson stopped speaking and his secretary paused with her pen still poised above the page.

'That's all. You can go now,' he snapped, suddenly tiring of the games he played with the unfortunate woman.

'Sir.'

She backed away, loathing the way his eyes ravished her body. She wanted to go home and scrub herself until her flesh was red and painful. How she despised him.

I hope Anna is up in Barrow or some other forsaken place and can't meet the jerk, she thought as she closed the door of the office quietly behind her. Anna must have been drunk or brain-damaged when she agreed to marry that piece of slime.

The secretary pulled a tissue from her leather folder as she waited for the lift. She surreptitiously slipped her hand into her blouse and wiped the breast and nipple Dawson had touched.

As the door closed, Ted swung his legs from the table, adjusted his trousers and crossed to the bar. He held the decanter over his glass until the whisky filled half of the tumbler.

'Here's to you, Dawson,' he toasted himself. The phone rang. He swore and lifted the receiver.

'Sir. It's Claire from the Iditarod Centre. She says it's important.'

'Put her through.'

As Ted Dawson listened to Claire's explanation, he grinned.

'Thanks, Claire. Of course our sponsorship stands. In fact, I may be able to increase it. Yes, I will honour our commitment to the Damas team. You've done well. Thanks again.'

'Now to see if this is merely one of Anna's stories,' he said. 'Claire believes her, but I want proof.'

He ran his finger between the folds of skin under his chin, then slowly nodded. He fumbled in his trouser pocket and dislodged a black cellphone. This call would be private. His two bed-bunnies would spend tomorrow night alone; perhaps the next few nights. It was time for Ms Anna McInnes to perform her wifely duties as Mrs Ted Dawson. She could also grace his arm at the charity dinner. That should dispel the whispers circulating Anchorage that his wife was deeply in love with her Butler toyboy. The thought of demanding his marital rights excited Double Dick.

'To me,' he said, draining the dregs in his glass.

Anna McInnes Dawson was tired. She walked into Anchorage Airport with her head bowed. Her blonde hair, pulled back from her face in a tight French pleat, caught and held the glow from the brightly lit halls and passageways. She clutched two unopened envelopes in her hand. She recognized the handwriting on both, but had no wish to read them.

'Native whispers,' she fumed. 'There's always some truth in them, but by the time they are three days old, like fish, they stink.'

In Barrow she had heard that Natû and Patrick were overdue in Skwentna, and there was already talk of a search party. She longed to be with Scott to comfort him. Anna knew how close he was to his sibling.

'Damn,' she said, as a party of tourists bumped into her. 'I wish I hadn't told Claire that it was over with Scott. She will have phoned Ted and he'll be gloating, that's probably what this letter is about. I'll have to read the damn thing, but first, Scott's.'

Anna leaned against the wall and slit open the letter which Bud and Scott had left at the airport for her. Tears welled in her eyes as she read.

I have nothing but myself to offer you, but that will change once I have graduated . . . I now know that I need you to make my life complete . . . I will love you for ever. Scott.

Anna choked back a sob and ripped open Ted's letter. As she read the cold words her face hardened and then paled.

Oh, no, she wept silently, how could I ever have told Claire that Scott meant nothing to me? How could I have been so young and blind to marry Ted Dawson? I've messed everything up. I have to be the one to break the news. He must not hear it from anyone else.

Anna tucked Scott's letter tenderly into the pocket of her flying jacket. She tore Ted's into squares, which she then ripped up until it scattered into the bin like confetti.

'Hi, Anna.' Two pilots walked past her, their heavy flight cases bumping against their legs. Anna did not look up, but continued tearing the paper into tiny pieces.

'The guy who wrote that is in for a bad time,' laughed one of the men.

'Yeah, Anna is a great girl, but I wouldn't want to upset her.'

'She's as tough as any guy,' answered his friend, nodding at an air hostess.

'Tougher.'

Double Dick Dawson sat on the cream settee listening for the sound of Anna's car in the driveway.

He stood up and moved to the front door as Anna gunned the engine then switched off the ignition. She was still in her flying clothes, and her lips curled down in distaste as she saw her husband filling the doorway, blocking the entrance to their home.

His pale blue sweater served only to emphasize the bulge above his belt and the roll of flesh resting on the polo neck.

Anna walked up the wooden steps and as she neared him she smelled whisky, warm and sweet.

At it again, she thought.

Anna tried to squeeze past Ted without touching him, but his arm shot out and he swung her off her feet. Her first instinct was to kick him, then she remembered Claire's warning. She laughed. It was a poor imitation of a laugh, but it worked.

'Mrs Dawson, you look great, better than I remember,' he said. 'In fact, so good, I think a closer inspection is necessary.'

Anna felt sick. What she feared had happened sooner than she expected. The thought of having his hands exploring her body, the body she had given so freely to Scott, nauseated her.

'I have to bathe and wash my hair,' she said. 'I came here straight from the airport.'

'Sure. Don't be long. See you in the bedroom.'

Anna grimaced as she walked into the house. Ted had bought it for her as a wedding present. But Anna spent most of her time in her cabin, and came to the house only when necessary.

As she sat in front of the mirror combing her wet hair she searched in vain for an excuse to keep away from her husband. Eventually her hair was dry and hung in a heavy golden cape over her shoulders.

You have to do this for Scott, she told herself as she slowly opened the door to the bedroom.

This will make Ted believe that it is truly over. Scott need never know what I've done. It'll be my secret.

Ted lay sprawled on the bed. He was naked, and watched Anna with bloodshot eyes. An empty tumbler stood on the table beside the bed. Anna studied his soft body with distaste. She hesitated.

'Take off your gown, baby. I want to see you.' Ted slurred his words slightly.

Anna picked up a glass from the bedside table.

'Another whisky?' she asked, hoping that a large tot would put him to sleep.

'No. Come here.'

Anna moved to the bed as slowly and carefully as if she were walking across ice.

'Kneel over me. You know what I like,' he snarled, as she stood uncertainly beside the bed.

Anna steeled herself for the ordeal. She stifled a gasp as he swung her over his body with her taut, muscular buttocks pressing hard against his mouth.

'Go on,' he said. 'Or do you reserve that for your toyboy?'

At the mention of Scott, Anna lowered her head over Ted and soon heard him groan with pleasure. Anna watched him convulse dispassionately, then attempted to climb from the bed.

'Not so fast, Mrs Dawson,' said Ted, grabbing her leg. 'I haven't finished with you yet.'

Anna forced the revulsion from her face.

'Good,' she said. 'I've missed you.'

'Heard you had a young stud,' said Ted, studying her expression.

'What, that kid?' answered Anna derisively.

Ted grinned. He'd show her exactly what she had been missing.

Women are all the same, he thought. Think they can hold down a man's job and they get cocky. But it's a different story in bed.

Scott, thought Anna, this is all for you. How I despise him.

As Ted moved over Anna, she drove all thoughts of Scott from her mind. She did not want her love sullied. She was afraid that if she allowed the image of the tall, auburn-haired boy to intrude, she may think it was him and not Ted with her, and she wanted to hate the experience.

'There,' puffed Ted, raising himself and looking down at Anna. She turned her head as rivulets of perspiration streamed down his face and plopped into her eyes. The salt made her eyes smart.

Ted's breath was stale with whisky fumes, and thin, blond hair plastered his forehead.

Anna managed a weak smile.

'I must go to the bathroom,' she said.

'Was that good?' Ted called after her.

'Wonderful,' she answered as she locked the door. About as wonderful as a rutting moose, she added silently.

'Better than the Butler boy?'

'I've told you, he's only a kid.'

'Remember eight o'clock tomorrow night.' Her husband's voice was muffled and indistinct.

'I'm flying.'

'No, you're not. I've asked them to reschedule as we're attending the BP charity dinner.'

Anna bit her lip. She wanted to contact Scott as soon as possible, and find out if there was any truth in the rumours about Patrick and Natû. She also realized that she now had to tell him about Ted.

She had been lost in a make-believe world in their cabin, but Claire had wakened her to the possibility of someone telling Scott about Ted before she had a chance to explain the situation to him.

Anna walked into the sitting room as the clock in the corner struck eight.

'On time. That's good,' said Ted, rolling a cigar from one side of his mouth to the other. 'Thought you were going to wear the red dress.'

'No. It's in the laundry,' lied Anna. The red dress was only for Scott; she would not wear it for Ted.

'That black is great, if your boobs stay in,' he said, eyeing the plunging neckline.

'They will. I wanted to look good at the function.'

'You will. The guys' tongues won't stay in their mouths when they see the show you're putting on.'

He ground his cigar into a large cut-glass ashtray.

*

Ted made a show of walking round the long black Cadillac and opening the door for Anna. He was conscious of the television cameras and photographers from the newspapers swarming as thick as mosquitoes round the car.

'One pose, Mr Dawson,' called one of the men, lifting his camera.

Ted turned to face him. He wrapped his arm round Anna's tiny waist and managed to cup one of her breasts with a meaty hand. Before Anna could pull away, the flashlight blinded them.

'Thanks, that was great.'

'Any time,' shouted Ted expansively.

Anna drew away from his embrace and, lifting her long skirt, walked up the stairs and into the hall. She was furious that Ted had manoeuvred her into a position of intimacy in public, but she fixed a smile on her face and prepared to spend a long evening mouthing platitudes and avoiding her husband.

Chapter Fourteen

TRAPPER JACK eased himself into the old armchair opposite the window. He moved slowly, as unsteady as an invalid. Scott watched him in dismay.

Trapper is old, he thought, as Natû had. The knowledge chilled him. Trapper had been his childhood hero. He idolized the elderly man, but still thought of him as young and strong. The knowledge that Trapper was in the autumn of his years saddened and frightened him.

'Coffee, Trapper?'

Trapper nodded. Lost in thought, he stared at the window as if willing the majestic Mount Denali to throw off her cloud and show herself.

The strident call of the telephone jerked Trapper from his reverie. Before Scott could lift it, Trapper's hand closed over the black receiver. Scott understood none of the clicks in the language but he shivered as Trapper's usually expressionless face hardened. Trapper spoke for a long time without interruption. He replaced the receiver gently and turned to Scott.

'My coffee?'

Scott was stunned. He expected Trapper to discuss the call.

'Sugar?'

'We're out.'

'Let's go and get some.' Trapper shrugged on his old parka and led the way to the truck.

He decided to tell Scott and Bud about Patrick and Natû when the Owens family found them.

They are still young, and the blood runs hot in their veins. If I tell them now, they'll go racing off to Yentna Station and we'll have four people lost, thought Trapper as he and Scott climbed into the truck.

'Don't answer the phone if it rings,' Trapper shouted to Bud, who was mixing dog food. 'It's my cousin in Skwentna and she speaks no English.'

'Okay. Buy some gum, Scott,' Bud replied, and turned his attention to the dogs.

Trapper left Scott to buy the sugar. He took the truck to be refuelled. When he returned, he walked up and down the aisles looking for Scott. He heard Scott's voice behind him.

'Ready to roll, Trapper.'

Trapper looked at the trolley brimming with food.

'Sugar and gum?' he laughed.

'It all looks so good, especially when it's cold out. Patrick and Natû will enjoy the cookies and chocolate bars.'

Trapper smiled.

'Okay. Let's see if we can pay for it.'

Scott left Trapper to pay for the groceries and wandered past the cashier to the shelves that were crammed with dog food. Most of it was aimed at the mushers. He idly read the list of ingredients on a few packets, and then, plunging his hands into the front pockets in his parka, he strolled back to the checkout counter to help Trapper.

A stand holding the daily newspapers and popular magazines caught his attention. He paused. There was something familiar about the half-hidden face on the folded newspaper. Scott pulled it from the rack. The world spun. He thought he was losing his senses. *Mr and Mrs Ted Dawson photographed as they were about to enter the BP charity dinner in Anchorage last night.*

Scott studied the photograph closely, there was no mistaking Anna's face and body. As he scrutinized the woman he loved, he noticed Ted's hand cupping her breast.

'No!' he shouted and ripped the paper in half. He let the one section fall to the ground and held the piece showing Anna's head and the self-satisfied smirk on Ted Dawson's face.

'Hey,' called the woman at the checkout counter.

'It's okay. Put it on the bill,' said Trapper softly. 'He can't help it. Gets like that sometimes.'

The woman nodded. She was used to strange behaviour. Wild countries often attracted wild people. She motioned for the young boy to continue packing the groceries into bags.

Scott remained standing with his back to Trapper clutching the torn newspaper, oblivious to the disturbance he had caused.

'Come,' said Trapper, pulling him towards the door. 'We'll talk in the car.'

Scott followed him blindly, stumbling over the sill of the sliding doors.

'Get in, I'll drive,' said Trapper as he tipped the store boy and opened the blue door of the truck.

They drove in silence. Trapper waited for Scott to speak. The young man sat brooding. He punched the wadded ball of newspaper repeatedly into the palm of his open hand, as if smashing Ted Dawson's face.

'Take it easy, Scott,' warned Trapper eventually. 'You can't manage dogs and a sled with only one good hand.'

Scott punched the paper ball once more, then slumped back in the seat.

Trapper glanced at him. The boy's eyes were closed but his tapered fingers turned the wadded paper round and round, trying to smooth it out.

Two faces appeared as Scott spread the wrinkled sheet across his knee.

Trapper recognized Dawson's fleshy face. The woman seemed vaguely familiar, but he did not know her. He forced his mind to focus on the shining white snow stretching as far as the eye could see. Unblemished. Pure.

He smiled and tugged his drooping moustache. It worked. By clearing his mind of trivia, he remembered Anna. She was the pilot who flown him to Deadhorse and Anchorage.

'Want to talk about her, Scott?' he said. 'Sometimes it helps sort things out in your head.'

Scott shook his head in denial, but started talking.

'Married? How can Anna be married? She would have told me. We love each other, and love has no secrets.'

Trapper nodded, and moved the wad of gum to his other cheek.

'She does love you, Scott. I could see that when she came to the cabin.'

'Then why lie? And about something as important as marriage?'

'Perhaps she is not happy in her marriage. Unlike our people, you can't just walk out and find someone else. Once you've signed your certificate, it's a long and ugly process to break the contract.'

'But look at the pig she chose,' said Scott, close to tears with shock and anger.

'Why choose him?' He hit the paper with his fist. It tore, leaving Ted with one eye and half a mouth.

'Perhaps she was young. He is powerful. Power and money are both strong aphrodisiacs for young women. They usually mature, then regret it.'

Scott opened his eyes and stared at the black trees as if seeing the world for the first time.

'Anna's no bimbo. She is an intelligent woman. No, Trapper. Your theory may work for a kid, but not Anna. There is no excuse. She used me and lied to me.'

'Men and women often lie to one another. They are different creatures trying to live together. It is difficult. If they came together only to mate, then went their separate ways, like many of our animals do, there would be more peace between the sexes.'

In spite of his anguish, Scott managed a thin smile at the picture painted by Trapper.

Trapper saw the smile and relaxed.

The worst is over, he thought. He'll survive this. Young love is always painful. The experience either breaks them or makes them stronger. Scott will be more careful next time. Perhaps his head, and not his genitals, will lead him.

Scott picked up the shredded newspaper and studied Anna's

face as the truck bumped down the track to the cabin. He swallowed hard as the truck jerked to a stop. Quickly he stuffed the paper into the pocket of his parka. He was not ready to let Bud see Ted and Anna Dawson pictured as husband and wife.

I'm lucky that Patrick and Natû are on their way to Rohn, he thought. I'm not ready for a 'big brother' lecture.

Trapper piled packets into Scott's arms until he could barely see over the top.

Bud joined them, kicking the mud and slush from his boots on the bottom step.

'Sugar?' he said quizzically.

'Those food markets are honeypots,' answered Trapper. 'Once inside, things just stick to your fingers.'

'So I see.'

Bud relieved Scott of some of the packets, tottering from side to side as he climbed the steps.

'Any phone calls?' asked Trapper, as the young men tumbled the packets onto the kitchen counter.

'Only one, but I didn't answer.'

'Good.'

Trapper crossed to the phone, dialled quickly then listened for a long time. He said a few words, put the phone down gently and turned to Scott.

'Now that we have sugar, where is my coffee?'

Chapter Fifteen

MUKTUK PETERS cursed as he pulled the tray of cookies from the oven. The fingertips of the old oven glove had worn thin and the hot metal stuck to his skin.

He let the tray drop on top of the wood stove and ran outside, where he dug his fingers into the snow.

The pain eased as the cold stopped the heat penetrating deeper into his flesh.

'Need every finger I have for the Iditarod,' he groused as he climbed up onto the deck in front of his single-room cabin.

Muktuk lived alone. Native whispers said that he once had a wife, but she left him after a few months to find another partner. Rumour also said that her desertion accounted for his morose nature and flashes of terrifying temper.

Those who knew the shambling giant of a man with thinning red hair and grey ousting the rust in his wispy beard, admired his knowledge of the country, his hunting skills and his control over unruly and overexcited dogs.

Many a musher wished they had Muktuk's skill at untangling two teams of fighting dogs.

Watching him unclip the main troublemakers, tuck them under his arms and carry them the length of the gangline as easily as if he was holding a pair of puppies, silenced not only the other dogs but any spectators. The fighting dogs looked up at the huskies' legs dangling helplessly in the air above them, and they all listened as Muktuk warned the ones under his arms what would happen if they caused further trouble.

They seemed to sense that Muktuk was bigger and stronger,

and would take no nonsense from them. His team seemed to give the least trouble in races.

Rookies fought for the honour of working with Muktuk and his dogs.

Muktuk ran his undamaged fingers through his straggly beard and pulled his red cap well down over his ears. He smelled the air. Snow was coming. His dogs, realizing that he had not come out to run them, curled up on the roofs of their huts and watched him reproachfully as he closed the door of his cabin.

The revving of a snowmobile in his driveway alerted and irritated Muktuk. Those machines annoyed him even more than the swarms of stinging insects that plagued both people and animals during the short, warm Alaskan summers.

He stuffed a whole cookie in his mouth and grimaced as he tasted the bitter burned edges. A quick gulp of tea helped clean his mouth. He shook another cookie from the tray, snapped off the blackened pieces and flung open the door.

'Out!' he yelled. 'Take that noisy junk out of my yard at once.'

Hearing the anger in his voice, his dogs joined in, howling a chorus to his commands.

'Message for you from Kiluk Owens,' shouted the young man. He left the engine running in case he had to retreat in a hurry.

Muktuk refused to have a telephone installed in his cabin.

'Run to answer a piece of black plastic? I'm no damn dog to listen to commands. People want me, let them find me.'

Everyone in the neighbourhood knew of Muktuk's aversion to phones, but there were few volunteers when messages needed to be sent to him, as they were well aware of his unpredictable temper.

'Switch off that noise and come here.'

The youngster stroked his snowmobile as he clambered down, seemingly afraid that he might not see it again.

'Rookies,' snorted Muktuk as he listened to the story. 'Alaska will teach them. She soon sorts out the weak from the strong.'

'So you'll come?' queried the young man, eager to be back at the Owens's cabin.

'Yeah. Guess so. Who else can find them?'

'I'll tell Kiluk. Thanks.'

'Push that stinking thing until you hit the road. Don't need the smell or noise in these parts.

'Sure thing.'

The youngster put all his weight behind his snowmobile. Apprehension gave him extra strength. Soon a dull roar was all that cut the silence.

Muktuk broke a cookie in half and gingerly tasted it. It was good without its band of burned flour.

'So you get to run,' he said to his dogs. They barked and howled as they watched him collect the harnesses, gangline and tuglines. The dog lot was a maelstrom of excitement. Huskies spun round their pegs like furry tops in excitement, others sat and howled, but none remained lying down. They were all eager to run.

Muktuk smiled as he walked between the boxes, choosing the dogs he wanted.

'Okay, Delilah, you lead with Shark today,' he said, walking a small bitch with marble-brown and -blue eyes away from her box. 'But no lifting your tail. I want no honky-tonk from you.'

The bitch trotted happily beside him. She seemed to enjoy the anguished howls of the huskies still chained to their pegs.

'Remember what I said,' warned Muktuk as he fitted her into a harness. 'You come on heat in the middle of this run like you did when we ran to Nome, and I'll give you to the first rookie who is stupid enough to take you.'

Delilah grinned up at him and fanned her tail. 'You've been warned, you little tart,' said Muktuk as he fondled her pointed ears and trudged back to select the rest of the team.

The dogs screamed at him like children begging for candy as he walked from hut to hut. Finally the dogs he chose were harnessed. Their neck- and tuglines were clipped onto the gangline. They stood proud and tall as if posing for the press.

'Let's go.'

Delilah led the team proudly with Shark. The gangline was tight and each dog pulled well. They understood that in the dog hierarchy, Muktuk was the dominant male even though he only had two legs.

The village of Skwentna was confusing to mushers and Iditarod racers alike, as turn-offs and side trails webbed the main route. But Muktuk saw only the main route.

'Haw!'

Delilah, as obedient as a pampered lapdog, turned the team immediately to the left. Shark followed seconds later.

Delilah did not hesitate. She ran as if directed by a compass. She seemed to feel that if she performed well, she could be the chief lead dog.

'Hike!' commanded Muktuk. He smiled as he felt the extra surge of power from the dogs, and the sled jumped forward.

'This year we'll be in the top ten,' he boasted.

As if they heard and understood him, each dog raced across the snow, tongues lolling and tails held high.

Muktuk breathed in deeply as the dogs ran the sled along the narrow trail. The whisper of sled runners on snow, the wind in his hair, the purity of the air made him drunk with happiness. He only found peace when he was with his dogs on the trail. He became an animal, part of the environment.

Muktuk sensed a sudden restlessness in Delilah. 'You come on heat and mess up this run, and I'll waste you,' he shouted.

The wind ripped the words from his mouth and flung them back towards Skwentna, where Herbie Owens and the youngster were preparing snowmobiles to follow Muktuk. Neither wanted to be too close to the sled. The hundred-odd inhabitants of the settlement were all aware of Muktuk's dislike of the machines, which had almost replaced sleds and dogs.

Suddenly a foul, sour stench flew past Muktuk. He sniffed but it was gone.

The dogs were excited and lifted their noses into the wind.

'Skunk,' said Muktuk, chewing a piece of beard that had blown across his mouth.

'No, you don't,' he roared at Delilah as he saw her starting to turn from the trail. 'Why don't you behave like Shark?' Shark, hearing her name, looked at Muktuk over her shoulder. Her lips lifted in a sneer. She was seldom singled out for praise, though Muktuk would not run the race without her.

Muktuk pounded beside the dogs. He followed the gangline to where the little bitch was about to indulge in her passion for skunk meat. He grabbed her neckline. Delilah's feet scrabbled at the air helplessly as he swung her back onto the track.

Shark bared her teeth at him and snarled.

'You'll get the same treatment if you try any nonsense,' he threatened.

Muktuk ran easily beside Delilah, forcing her to remain on the track and run beside Shark, keeping the gangline tight and the rest of the team in place.

He glanced back over his shoulder as he ran, making sure the other dogs were not trying to follow the tantalizing stench of skunk.

'Should only be out at night, you stinking thing,' he called to the nocturnal animal he could not see.

Delilah suddenly tried to peer round his legs as he ran.

'Yeah, go that way and get a squirt of skunk juice in your eyes,' he shouted. 'You are supposed to be the brains of the team, and you don't know what it does when it is attacked and lifts its tail.'

Muktuk bumped her hard, and Delilah gave up her attempts to see the skunk, but she kept lifting her head and sniffing hopefully.

'Fool dog,' he growled, then, satisfied that the skunk was way behind them, he loped back to the sled.

'Hike. We're out here to find rookies, not skunks.'

Sockeye lifted his nose from its warm cushion in his fluffy tail. He smelled the air carefully, looked at the rest of the team curled into mottled white, black and brown balls, then snuggled his nose back into his thick hair.

Suddenly Sockeye jumped up. The smell was closer and it excited him.

He alerted the other dogs, but Patrick had tied their necklines and the gangline to tree trunks to make certain they could not move while he ran White-out and Bud's team towards where he hoped they would hit the trail. Leapfrogging the teams through the forest was exhausting, as he had to keep within earshot of the team left behind.

Sockeye was the only dog who had any freedom of movement. As Sockeye watched, a shadow slid between the trees in the forest. It moved silently and slowly as if afraid of being detected. All the dogs were now standing staring into the gloom. One of the stumps seemed to move.

A vixen, almost the size of a husky, moved into the open. The dogs bayed their interest and arousal. As if conscious of the commotion she was causing, the female fox walked slowly around the dogs and finally stopped in front of Sockeye.

Sockeye and the vixen managed to overcome the problems of harnesses and tuglines and were firmly locked together when a crashing in the brush startled them.

'Sockeye! You stupid damn dog. I leave you alone and what do you do? Find yourself a fox in heat who is probably carrying rabies, but you're so damn randy you don't care. If she bites any dog in Natû's team I'll kill you, and that's no idle threat.'

Patrick patted his pocket where the magnum should have been, then remembered that he had left it with Natû.

He realized that he could do nothing until the mating was over, but the thought of Natû lying alone and helpless in the sled until he returned made him reckless. He searched for and found a thick branch.

He strode towards the panting Sockeye. Patrick kept a wary distance from the vixen. He hated injections more than Bud, and had no desire to undergo the ordeal that Bud had just completed. But as she heard him, the vixen tried to turn and run. There was only fear in her yellow eyes.

'Relax,' said Patrick softly. 'As long as you remain together like this, I can do nothing.'

146

Patrick watched them for a moment, then sat down heavily on a log. He prepared himself for a long wait.

The rest of the team lost interest once the vixen chose Sockeye. Eventually the dogs engorged sexual organs relaxed. Even as Patrick watched, the vixen vanished, a thread of smoke between the trees.

Patrick sat for a few moments staring at the place he had last seen her. It was not only the spectacular and often terrifying beauty of the mountains and glaciers which held him enthralled, but moments like this, when he felt humble to have witnessed the courage of a wild creature.

She left the safety of the woods and came to the dogs and sled, which must stink of man, just to mate, he thought.

Patrick put both hands on his knees, stood and rolled his shoulders to release the tension of running a relay through the trees with two sleds.

'Now let's get Natû out of this neverending spruce forest and onto the trail.'

He whistled, a soft, low call. The dogs understood. They uncurled and went into full stiff-legged stretches as if on show.

'Line out.' Sockeye behaved impeccably. He held the gangline taut while Patrick untied and collected the ropes he had used to keep the team immobile.

'Let's go.'

Sockeye seemed to follow a nonexistent line of fluorescent Iditarod markers through the trees. Occasionally he put his nose to the snow, lifted it and pulled the team behind him.

'Your wild lady friend did you some good,' said Patrick as loud barks greeted them.

Sockeye stopped beside Bud's sled and howled a song of greeting to Natû.

'Sockeye, you crazy dog,' she whispered.

Patrick bent over her, tucking her hair into her hood. He was worried; the blood seemed to have drained from her face while he was fetching her team. Pain glazed her eyes and narrowed her mouth.

Don't let her have abdominal bleeding, he thought. I must get to Skwentna and find help. I'm sure Trapper's friends will know someone who can examine her and do something.

'Now I'll take you out with Bud's fast team, Natû,' he said, tenderly stroking her cheek.

Natû held her breath as pain, as insidious and threatening as hunting wolves, crept across her lower belly.

'No,' she said firmly as the pain released its hold. 'I'm feeling fine. Let's leapfrog the teams till we find the trail. Then we can stake my team on the trail and run for Skwentna with White-out and Bud's fast dogs. My team will be easy to find on the trail. It'll take for ever to find them in this spruce if you leave them staked here.' Sockeye howled again, as if in agreement with her.

Patrick shook his head. He wanted Natû on the trail and out of the forest with the fast team.

'Please,' she pleaded.

'Okay,' Patrick sighed, hoping that the trail was close.

Sockeye continued to surprise Patrick. He wound through the maze of trees with confidence. The trees cut out the weak light. Patrick had no idea where they were: he relied solely on Sockeye.

Suddenly Sockeye's tail shot up like a starter's flag. He no longer trotted. He strutted with his head held high.

'Not another vixen in heat,' said Patrick quietly as the dog ran down the slope and out onto the trail. Sockeye barked in triumph and looked back at Patrick.

'Don't you trash-talk me, dog,' shouted Patrick. 'You were as lost as I was. It was just good luck that you fell into the trail.' But he could not be angry.

It seemed Patrick took for ever to tie the team down before he could trudge back to Natû. The amazing repertoire of wolfsongs told him exactly where they waited. Whenever they stopped singing, Natû would howl softly, and within minutes the whole team was in full voice.

'Well done,' teased Patrick as Natû ended a lonesome howl. She looked embarrassed.

'It was one way to make sure you found us,' she defended herself. She smiled weakly at Patrick. 'Let's go,' she said.

The pains had subsided again and Natû was able to relax a little in the lurching sled.

They moved slowly around the trees. White-out easily followed the trail marked by Sockeye.

Suddenly the silence was shattered by a deafening cacophony of barks and howls. Natû listened, then said, 'They are challenging something. Those barks are invitations to a free-for-all fight.'

Patrick grimaced.

'Huskies must be the most lovable and impossible dogs in the world. It's that mad wolf strain in them.'

'It's what gives them their extraordinary endurance and makes them want to run,' answered Natû, still reading the howls and screaming barks.

'It also makes them fight. Usually anything and anyone,' said Patrick.

Chapter Sixteen

SHARK AND Delilah were pulling strongly, happy to be running. Shark had eventually realized that on this run she had to share the lead with Delilah, and had stopped trying to savage her, though she still challenged her to a future fight.

Delilah did not deign to reply. She merely fanned her tail and looked back at Muktuk with love in her marbled eyes.

Suddenly Shark stopped running. She jumped up and down snarling and barking, screaming messages to Muktuk. Muktuk saw the loose tuglines and slack gangline and raced up to his lead dogs.

'No you don't,' he bellowed. 'You leave my dogs alone, you damn big-nosed idiot.'

The moose that had contested the right of way and chased Natû's team into the spruce forest was once again standing in the middle of the trail. He had found no Alaskan willow. For the second time he had found a dog team in his way.

This time he charged straight for Muktuk's team. His feet were flying, and Muktuk knew what damage one of those hoofs could cause if they hit his dogs.

Shark challenged the moose to do battle. Spittle flew from her mouth as she strained to free herself from her harness. At last she had found a worthwhile opponent.

Muktuk ran in front of her blocking her view. In her anger at losing the moose, she sank her teeth into his calf.

The sharp report of a 44 magnum shocked her into silence. The moose moved forward a few slow steps, then hit the snow as hard and fast as an imploding building.

Muktuk walked towards the huge ruminant. Its neck was

twisted so that the flattened antlers dug into the snow. He studied the red patch bleeding into the snow. The eyes staring up at him were lifeless and beginning to glaze like crackled porcelain.

'Damn moose,' he said, 'that'll learn you to tangle with my dogs.'

The smell of blood and moose excited Shark even more than the rare opportunity to bite Muktuk. She released her hold on his calf and strained to reach the dead animal.

Muktuk ignored his aching calf and pulled her around the moose, holding her well away from his ribs in case she tried to sneak another bite.

He ran ahead with his two lead dogs until the team and sled were well past the tempting meal.

'Come back later for that moose,' he muttered. 'Can do with more meat for winter.'

Muktuk ran in front for a while, enjoying the exercise. Shark bared her teeth at him and Delilah smiled, a fawning grin.

She delighted in being allowed to share the lead with Shark, though she was aware that Shark was still dominant.

'Whoa!' roared Muktuk, finally wiping his forehead with the back of his glove. He was breathing deeply, and the odour of garlic hung heavy around him. It was his panacea for all ills. Skwentna residents admitted that Muktuk Peters was never ill, though some doubted that it was because of the copious amount of garlic he consumed.

He fed his dogs garlic, and there was no dissension that they were the strongest, healthiest dogs in the region.

'The damn-fool rookies may be lost,' muttered Muktuk when he saw Sockeye and Natû's team firmly staked to the side of the trail, 'but the dogs are okay.' He dropped the brake and snowhook on his sled and walked the length of Natû's dog team, assessing her dogs quickly and expertly.

'Some good flesh there. Good, tough village dogs and a lot of wolf. Plus some expensive kennel-dog flesh, probably paid for by BP,' he said. 'Pity to waste it on a rookie. Though Trapper's daughter can hardly be called a rookie.'

He walked back to his team, who were straining to reach Sockeye.

'Quiet!' he yelled.

One of his large wheel dogs, a black, wild-eyed troublemaker, defied him and continued to bark invitations to a fight.

Moving surprising lightly and quickly for a large man, Muktuk reached him and lifted him up until their eyes were level.

The dogs eye's, one blue and one brown, stared at him, but eventually it broke the stare and Muktuk dropped him to the ground.

Both teams were now quiet.

Muktuk trudged to where runner tracks emerged from the forest. He looked back at the two teams stationed on either side of the trail.

'I'm going into the spruce. If one of you as much as wags a tail, you'll be skinned and made into dog food. Got it?'

The dogs all sat quietly staring at him, only Shark, his experienced lead bitch, still showed her teeth. The rest seemed to understand and respect his strength.

Muktuk climbed the bank. He walked slowly, moving from sled mark to sled mark as if feeling his way in a blizzard. He stopped every few minutes to listen, but Muktuk knew that all one heard when huskies ran was the whisper of sled runners. In the spruce he hoped to hear the crash of brush and undergrowth.

There. He stopped and stepped behind a tree trunk. The noise he heard could have been a moose searching for food in the snow. It was coming closer. Muktuk strained his eyes. There was something snaking through the trees. It was low and small. Certainly no moose. It was a husky.

'Natû!' he shouted. His voice swung on the bare branches and stayed in the forest.

'That can only be Muktuk Peters from Skwentna,' said Natû. 'They must have sent him out to find us.'

Patrick's first reaction was one of annoyance. They were so close to the trail. He had found Natû and brought both dog teams through the spruce. Now legend would recount it as Muktuk's rescue.

He then realized that Muktuk could lead them straight to the Owens and help. He would not have to worry about the maze of trails leading in and out of Skwentna.

Muktuk stepped out from behind a tree as White-out approached him.

'Natû. Are you all right?' he said gruffly. He found it difficult to express concern or sympathy.

She nodded, and Patrick gestured to Muktuk that they should continue.

'You did good,' said Muktuk, then fell in behind the sled with Patrick.

'What is it?' he asked, breaking into a slow jog to keep up with the sled.

'Don't know. Could be smashed spleen or some other internal organ. I've been watching her. She cramps up. I think she's right. It is her stomach.'

'Kiluk stands in for a doctor in the village, she'll sort it out. We'll have Natû fixed up. If she's Trapper's kid, she's tough. Don't worry.'

Patrick nodded and concentrated on keeping the sled as steady as possible. As White-out neared the trail, Sockeye's team greeted him with the hysteria usually reserved for the start of the Iditarod.

'Crazy dogs. Greet each other one minute and tear each other apart the next. Goddam wolves,' groused Muktuk. 'Remember this: trust only one dog. Your lead. It is your life.'

Patrick nodded again. 'Sure thing,' he said.

'I've a mean little bitch,' continued Muktuk. 'Has teeth like a shark, and isn't shy to use them. Even rips into me. Hate the swine, but she can sense trail under three foot of snow. Smells suckholes before she is near them. Has never led my dogs into water.'

Muktuk cleared his throat and spat the phlegm onto a shrub frosted with snow. It hung in the branches for a moment, like a flat slug, before dropping to the ground. Natû averted her gaze and turned her face into her hood. The wolverine fur covered her cheek, and she thought of the sled ride to the cabin after her and Bud's wedding party at the Captain Cook. It all seemed so long ago. A tear of self-pity trickled down her cheek and she licked it before it froze on her skin. It was salty in her mouth.

She could hear a low murmur of men's voices behind her.

'Today I'm running her with Delilah, another sort of bitch,' said Muktuk. 'Hope Shark can teach Delilah trail skills. The tart already has all the others.'

Don't let Muktuk see you cry, she admonished herself. You're an Inupiat. Remember that. You come from people who live on a land mass as close to the North Pole as one can get without being a polar bear and wandering on the ice pack.

'Okay, Natû?' Patrick's voice blocked out her thoughts.

She swallowed and steadied her voice.

'Sure, fine.'

'She's one helluva girl,' said Patrick.

Muktuk nodded. He preferred a life uncluttered by women. The baggage and trouble they brought with them was not worth the short pleasures of having them. He spat again. This time the sled runners smeared the viscid mucus into the snow. Natû did not see it and gag.

Natû was about to thank Oline for listening to her plea and stopping the pains, when her belly seemed to tear inside as the sled hit the bank and bounced down onto the trail.

She gasped and pressed her hands down on her stomach.

Patrick handed the sled to Muktuk and ran to White-out in the front. He held him still as Muktuk brought the sled onto the trail.

'Whoa,' shouted Muktuk as he dropped the brake and snowhook before going up to Natû.

Muktuk had not had a good look at Natû in the dim light of the forest, but out on the snow he read the pain in her eyes.

'Patrick,' he called, 'follow my team. Let's go.' Patrick, alerted by the alarm in Muktuk's voice, left White-out, released the brakes and hooks on the sled and was soon close behind Muktuk. The trail they were on was well travelled. Muktuk ignored the misleading turn-offs and headed directly for Skwentna.

'Whoa!' Suddenly Muktuk's team stopped. Patrick could see no reason for the unexpected halt, but stopped his team.

'Get those damn things off the snow. Lock them up in the barn where they belong.'

Patrick stared at Muktuk in amazement. The sane musher had turned into a raving madman. He was stamping his feet and punching the air with his fists, while colourful language exploded the silence.

Only Shark, one of his lead bitches, seemed to understand his anger. She bared her teeth and joined his outrage with dog talk and threats to tear the snowmobiles and riders apart.

The two dog teams sat in the snow seemingly amazed, but prepared to enjoy the performance.

Suddenly, over the rise appeared the reason for Muktuk's anger. He had heard the snowmobiles long before Patrick. Seeing the vehicles only increased Muktuk's rage. The three men on the machines could not hear what he was saying, but his intentions were clear.

The older of the three climbed from his machine, bent over it and it was silent. He walked to where the teams were. 'Muktuk,' said Herbie Owens, his voice soft and placatory. 'Only brought the fool things so I could be free to run one of the teams back.'

Muktuk calmed down immediately. He liked Herbie Owens, and respected his craftsmanship. A man who could make racing sleds was someone he could relate to.

'Where is the other team?' asked Herbie, crossing to where Natû lay in the sled bag.

'Hold on,' he said to her. 'Kiluk is waiting. Everything will be all right.'

'Way back near the turn-off to Duck Lake,' answered Muktuk, mollified by the reason for the presence of the machines he detested.

'You go on with Natû. It'll be quicker for me to find the dogs by snowmobile than walking.'

Muktuk merely nodded.

'Let's hike,' he called.

Shark took a last bite at the dog behind her and started pulling.

Herbie waited until the dog teams were out of sight before trudging back to the snowmobiles. The two youngsters still sat on the one, huddling as close as a pair of ptarmigans in winter. The machine was idling. They had been ready to turn and head for Skwentna if Herbie failed to placate Muktuk.

'One of you come with me to find the dogs. I'll run the team back and you can take the machine. Oh, a word of advice: don't try to overtake Muktuk. Let him get the dogs into the village first.'

The youth who had chosen to go with Herbie to find Sockeye and Natû's team called to his friend as he climbed onto Herbie's machine.

'Wait for me. We'll drive there together.'

'Strength in numbers?' mocked Herbie gently. 'It's a good idea. You can't trust those machines. It's unwise to be out on your own.'

The boys sighed. Were they about to have another boring lecture about freezing to death in a snowstorm because machines were likely to run out of fuel or develop mechanical problems, leaving you stranded in the middle of nowhere? Were they to hear that, unlike dogs, machines are cold and inedible, useless to a man depending on them for survival?

'Besides,' continued Herbie, 'you may run into Muktuk, and I won't be there to sweet-talk him. He was only warming up when we arrived.'

The bored smiles reserved by the young for lectures by the old vanished. Within minutes, both snowmobiles were ready to head for Duck Lake and Natû's team.

Chapter Seventeen

ANNA FLUNG open the door to her cabin. She looked around the empty room as if expecting to see Scott. But only the stale smell of dead ashes and blackened logs in the cold fireplace greeted her.

She crossed to the basket holding logs chopped by Scott. Choking back a sob, she threw them into the grate. A cloud of grey ash enveloped and choked her. She knew she should clean the grate before laying a new fire. She coughed and sneezed, then sat back on her heels. Tears streaked rivers through the ash, and as she knuckled her wet eyes and cheeks, her hands were tattooed as if for some archaic ritual of grief.

'Oh, Scott,' she sobbed, 'what have I done? We had it all.'

Eventually, nauseous with crying, Anna walked into the bathroom. She stared at her red-rimmed eyes and her cheeks streaked with tears and ash. She held her face in the basin of cold water until she felt that she was drowning. Anna groped blindly for a towel.

Suddenly she spun round.

'Scott,' she called, but there was no answer. Yet he was in the room. She could smell him, smell his aftershave. She wiped her eyes harshly. There. Scott was here. She could not mistake the smell of his body. Shakily, Anna looked at the towel in her hands. She was holding Scott's t-shirt.

A car hooted outside. Cradling the damp shirt to her cheek, Anna walked to the door. If that's Ted, she thought as she moved through the front room, I'm asking for a divorce. He is not going to touch me again.

Anna opened the door a crack.

'Claire,' she said in surprise. 'What are you doing here?'

'We need to talk. Can I come in?'

'Sure,' Anna opened the door wide and Claire wrinkled her nose at the stale smell.

'I'll have the fire going in a minute. Will you put water on the stove for coffee?' said Anna, as she bustled round cleaning the grate and re-stacking the logs.

Soon the two women were warming their legs in front of the fire, while their fingers absorbed the heat from steaming mugs of coffee.

'Now tell me, Claire, what was important enough to bring you out here?'

'Whispers again, Anna.'

'About?'

'Patrick and Natû.'

'Patrick? But Natû is married to Bud. They haven't . . .?'

'No. Natû wanted to run her Iditarod team to Rohn. Give them a taste of the trail. As you know, Bud can't run yet. He's waiting for the doctor's okay. So Patrick offered to take Bud's team. That way, Natû was not alone and Bud's dogs got to run.'

'And?'

'Whispers reached Wasilla yesterday that Natû and Patrick have not made Skwentna. A search party is being organized by the Owens.'

'Yes?' Anna sipped her coffee and stared at her friend over the rim of the mug.

'Whispers also say that Trapper is the only one speaking to Kiluk and Herbie Owens. I think he's worried about what Bud and Scott will do or attempt to do, if they are told that Patrick and Natû are in trouble.'

Anna thumped her mug on the low table, and the dregs soaked into a flight manual she had thrown down when she came in.

'I must go to Scott. He never stops talking about Patrick. He hero-worships his brother.'

'Anna,' continued Claire, 'remember, it's only whispers. The whole story could be wrong. In fact, Patrick and Natû could be lunching with Kiluk and Herbie right now.'

'That's why I must go and talk to Trapper and see Scott,' said Anna, jumping up and flinging a bag over her shoulder.

'If you would only have a phone here, life would be much easier,' admonished Claire.

'Yeah, easier for everyone to reach me. No thanks.' Anna turned back as she reached the door.

'You're a star to drive all the way here and bring me this news,' she said.

Claire smiled a little sadly, and splayed out the end of her thick plait that was heavily streaked with grey.

'They say that in Africa messages are heard in the beat of drums. Here, I often feel that whispers are carried, and probably changed, by shamans flying at night.'

'However they do it. Drumbeats, or shamans flying on the night air – stories certainly travel,' agreed Anna.

'Oh, Anna,' said Claire, 'one last thing. Ted has increased the sponsorship for the Iditarod, and the Damas team are definitely in.'

Anna's face closed. For a moment Claire was sorry she had broached the subject of Ted Dawson.

'We all saw your photograph in the paper. We know you persuaded him to change his mean little mind. Thank you, Anna.'

Anna felt queasy when she thought of Ted's meaty hands exploring her body, but she forced herself to smile.

'No sweat,' she said.

Both women stood up. Anna walked quickly outside. She needed fresh air to quell the nausea brought on by Claire's news. Claire quickly checked that the dying fire was safe enough to leave and joined Anna outside.

'Thanks.'

Claire put her arms around Anna and hugged her.

'Good luck.'

Anna lifted her hand in farewell as she reversed down the rutted track.

The three men in the cabin were buried in gloom, as deep and suffocating as a snowdrift.

Scott stood for hours in front of the window, hands thrust deep into his pockets, staring sightlessly at Mount Denali. He rocked back and forth on his heels, as irritating as a metronome, until Bud wanted to shake him and make him talk.

Trapper was deaf to all questions. He stationed his chair midway between the telephone and the front door. Occasionally he glanced across at Scott, opened his mouth as if to speak, then closed it and returned to caressing his moustache and combing his beard with his fingers.

Bud walked to where he could see the clock on the wall. It was a wedding gift. He and Natû hated clocks, so they tucked it out of sight between two cupboards in the small kitchen.

'Time to shovel dog shit,' he said, trying to sound enthusiastic. 'Coming, Scott?'

Scott continued to rock, and ignored the question.

'Bud should have help,' said Trapper shortly. 'He took a knock with the rabies treatment. I want him to get back to work and running slowly.'

Scott turned to look at Trapper as if awakening from a nightmare.

'Sure,' he said. 'I wasn't thinking. Sorry, Trapper.'

'It's okay, Scott. I understand.'

Trapper watched Scott stumble from the room. Life is hard when one is young and idealistic, he thought. But he'll learn to roll with the blows. Soon the boy will avoid sucker punches.

'Lighten up. The gum couldn't have been that bad,' said Bud with a grin, throwing a shovel to Scott.

Scott caught it deftly.

'It wasn't the gum.'

'Want to talk?' asked Bud, leaning on his shovel.

Scott fondled the upright ears of a husky standing tall on its hut.

'Nothing to talk about, but thanks.'

Scott liked Bud, but was not ready to share his private hell.

Perhaps when Patrick comes back, he thought. Though his cure to all ills is to find me a hot babe. Women are the one thing I don't need in my life. Unbidden, the mental picture of Ted's hand cupping Anna's breast filled his vision.

'Hey!' called Bud. 'We're not digging for gold. Remember the last gold rush was on a tributary of the Haiditarod river. That was way back in 1908, sometime. We're only scraping the muck off the top.'

But Scott vented his anger and frustration on the dog lot. Snow and earth flew around him as he shovelled the faeces into the sled.

Bud watched for a while, shook his head and worked on steadily and calmly.

Chapter Eighteen

NATÛ CLENCHED her teeth and closed her eyes. Pain rushed on her, shook her and retreated. She wanted to scream, to shout for Patrick to stop the bumping sled.

'I'm Inupiat,' she whispered. 'Oline, you knew pain. This is nothing. I do not have Nanuq burying his teeth into my flesh and ripping out chunks to eat. You were old, and you knew what would happen. Let me share your courage.'

She gasped as pain as sharp and curved as an ulu, the traditional Eskimo knife, rocked into the walls of her stomach.

Muktuk heard White-out closing on his team.

That rigger husband of Natû's sure has a fast team, thought Muktuk. Put a few Iditarods under his belt and he'll be someone to watch.

The small settlement of Skwentna appeared. The dull thud of a generator seemed obscenely loud as Patrick looked down to where the river lay below them in frozen coils of silver. He was trying to memorize as much as possible for when he ran the race, but already the trail had blurred.

'Haw!'

Muktuk's team swung left and stopped outside the Owen's cabin.

Kiluk came hurrying to the sled. She zipped open the bag and spoke to Natû in their native tongue.

'Quick,' she ordered Patrick and Muktuk, 'lift her carefully and put her on the bed in my room.'

Natû's shoulders shook with sobs as the men left and closed the door. Kiluk held the young woman to her, and Natû snuggled up against the warm, soft bosom. Kiluk rocked her gently until she was calm.

The room was warm and Natû felt safe. 'Now let's examine you,' said Kiluk Owens as she unzipped Natû's sled suit. She ran her hands deftly down and across Natû's ribs.

'Probably bruised, but I cannot feel anything broken,' she said. 'No, your ribs are not the problem. Did you know you were pregnant?' she asked as she stripped off the pants. She studied the blood that streak Natû's thighs. She shook her head when she saw dark red clots of blood and felt the wet suit pants. She threw them in the corner.

Natû watched Kiluk, then nodded.

'I thought so,' she said in a small voice. 'But I so wanted to run the Iditarod.'

'That mad, crazy race changes everyone who runs it,' said Kiluk. 'They are never the same again. Once they have challenged death to a one-on-one fight and have seen scenery dreamed of only by angels, they long to experience it again and again. Some do. Others have only the memories to keep them unhappy until they die.'

She clucked and turned away from Natû. 'You, it seems, will run your race, but alone.'

'No. No. No!'

'You cannot have all your wishes in one sled, Natû.'

Those were the last words Natû remembered.

The stabs of pain Natû had endured on the sled were only the outriders.

Kiluk allowed no one into the room. Natû did not scream as the placenta separated from the uterus. She made no sound as the foetus, curled in its watery sac, passed from her body.

Kiluk studied the foetus and shrugged. It was a girl. As her hard hands massaged Natû's stomach in firm downward movements to expel the afterbirth, she remembered stories told by her grandmother of early Inupiat tribes, particularly the Netsilik, who killed baby girls at birth, as the nursing period was an obstacle to a new pregnancy and the hope of producing a son, a hunter, one who could feed the family during the Stygian winters.

'There,' grunted Kiluk as the afterbirth slid into a bowl.

She covered the yellow plastic bowl and hid it under the bed. Later she would do what must be done with the foetal remains.

She wiped the sweat from Natû's face and dabbed at the blood on her lower lip, where Natû had bitten down to prevent herself from crying out loud.

'You'll feel much better now that it's all cleared out,' she said, emotionlessly.

'But the baby. Bud's baby,' whispered Natû. 'How do I tell him, Kiluk?'

'You don't.'

Natû stared at Kiluk in horror.

'I can't lie about his child.'

'Did he suspect that you were pregnant?'

'No.'

'Did anyone? Trapper? Anyone at all?'

'No. I'm sure they didn't.'

'Then, little Natû, listen to me carefully,' said Kiluk, licking a patch of toilet paper and sticking it on Natû's lip to stop the bleeding.

'Keep as quiet about this as you did during the labour pains to expel it.'

'But it was a baby,' said Natû.

'Not if it couldn't breathe on its own after the birth trauma,' said Kiluk firmly.

Natû closed her eyes and Kiluk let her lie in silence for a while.

'Think about it, Natû. How is telling Bud going to help him? He will be hurt, maybe angry. Few men can take bad news. They usually run from problems.

'That is why we women have to tell them only what they can absorb and handle. Be strong. Strong enough for both of you.'

Natû pinched the bridge of her nose until her eyes watered. She would be strong. She would not cry. It was her fault she lost the baby. Kiluk was right – why should Bud suffer? The thought of Bud hating her finally tipped the scales.

'Okay,' she said. 'But what about the men out there?' She gestured to the main living area.

'They know nothing. You have badly bruised ribs and stomach, and will need to rest for a few weeks,' answered Kiluk, tidying the room and opening the window to release the sweet-sour smell of blood.

'But I'm coming to Rohn.'

'No you are not, unless you want me to tell Trapper and Bud how foolish you've been,' said Kiluk harshly. 'You've lost a lot of blood, and may have to have a transfusion or iron tablets. I have a cousin who is a doctor at our new medical centre on Tudor Road. It's an easy twenty-minute drive from Chugiak.'

Natû shook her head and Kiluk frowned.

'Be sensible. If you want to run the Iditarod, you have to build up your strength. Have a check-up. Sepsis can set in after a miscarriage. I think everything is out, but I can be wrong. It costs nothing, and no one will know.' Kilak paused. 'If, of course, you are not serious about the race, then don't go and see him. Stay at home and watch television as others experience the trail.'

Kiluk smiled inwardly as she watched the expression on Natû's face change. It had worked. Natû would go to her cousin for a check-up.

She is a strong girl and can handle an early miscarriage, Kiluk decided as she prepared to face the men.

'Lunch,' she called as she bustled into the main room.

'Natû?' chorused Patrick and Herbie.

'She's fine. Badly bruised ribs and stomach. Nothing serious that I can find. A little rest. Lots of red meat, and she'll be lost in a spruce forest again.'

Patrick pulled out a wooden chair and slumped into it. He had not realized how worried he was about Natû until Kiluk pronounced her well.

'We had better phone Trapper,' said Herbie, seating himself opposite Patrick at the table. Kiluk clucked to herself again and padded across the room. Before she could lift the phone it crackled, and its shrill call made her start.

'Trapper?' said the men.

'Probably,' answered Kiluk as she lifted the receiver to her ear.

Chapter Nineteen

TRAPPER WAS engrossed in the story Kiluk was relating.

'No. Muktuk says they were almost on the trail when he found them. Yes. Natû is fine, bruised and a little shaken, but remember, she's Inupiat.'

Trapper heard the door open but did not turn round. Anna McInnes stood in the entrance, uncertain as to whether she should walk in.

'Shut the door!' snapped Trapper, as he felt the cold air across his face.

Anna obeyed silently.

'It's okay, boys. They've found them,' said Trapper, thinking he was talking to the boys. 'Kiluk says Natû should be flown out. She has bruised ribs. She fell off the sled or something.' Trapper was surprised that Kiluk had not mentioned the pregnancy. I was probably reading signs that were not there, he thought. Bud would know, and he has said nothing.

'Patrick can run the one team back, but we need someone to run Natû's team,' he continued.

'I can fly Scott up to Skwentna and he can run the dogs. I'll bring Natû back. I have a few days free.'

Trapper swung round at the sound of the female voice. Anna still stood in the room, but the door was now closed behind her. Trapper's eyes seemed to vanish in the folds of skin around his eyes as he studied the face he had seen so recently on the piece of newspaper clutched in Scott's trembling hand.

*

Scott and Bud trudged up the hill to the flat top where the dogs' huts were placed. 'Another load should do it,' said Bud, cheerfully bumping his empty sled behind him.

As they crested the rise, Scott stopped as if confronted by a rutting moose. A deep red Mercedes, splashed with mud where it had raced through slush, was parked close to the cabin. Anger fought the sudden surge of excitement and left him feeling nauseous.

'Anna,' he whispered.

Unaware that Scott had stopped, Bud chatted on as he walked to the pile of faeces waiting to be dumped in the trash hole at the base of the hill.

'You go inside and rest, Bud. I'll do that,' said Scott, pounding across the lot to join him. 'You heard Trapper say that you were not to overdo things.'

Scott gave Bud a shove towards the cabin and started filling the sled, eager to be out of sight of the cabin and the proximity of Anna McInnes Dawson.

Bud shrugged. Scott had been behaving strangely for the past few days, but if he wanted to complete the job, and slither around in the melting snow and mud churned to a mush by the dogs circling the pegs, then he was ready for a mug of coffee with Trapper.

He wanted to find Trapper alone to ask if Natû and Patrick were at Skwentna. He was eager to talk to Patrick to find out how his dogs were running. It would be good to hear how White-out was behaving, though he knew Natû would have no problem managing her team.

It seemed strange that Trapper avoided discussing the run to Rohn.

I suppose it's normal for a father to worry about his daughter, Bud thought. He climbed the steps, not noticing the sleek red car.

The sound of a woman's voice brought him to a halt outside the door. He did not recognize the voice.

'I cannot speak for him, but I don't think he is ready to see you,' said Trapper firmly.

'Oh, I understand, but it was all a dreadful mistake. I must explain it to Scott,' pleaded Anna. 'I can fly to Skwentna today and bring Natû home,' she continued.

At the mention of Natû's name, Bud flung the door open and swung into the room. He almost knocked over the slim woman standing with her back to him, pleading with Trapper.

'Natû? What's wrong with her? What has happened?'

His eyes flashed as he strode across to Trapper, and he seemed to be unaware that he was clenching and unclenching his fists as he walked.

'Sit down, Bud. Natû is fine.'

Bud relaxed slightly.

'Then why does this woman want to fly to Skwentna? And who is she?'

'Anna McInnes is my name. I'm a pilot with Alaska Airlines, and I hope still a good friend of Scott's,' answered Anna quickly.

Bud looked at Anna closely for the first time since entering the cabin. She held her head high and returned his gaze steadily. Scott's sure found a looker in this one, Bud thought. Wonder what happened?

Bud held out his hand to Anna. The glove was caked with mud, but Anna did not hesitate. She held it in a firm grip.

'Hi. Scott has spoken often of you and Natû. I feel that I know you,' said Anna with a smile.

'Can't say the same,' replied Bud.

This woman is probably the reason for Scott's stinking mood, he mused, enjoying the way her face was transformed from mere prettiness into deep beauty when she smiled.

Trapper watched the interaction between Anna and Bud.

In Inupiat society, this woman would probably transgress her husband's rights and give herself away instead of waiting for him to lend her. But I think she has a serious problem to face with Scott.

Trapper gestured to the door.

'You came to speak to Scott, Ms McInnes. He is in the dog lot.'

'Bottom of the hill, dumping shit in the trash hole,' explained Bud.

Anna merely nodded and turned to the door. 'I'll go and find him. My offer stands.'

Trapper tugged at his beard. He admired the way she came into what she must have known would be an unpleasant situation.

Bud towered over Trapper.

'Now tell me about Natû and Patrick,' he said. 'Is that what all those phone calls were about between you and Kiluk Owens?'

Trapper nodded in assent.

'Sit down.'

Bud listened attentively, asking only a few questions.

'I can fly to Skwentna with McInnes and run Natû's team back,' he said, when Trapper had finished the story.

'You have recovered remarkably well, but if you do the run now you will not have this as your rookie year in the Iditarod,' said Trapper. 'And who knows if BP will sponsor you again next year? You have a wonderful opportunity. Don't blow it. Scott can go. He and Patrick need some time together to talk. Patrick is the one person Scott can trust, and allow to see his pain.'

Anna breathed in lungfuls of the cold wet air as she walked through the dog lot looking for Scott.

Mist drifted across the lot, obscuring then opening sections of dog huts. Anna felt as if she was wandering in a dream. How could she find Scott? The dog huts were obviously set on the flat top of a small hill, but she could not see the sloping edge, and she had no idea which side they would use for burying trash.

Think, she ordered herself. Obviously it's the side which is as far away from the cabin as possible. Then I'm walking in the right direction. Where the dog huts end, the slope must start.

Anna walked on, lost in thought, composing and rejecting speeches for Scott. Suddenly she stood looking down into a void, but sled marks stood out clearly in the mud.

'This is it. Now to see Scott.'

Anna did not realize how slippery the snow was. The bucket sleds, heavy with faeces, had gouged a muddy slide down the hill.

Anna was looking around for Scott. She screamed as her feet shot out from beneath her and she hit the ground. She found a bare bush and hung onto it to pull herself up, but the roots gave way as the bush took her weight, and she landed on the base of her spine.

'Damn. I'm obviously not going to be able to stand, and I'm damned if I'm crawling. I'll toboggan on my bum like we did as kids.'

Anna tucked her feet close to her bottom and pushed herself down with her hands. To her delight, it worked.

'It may not be graceful, but I'll make it,' she said, gritting her teeth.

Scott sat hunched over beside the empty metal sled. He rested his head on his knees and tried to pretend he had not seen the red Mercedes.

The cold seeped through his clothes now that he had stopped working and was sitting still. He regretted having thrown off his parka in the frenzy of shovelling, but he was not returning to the dog lot until he heard Anna's car leave.

Mrs Ted Dawson and I have nothing to say to each other, now or ever. The words ran through his mind, as monotonous as a mantra. He clung to them as if they were a lifeline to sanity.

Anna finally reached the bottom of the slope, rolled onto her knees and stood up. She saw the silver gleam of the sled before she saw Scott. He was still huddled with his head buried between his knees.

She wanted to call out to him, but found that, like a asthmatic, she was battling for breath. Her heart pounded in her ears and deafened her.

She longed to run into his arms and feel his strength as he held her to him. Anna needed to bury her face in his chest, feel his kisses on her neck and forget the horror of the past week.

Suddenly Scott lifted his head as if sensing someone near.

171

Anna's voice cracked as she tried to talk; there was so much to tell him. But his eyes were those of a stranger.

'Mrs Ted Dawson and I have nothing to say to each other, now or ever,' he said coldly. He lifted the sled handle and pulled it easily up the slope behind him. He did not look back to see if Anna was following, or whether she could climb up the hill.

Anna's eyes filled with tears and her full bottom lip quivered.

'I won't cry,' she said fiercely, wiping her eyes.

'Ted won't win this one. Scott will listen to me. How can he refuse to talk to me when he hasn't even heard my story? If he still feels this way once I've explained things to him, then I'll accept it, but not before. I love the fool. Can't he understand that?'

Anna started up the slope trying to put feet into the steps made by Scott as he trudged to the dog lot. Anna was sweating and out of breath when she saw the first wooden dog box. Scott was nowhere to be seen.

Anna's face set in an expression of cold determination, and she walked to the cabin. Her footsteps dragged as she neared the door.

'Do you want to be humiliated in front of Trapper Jack and Bud?' she said to herself. 'I want Scott, and if that means more of the "Mrs Ted Dawson" routine, fine, I can take it.'

The three men spun round as Anna strode into the room. She stood still and tall, but looked like a bedraggled husky pup after its first training run. Mud streaked her clothes and face into hunter's camouflage. Her eyes were rimmed red with tears and the cold, but her voice was firm. She ignored Scott and Bud and spoke to Trapper.

'Have you accepted my offer? I'm a good pilot; your daughter will be safe with me.'

Trapper looked at Anna carefully. Obviously the meeting with Scott had not been a happy one.

'What's wrong with Natû?' Scott asked Trapper, still ignoring Anna. Trapper held up his hand to stop Bud explaining. Scott paced up and down the room as he listened to Trapper.

'I'll phone Bruce. We can leave from Birchwood as soon as he's ready.'

'You can't,' said Anna shortly. 'Bruce is in Hong Kong and won't be back for another four days.'

For the first time, Scott turned to face Anna. His eyes were flat and hard with dislike. Anna had not thought of the possibility that Scott could hate her and never want to see her again. But now, as she searched for a sign of the man she loved and found only indifference, her defences crumbled.

She turned and walked quickly to the door. She would not weep in front of the three men.

'Miss McInnes,' Trapper's voice stayed her hand on the door knob.

'Natû is my only child. I would be grateful if you brought her here.'

'No sweat.' Anna opened the door.

'Oh, Miss McInnes, they need someone to run Natû's team back with Patrick. Bud needs rest. Would you take Scott?'

Anna looked back over her shoulder, oblivious to the picture she presented, the back of her slacks plastered with mud, soiled as a baby's diaper.

'I'll be at Birchwood in two hours. Have whoever you are sending waiting there.'

The door slammed behind her.

'Trapper, I can find another pilot. Give me an hour or two,' pleaded Scott.

'We have a pilot. Natû needs to be checked by a doctor at our new hospital. Kiluk has already phoned and made the appointment. Be at Birchwood.'

Scott had only heard that tone in Trapper's voice when he and Patrick were very young and had transgressed some social custom or did not pay due respect to the animal they killed.

'Birchwood it is,' he agreed.

*

Anna walked along the line of aircraft battened down at Birch-wood. She studied each light plane as she passed, putting a face and name to the person who owned the machine.

Eventually she stopped beside a Cessna 180 and patted the orange and white striped tail. She busied herself walking around the plane, doing external checks. She deliberately did not look at the airport entrance to see if Scott was coming.

He was familiar with the airport and could find her. Crunching gravel and a glimpse of familiar boots beneath the belly of her plane told her of Scott's arrival. She caught her breath, and the familiar surge of excitement which flooded her body every time she saw Scott tingled along her nerves.

She waited for him to greet her, but as the silence lengthened she tried to ignore his presence and continued with the pre-flight checks.

The plane shook as Scott kicked the tyre on his side.

'Don't worry, I've already checked the wheels and tyres, they're fine,' shouted Anna, tucking a strand of blonde hair under her cap.

Scott did not answer. Instead he walked around the nose of the aircraft, opened the door and flung a small backpack onto the back seat.

'Into the hold, please,' commanded Anna coldly. Scott slammed the door and walked back to obey her. The rigid set of his shoulders told Anna he was angry.

Tough, she thought. As long as I'm the pilot of this aircraft, you, Mr Butler, will do as I say.

Anna dragged out the checks as long as she could, but finally she swung herself into the plane. Scott followed closely and strapped himself into his seat. He automatically looked at the windsock. The wind was strengthening; the windsock now stood at almost ninety degrees to the pole.

His eyes followed Anna's slender fingers as she touched each instrument lightly after checking it. He wanted to take her hand and hold it to his mouth, but the mental picture of her and Ted, which refused to fade, refuelled his anger. He turned and looked down to where the gravel was flying as the plane turned to taxi onto the runway. Anna held the microphone close to her mouth, giving details of their destination and ETA.

Scott deliberately kept his face turned away from Anna, and stared out at the trees growing ever smaller as the plane climbed to cruising altitude.

The angry silence became oppressive in the small cockpit, and Anna took a deep breath.

'I'll fly along the Iditarod trail to Skwentna,' she said. 'It's the easy part, but its interesting to study the terrain from the air.'

Scott grunted but still did not look at her. You're hurting, she thought, but so am I, Scott. So am I.

Anna studied the instrument panel in front of her. It was humiliating to have all her overtures ignored.

It's your fault, she told herself. You've taken away his pride and he wants to hit back at you. He can't do it physically, so he's making you suffer mentally.

She sighed and glanced out of the side window. Put up with it, Anna, she thought, as she watched the unending vista of lakes and rivers dance with the forests and hills.

Scott coughed and Anna turned to face him, hoping that he was about to speak to her, but he kept his lips clamped tight; only the twitch of a muscle in his cheek told of any emotion.

Anna turned back to her flying and pretended to study the instrument board again.

Anna matched his silence until the winding Skwentna and Yentna rivers appeared, lying like discarded tinsel below the small village.

'Alaska range ahead,' said Anna, pointing to a barrier of dark mountains barring the way to the Interior. 'You have to climb over three thousand feet to cross them at Rainy Pass during the race. That, of course, is if you survive the mad ride down the canyon carved out by the Happy River.'

Anna glanced at Scott, but he sat staring stony-faced at the Alaska range.

The village came into view, and Anna knew that once they

landed she would not have the opportunity to be alone with Scott. She had to make him speak to her.

'Scott, I know that you are angry. You have every right to be furious. But I should be given the opportunity to explain things. I love you so deeply. Please listen.'

'You have nothing to tell me, Mrs Ted Dawson,' he answered coldly. He deliberately studied the landing strip.

Anna sucked in her lower lip. She concentrated on landing the plane. It touched down and stuck. Anna taxied to where Patrick and Herbie were waiting. They turned away as sand and grit flew up around them.

As the plane stopped, Scott flung open the door and jumped down. He hurried over to greet his brother.

'What's wrong, kid?' Lovers' quarrel? No goodbye kiss for the lady in red?' teased Patrick. Then, seeing the look in Scott's eyes, he desisted from teasing him further. I knew it would happen, he thought, as they trudged to the rusted van owned by Kiluk and Herbie.

I was right. She's not his type. Now he wants to kill someone. It may as well be me. He has to talk, and get rid of the steam inside him. I'll tackle him on the run home. I'll get him to tell me what a bitch she has been to him.

Anna watched the two brothers embrace, and finally tears shamed her. They ran unchecked down her cheeks. She bent down, pretending to look for something in her folder between the seats.

The door opened.

'Scott?' she said, raising her tear-stained face to the opening, but it was Patrick leaning into the cockpit.

'No, but will I do?' he asked. He swung himself into the seat, not waiting for an answer.

'My brother is going through hell, Miss McInnes. The last time I saw him cry was when he was five and fell out of a tree, breaking an arm and fracturing a few ribs. I think you should know that I don't like people who use my brother and hurt him. That means you.'

Anna sniffed and wiped her nose on the sleeve of her jacket.

'Nor do I,' she said. 'I hate myself, but he won't let me explain. I tried all the way over here. He won't talk to me.'

Patrick suddenly felt sorry for the woman he was prepared to hate.

'Try me,' he said. 'I'll listen.'

Anna looked to where Patrick and Scott were standing talking.

'We have time. The Owens are bringing Natû in a friend's truck. It's new and has better suspension than theirs. They don't want to bump her if they can avoid it.

'Natû?'

'Don't worry,' he said in answer to Anna's unasked question. 'Kiluk says Natû will still run the Iditarod. Now tell me why you and Scott are so damn miserable.'

Patrick put his hand over Anna's, which was cold and trembling.

His touch unlocked the hurt and horror.

Between sniffs, Anna told him about her sham of a marriage to Ted Dawson, her love for Scott, her fear that she had lost him. She pleaded with him to intercede on her behalf.

'He won't talk to me. He hates me. But he may listen to you.'

When at last she finished, Patrick sat in silence with his head bowed. In spite of his initial dislike of Anna, considering her too sophisticated for Scott, he believed her story and felt sorry for the woman begging him to help her win back Scott's love.

She looked completely different in jeans and a flying jacket, with tears still running down her cheeks. She reminded him of Savannah, his sister, running to him when she was hurt.

Patrick scrabbled in his pocket and pulled out a green and orange check scarf which he used as a neck warmer when running sled dogs.

'Here, wipe your eyes,' he said gently. 'The Owens have arrived. I don't want Kiluk thinking that I've made you cry. She'll kill me. Kiluk is a tough lady, and I'd like to remain friends with her.'

Anna smiled tearfully and scrubbed at her face. Patrick was about to climb out of the aircraft when, on impulse, he leaned over and kissed Anna on her still damp cheek.

'I'll talk to my young brother,' he said. 'We've a long run back to Chugiak. I'll see what I can do.'

Anna tried to smile her thanks, but burst into sobs of gratitude instead.

'Now, now Anna. If you wet that scarf again I'll not be able to use it on the run.'

Anna found a tissue in her trouser pocket, blew her nose and handed Patrick his scarf.

He flung it carelessly over his shoulder and jogged to where Herbie Owens had parked the truck.

'Why is Anna not coming over to say hi?' asked Kiluk, as Patrick opened the door for her.

'I think she's in a hurry to get Natû back and into hospital. She also said something about the weather,' lied Patrick.

Scott looked up at the sky and checked the windsock.

'Looks okay to me,' he said.

'Sure, it will be. I think her main worry is Natû.'

'She is a good girl, that Anna McInnes, said Kiluk, watching Patrick help Natû down from the truck.

'Always ready to help. Everyone likes her up here.'

'Don't you mean Mrs Anna Dawson?' asked Scott bitterly.

Kiluk spun round. Her eyes glinted. She was angry. Both Patrick and Herbie busied themselves by placing a protective arm under each of Natû's shoulders.

'Has Trapper not taught you never to judge a man until you have walked a mile in his shoes?' she snapped. 'Have you tried on Anna's shoes?'

Patrick smothered a smile at the thought of Scott teetering in the high-heeled sandals Anna had worn to the wedding. He quickly pulled on a sombre mask to cover his lapse.

'If you blondies were sensible like us, you would only marry when babies arrive,' said Kiluk.

Patrick thought he felt Natû stiffen at the mention of babies.

She is probably in more pain than she shows, he thought.

'Come, Natû, let me carry you to the plane,' he said, scooping her up in his arms like a baby. She did not protest. It was comforting to be cradled.

Herbie put his hand on Kiluk's arm to stay her tongue. He should have known better: his wife had not earned her formidable reputation by being gentle when she felt something was unjust.

Kiluk had noticed Anna wipe her eyes with the brightly checked scarf, and had seen Patrick kiss Anna gently on the cheek.

Native whispers had told her of Scott and Anna's romance. They also told of Anna's return to Dawson's side in public.

Kiluk did not like Dawson or the oil company he managed. Neither did she like his treatment of his employees. She smiled as she thought of his dismay if he knew what the whispers said of him.

In the pockets of the vast, magnificent wilderness where man has settled whispers, like mosquitoes, fly and sting.

Natû pressed her face to the window and waved as Anna turned the plane for take-off.

'Scott looks like a child caught doing something wrong,' said Natû, watching Kiluk wave her finger as she talked.

Anna glanced across at the small group clustered round Kiluk, then turned her attention back to the runway and the plane.

'Kiluk is giving him one of her famous, or should I say infamous, lectures. As a child I was terrified of doing anything to annoy her. Oline was never angry. Inupiats never smack their children. I wish Oline was here with me now.'

Even though Natû dropped her head quickly and her thick, black hair curtained her face, Anna saw her mouth tremble and her eyes fill with tears.

'Are you in pain, Natû? Do you want to return to Skwentna and rest until you feel stronger? I'll come and fetch you whenever you're ready.'

'No, I'm fine. Sorry.'

Anna peered at her, but Natû had closed her eyes and appeared to be asleep.

Anna took a last look at the van still standing to one side of the strip.

The small group sat in the van watching as the Cessna bumped down the strip, lifted, wavered like a damaged butterfly in the wind and then turned on a heading for Birchwood.

'That's it then,' said Kiluk. 'Bunks are ready. Chilli moose is on the stove. I'll phone and tell Trapper that Natû is on her way home.'

'He's probably at Birchwood already,' laughed Patrick.

In the plane, Natû sat in silence with her head bowed.

If she's Trapper's daughter she can probably sit silent and motionless for hours, thought Anna as the plane cut through the clear blue sky. She remembered the countless stories Scott had told her of his childhood with Trapper.

Time flew by swiftly, as unnoticed as the wild beauty beneath them. Anna relived her memories with Scott.

Natû thought of Bud, and her chances of running the Iditarod.

Chapter Twenty

TRAPPER STOOD beside his truck, squinting into the light. He seemed oblivious of the wind whipping his beard across his parka like windscreen wipers. He had driven to Birchwood Airport as soon as he'd received Kiluk's phone call.

He had to see his daughter, and find out if she was pregnant. The thought of having a grandson filled him with delight. He would have a young soul to mould and a boy to turn into a true Inupiat, before it was time for him to leave and meet his ancestors.

A truck drawing up beside him diverted his attention away from the sky.

'Hi there.' A woman in her early forties, with a thick plait hanging out of her knitted cap like a cat's tail, walked towards him.

'I'm Claire, part of the team at Wasilla Iditarod headquarters.'

'Trapper Jack,' said Trapper gruffly, and returned his gaze to the skies.

'A well-known name up here,' said Claire, studying the squat, bulky figure with a mouse-eaten beard. 'Wish we had more like you to fight for the land.'

Trapper favoured her with a brief smile, then scanned the heavens.

'Anna won't be landing for at least another twenty minutes. They have strong headwinds. I'm so pleased that your daughter is fine.' Claire found that she was babbling. She had not expected to meet Trapper, who was a legend up in the Forty-ninth state. 'I've always wanted a daughter but could never find a man, at least not one to father my daughter. Now,' Claire looked down at her dumpy body and flicked her plait away from her shoulder, 'now it's too late for those crazy dreams. So I baby dogs and mushers. It keeps me busy.'

Suddenly Claire stopped talking, afraid that she was boring Trapper.

'Sorry. I don't usually run on like this.'

'That's okay, worry loosens the tongue, and I think you are worried about Anna,' said Trapper.

He instinctively liked this homely woman. Perhaps he could learn more about Anna and Scott from her.

'I've a flask in the truck,' he said. 'How does hot tea sound?'

'Better than champagne, today.' Claire followed Trapper to his truck.

Soon they were seated inside, sipping strong black tea.

'Thanks,' said Claire, running her finger round the stained rim of the top of the flask which she was using as a cup. 'It's better in here. That wind was showing its strength, and unlike the mushers I do not enjoy fighting it.'

'I hope Miss McInnes enjoys flying in it,' said Trapper, bringing the conversation round to Anna, the person he wanted to know more about.

'Oh, Anna's a star. She's a top-drawer pilot. Don't worry about your daughter. She's safe in Anna's hands.'

Trapper topped up Claire's cup.

'This Miss Anna McInnes. I saw her photograph in the paper recently at a charity function. I believe the article referred to her as a married woman?'

'She is. Well, sort of. Anna and I have been friends since we were kids. Her dad was a flying instructor in the Lower Forty-eight. They were a decent, hard-working, middle-class American family.'

'The backbone of society,' interjected Trapper, spooning more sugar into his tea.

'Yeah. Anna was a clever kid. She had looks and brains, things which are seldom handed out together.'

Claire sighed and twirled the end of her plait.

182

'I envied her. Then came the crash. Her father was flying his family to Denver to visit relatives. A sudden storm hit. The plane went down. Flames attracted rescue workers. Anna was the only survivor. Her relatives gave her a home.'

Claire drained her cup and placed it on the rubber mat at her feet.

'I didn't see Anna again until she appeared here in Alaska. She came up to fly for Mark Air, which as you know went bust. That's where she met Ted Dawson, on a flight to the Prudhoe Bay oilfields. In those days Dawson was a slim, good-looking young executive with his feet on the ladder to success. But he was older than her, with a reputation for collecting women.'

Claire stopped talking and peered forward, looking up at the sky.

'Go on.' Trapper did not want Claire to stop talking; he wanted to know more about Dawson.

'No one knows why she threw herself away on Ted Dawson. Perhaps looking for a father figure. Perhaps financial security. Whatever the reason, it was a disaster. He no sooner had her, when his fingers became sticky again. We all hoped that her affair with the Butler boy would break Dawson's hold over her. But Double Dick is tricky. He blackmailed Anna into playing the wife again.'

'Blackmail is a very strong word.'

'What he did was mean and nasty and it worked,' said Claire. 'I pretended to believe Anna when she said it was over and Scott was only a fling, but the emptiness in her eyes told me she was lying.'

'Tell me.' Trapper emptied the thermos and listened intently as Claire spoke.

At the end of the story, he nodded, patted his moustache in place and climbed out of the vehicle.

'She's here,' he said.

Claire went to stand beside him. The sky was empty and the whistle of the wind was the only sound to break the silence.

They stood for a few moments and Trapper pointed.

'See, there it comes.'

Claire was not certain whether the spot was merely due to eye strain or was in fact an aircraft. The soft drone, gradually increasing in intensity, proved Trapper to be right.

Chapter Twenty-One

'BIRCHWOOD AHEAD,' said Anna touching Natû lightly on the arm. Natû opened her eyes.

'Who is that waiting with Trapper?' she asked.

Anna prided herself on her eyesight, but she could not even recognize Trapper Jack. He was merely a small stick figure in the distance.

She shook her head.

'Ready for touchdown?' asked Anna. 'I'll make it as soft as I possibly can.'

True to her promise, the wheels kissed the ground and clung as if to a lover's lips.

The plane taxied to a stop where Claire and Trapper stood waiting.

They both hurried to the door and helped Natû down. Natû waited for Anna to climb out, then hugged and thanked her. She gave them all a wan smile, but walked steadily to the van. Claire helped Natû into the truck, then crossed to the plane to talk to Anna.

If an Inupiat woman can give birth in winter alone, and chew through the umbilical cord to separate the baby from the placenta, then I can behave normally after a simple miscarriage, thought Natû as she watched Trapper approach the van.

These thoughts gave her the strength to smile and talk to Claire and to her father, but they also emphasized the emptiness she now felt.

Natû had hugged the secret of her baby to herself for so long, that she felt as if part of herself was gone for ever and would never be replaced.

185

Who am I going to talk to now when I run the team? she asked silently. Baby, we will not run under the burled arch in Nome. We will not finish the race together.

'All right?' Natû started. She had not realized that Trapper was talking to her.

She nodded, not knowing what she was agreeing to.

Stop it, she commanded herself. Kiluk said it is not a baby until it can exist outside the womb on its own, and it could not.

'Kiluk has made the appointment,' said Trapper. Natû blanched. Was her father reading her mind? How did he know she was thinking of Kiluk?

Natû nodded again.

It was wise of Kiluk to insist that I drive Natû straight to our hospital for a check, thought Trapper, glancing at his daughter from the corner of his eye as the truck bucked over the gravel road.

She is very pale and quiet, and moves with the stiff joints of an old woman.

Trapper sat in the truck waiting for Natû. He had walked into the hospital with her, but as usual the antiseptic smells and soft squeaking of rubber-soled shoes made him nervous.

He sat as unmoving as if on sea ice, waiting for a seal to surface for air at one of its aglus. Stoicism and patience were the two great strengths of the Inupiat people, and Trapper had an abundance of both.

Natû lay with her knees bent high and legs spread open.

'Kiluk is an excellent midwife,' the doctor pronounced as he finished his examination of Natû.

'I think we'll do a vacuum, in case anything is still in the womb, and perhaps in this case a course of antibiotics as well.'

'My father is waiting and does not know,' said Natû.

'Sometimes ignorance is advisable. We'll keep it that way. I'll say I need you for observation. He can collect you in the morning.'

186

'Thank you,' whispered Natû. This would give her time alone before facing Bud.

'Doctor,' called Natû as he was about to open the door.

'Yes?'

'I want to run the Iditarod in March. This won't stop me, will it?'

He came and sat on the edge of Natû's bed.

'A few years ago I would have said the Iditarod was too formidable and dangerous a race for women to even think of entering. I certainly did not believe that a woman could ever complete the thousand and nine miles to Nome.'

He smiled.

'As usual, your sex has proved me wrong. Not only did women enter and complete that killer race, they also won it. They beat the best men veterans, repeatedly. When Mother Nature fashioned women, she built in extra endurance and survival traits. The leftovers she gave to men.'

Natû laughed. It was the first time she had smiled or laughed spontaneously since Sockeye bolted into the forest.

'Thank you,' she said. 'I needed to hear that.'

'Tight lines and a good trail, Natû. I have no doubt that you will be in the starters' chute for the race. I'll watch out for you on television, and Kiluk will have the radio blaring until they take down the widow's lantern from the arch in Nome when the last musher staggers past.'

He walked quickly to the door.

'Sleep now. Sleep is the greatest healer.'

Natû walked to the entrance of the hospital. She had recovered quickly and felt well and strong. She expected to see her father, but a tall, muscular man stood near the door. Black hair curled into his neck.

'Bud,' she shrieked and ran to him.

Bud opened his arms and waited for her to reach him. He

enfolded her and held her close. Natû wrapped her arms around him as if she would never let him go.

'Natû,' he whispered as he bent down and kissed the top of her head. 'I thought I had lost you. You are my reason for living.'

Natû looked up at Bud in surprise. She knew that he loved her, but he usually did not express his feelings in such flowing terms.

'Come,' he said. 'Don't cry or they won't let me take you home. They'll say you need to stay for further observation, as I'm obviously a wife-beater.'

Natû sniffed back her tears of joy.

'Let's go quickly,' she said.

Kiluk's cousin watched them climb into the truck, then he turned to follow the nurse who had been sent to find him.

'Good luck, Natû,' he whispered. 'I've a feeling Trapper will be proud of his daughter in this race.'

Chapter Twenty-Two

PATRICK SET a gruelling pace once they twisted their way out of Skwentna. He felt that Scott should rid himself of his anger with physical exercise.

Patrick allowed White-out to race ahead, urging Bud's team to try to outdistance Natû's team, driven by Scott.

The ruse worked. Scott accepted the challenge. 'Come on, Sockeye. Don't let that lot of fancy dogs beat you. You are native dogs. Running is your game. Get up! Let's hike!'

Scott jumped off the sled runners to lighten the load, and ran up the hill beside the sled.

Patrick looked over his shoulder and grinned. 'Run, kid, run,' he said. 'You'll be easier to talk to when you're tired.'

Shark heard the teams approaching before Muktuk did. She jumped up, alerting all his team, who were lying quietly waiting for him to butcher the moose and hopefully feed snacks to them.

Shark immediately issued a challenge to fight Sockeye, White-out and their teams.

'Quiet, you mean-tempered little bitch!' yelled Muktuk.

The tone of his voice was enough to make his team sit down again. But Shark was intelligent enough to realize that Muktuk would not leave the moose until it was cut up and packed on the sled.

She continued to snarl and bark insults at the approaching dogs.

Muktuk stood up. He had pushed the sleeves of his shirt and jacket above his elbows. Blood ran down his arms and dripped from his fingertips, patterning the snow with scarlet polka dots.

189

'One day I'm gonna skin you, just like the moose,' he threatened. 'Damn-fool dog. What do you think is out there? Another moose?'

Muktuk patted his pocket, making sure his revolver was in place.

Another moose would be good, he thought. I can stock up on jerky.

Both Muktuk and his dogs enjoyed chewing strips of dried moose meat.

Suddenly Muktuk spun round and looked behind him: White-out was coming over the rise, closely followed by Sockeye and Scott.

'Keep them dogs away from Shark and Delilah,' shouted Muktuk, but too late. Shark lunged at White-out, missed him and sank her sharp canines into the swing dog, a pure-bred Siberian husky, who ran too close to her.

Patrick dropped the brake and ran to pull Shark off his swing dog, who was ready to kill the little bitch.

'Take your team on by,' Muktuk yelled at Scott, as he ran to help Patrick. 'Nothing Shark likes better than a brawl.'

Scott understood and ran his team well away from trouble. He stopped with his team, making sure they couldn't pull the brake and join in the fun. He sat in the snow beside Sockeye, fondling his ears, which were pricked up like early-warning radar systems, interpreting the mixed howls and barks from the teams behind.

Muktuk and Patrick reached Shark at the same time. 'Let me get her,' said Muktuk. 'In this mood she'll tear into you.'

He swore as his lead dog left Patrick's husky and clamped her jaws over his upper arm.

Fortunately his rolled-up sleeves wadded into her mouth and stopped her teeth ripping open his flesh.

'Need that arm for the race, you fool,' he said, pulling her away and holding her in the air where her teeth snapped harmlessly and her feet paddled for purchase.

The boys left Muktuk calling Shark names they had never heard but filed away for future reference.

'It would be great to run to the Rohn cabin, stay overnight and then start back to Chugiak tomorrow,' mused Patrick.

'Fine by me,' answered Scott, but with more enthusiasm in his voice than Patrick had heard since Anna had dropped him at the landing strip and collected Natû.

'A few problems with that idea,' said Patrick thoughtfully.

'Kiluk phoned Trapper to say we were on our way home. He's had one upset with Natû and he doesn't need another with us,' Scott nodded.

'We're also headed for Yentna Station and Knik, not Rainy Pass and Rohn.' Patrick pulled up his checked neck warmer. 'Tell you what: last one into Wasilla buys pizzas and beers.' Patrick was gone before Scott could reply.

'Kiss your money goodbye – here I come, my big brother,' called Scott.

The hours passed in mesmeric silence as the boys concentrated on the trail and the dogs. Scott was happy pretending that he was running the Iditarod.

He was content to remain close behind Patrick until the outskirts of Wasilla, as Patrick and his team knew the trail.

I'll use your knowledge of this section of the trail, then overtake you before the town, pizza man, he thought.

Chapter Twenty-Three

THE FIRST Saturday in March seemed to rush on Natû, Bud and Patrick with the speed of a blizzard racing across the frozen Bering Sea.

Natû bent over the sewing machine until late at night sewing extra dog booties for Patrick's team. She and Bud both had one thousand pairs of booties, to ensure that each of their dogs would be well protected during the race. Their booties were all part of the donations under their sponsorship.

But Patrick had managed to collect only one hundred and thirty pairs, barely meeting the mandatory terms of eight booties for each dog running.

Natû was given a roll of polypropylene by an Iditarod fan, and she decided that as it was not given to her as part of the sponsorship, she was entitled to use it for Patrick. As the pile of bright red booties grew on the floor beside her machine, so her smile widened and her laughter became more frequent.

Trapper spent hours on the phone, cajoling small companies into providing harnesses and tuglines, plus the seven mandatory items required by the committee and the other recommended safety equipment.

Herbie and Kiluk Owens arrived to help train 'Trapper's team'. Herbie brought two of his beautiful sleds. A light toboggan-type sled to start the race, and a heavier, beautifully crafted basket sled which would be loaded with the mandatory and extra gear needed for the race after the second start outside Knik. Herbie believed that the safety afforded by a heavier sled when running along the coast with its sudden snowstorms, gales and blizzards outweighed the extra items the dogs would have to pull.

'That wind flips light sleds, dogs and mushers over like a kid waving a flag at the parade. Play safe, start light, then use the larger, heavier sled,' he advised Patrick. 'I'll fix up my own sled and get it to McGrath for you. Who knows, you may need it after Dalzell Gorge and Farewell Burn.'

'I'm not about to smash up that beauty you've just built. She has to last for the next ten Iditarods,' said Patrick seriously.

'And after that, when I get my chance to run,' added Scott.

Kiluk smiled. 'Herbie's sled will last as long as there are good mushers to ride them. He builds his to take punishment on the trail, not to collapse into a pile of nuts and bolts.' Her expression told what she thought of the modern sleds, that were bolted and screwed together.

'Talking of modern sleds,' said Trapper, turning from the phone. 'We've now got a track drag with carbide tips to pull behind the sled. It'll give you more control on descents and help grip on glare ice. The same company are giving us polycarbonate goggles, which will cut out over ninety nine percent of UV rays, and they are not smoked. And they've thrown in a headlamp, the same as Bud's, dual beam, lithium batteries and krypton bulbs.'

Patrick whistled softly. 'Thanks, Trapper.'

'A dog lover from Dallas phoned early today,' said Kiluk suddenly. 'She heard that we have the begging bowl out and wants to be sure that the huskies have foot ointment. So she has given us foot, anti-diarrhoeal, ophthalmic, antiseptic ointments and antibiotics for them. Oh, and she is adding sunblock, moisturizing cream, cold capsules and throat lozenges for your Patrick, plus a herbal mixture for diarrhoea.'

Patrick laughed.

'I almost forgot. She is also giving you glare liners, surgical gloves and a supply of chemical handwarmers. She says that she read 'Kate Pearson's Tip' in *Mushing* magazine, and wants to be sure that you can re-boot your dogs and apply foot ointment quickly in bad weather.'

'Bless all dog lovers,' said Patrick.

Kiluk glanced over at Natû, but she was still bent over her sewing machine. The pile of red booties was growing steadily.

'Muktuk arrives tomorrow,' she said.

'Lock up the snowmobile, Scott,' said Patrick. They all laughed except Scott. He loved the snowmobile he had rescued from a junk yard and painstakingly restored.

'You didn't say that when the dogs pulled it in training, before the snow fell,' he countered.

'Right. Muktuk was not here.'

Patrick turned to Trapper and Herbie. 'It'll be great to have a veteran with us,' he said. 'This will be his tenth Iditarod, won't it?'

'Yes, with that troublemaker lead bitch of his,' answered Herbie. 'The dog seems to get stronger with age. Last year she fastened onto the arm of one of the CNN cameramen covering the start. The guy missed filming the first musher away, and almost lost his job, plus his arm. Dog bites are bad things, go septic very quickly.'

Trapper sat at the table in the large central room ticking off items on the long list in front of him.

'We're getting there,' he said. 'The Inupiats in Barrow have frozen "water snacks" for us, whitefish and water and oil, to give the dogs at short rest stops. They have also sliced and frozen beaver meat, in case Patrick has real problems getting the dogs to eat. Dogs usually go for beaver when they reject everything else.'

'I can't believe how everyone is helping,' said Scott.

'The Iditarod is a great bonding of people. They forget their differences, and for two to three weeks the only important thing in Alaska is the race. But don't be fooled into thinking that every musher is there to help and give advice. Many will, but you'll find those who'll fill you with horror stories, look at your dogs and shake their heads. If you're not tough you'll start doubting yourself and your dogs. Don't. Remember, rookies are not expected to win, only to finish and live to run again.'

It was a long speech for Trapper. He had been strangely quiet since Natû returned from hospital. She noticed him watching her closely when she ran the dogs. But she was caught up in the giddy excitement, strain and stress which precede the world's toughest race. She had little spare time to worry about her father's silence. Her energy had returned, and she felt as strong and healthy as her dogs.

At night, the beautiful, haunting wolfsongs would either chill or thrill the mushers who were gathering in the bush for their final training and preparation. The huskies sensed the excitement and sang to each other, telling stories of the trail, boasting and taunting each other to feats of daring.

Scott, Bud and Patrick visited the camps and talked to the mushers, veterans and rookies alike. They amassed a wealth of detail, plus some horrific stories.

Trapper listened to the boys each night and sifted the information, discarding the disinformation and ignorance from the important tips.

One night, accompanied by the lonesome howl of their huskies, who recognized them as they approached the dog lot, Scott and Patrick trudged back from a musher who had set up camp close to their cabin.

'You'll have to put some fat on those bones of yours,' teased Scott. 'That guy works at the Arctic Sports Medicine Institute, and he says mushers must be tubby. You need at least nineteen per cent body fat to run a race where you'll lose about thirty pounds, as you burn off ten thousand calories a day.'

Patrick laughed.

'So you remember all the figures. He must have impressed you. Don't worry, kid. I'm like a piece of jerky – tough and long-lasting.'

Scott put his arm loosely across Patrick's shoulder.

'Watch yourself out there. Most of these mushers predict that someone is going to buy it soon in the Iditarod. I don't want it to be you.'

Patrick strained to see Scott's expression, but his face was shaded in the dark and his features were barely discernible.

'Now don't go believing everything they say.'

Patrick took a deep breath, uncertain as to whether this was the time to approach the subject of Anna. They had not spoken of her since their stop at Wasilla to eat pizzas, when he had told Scott the story behind the picture in the newspaper.

Scott seemed to believe him at the time, and Patrick was certain that his kid brother would contact Anna.

Anna had neither phoned nor appeared at the cabin, which made Patrick think that his explanations on her behalf had not changed his brother's mind. Scott had obviously not contacted her.

'I can't afford to buy it,' he said. 'Who would be here to sort out your love life?'

Scott grunted. It was a small, dismal sound.

'Love life? There is none.'

He thought of all the letters he had left in Anna's mailbox at her cabin and at the airport. None of them had been answered. Patrick was wrong. Anna had obviously been happily reunited with her wealthy husband.

No, I'll write no more letters, he thought. Light suddenly streamed out of the cabin door, lighting their way up the steps.

'Good news,' shouted Bud as he held the door against the wind.

'Close the door, all the Velcro strips are blowing away.'

Natû's voice carried clearly to where the brothers stood.

'Tell them when they are inside, not standing in a wind which will soon be a gale.'

Scott and Patrick were thrust into the room with the wind like a giant's hand on their backs.

'What news?' they asked together.

'We now have a donor for all the food for Patrick's team,' said Bud, 'not only the snacks.'

'Fresh frozen meat, oil and dry ingredients. And they are shipping it out to the dog drops along the trail,' added Natû, her eyes sparkling.

'Not only that, the donor has added cases of HEET, so you have kerosene, plus a cooking pot and a six-gallon insulated cooler to feed the team warm food along the trail.'

'Great stuff,' yelled Patrick, swinging Natû off her feet and away from her machine.

'Patrick, stop it. I only have a few dozen Velcro strips to fix to the booties and I'm done. Put me down, you crazy man.'

'This is marvellous stuff,' said Scott. 'Who is Patrick's donor?'

'Anna McInnes,' said Trapper. 'She arranged it with a firm in San Francisco when she was there a few days ago.'

San Francisco? Why is Anna down there? She is part of the Elite Iditarod Flying Team and should be here in Alaska, thought Scott.

Suddenly he realized why his letters had gone unanswered. Anna had not seen them.

'How long has she been in the Lower Forty-eight?' he asked Trapper, trying to appear nonchalant.

'You'll have to ask Bud, he answered the phone. He put it down as you and Patrick arrived,' answered Trapper, ticking off the items Anna had obtained from the list.

Scott felt ill. He could have heard Anna's voice. There was so much he needed to tell the woman he loved. He had to apologize, and to ask her to marry him once he was through with varsity and had found a job. He did not want to see her with Ted Dawson again.

He was sure that with Trapper's support, Jake and Casey would not object to his plans. His parents would love Anna, especially once they'd met her and realized that he did not intend to marry until he could support her. But he had to talk to Anna now.

'Where is she? Did she leave her phone number?' he asked Bud eagerly.

'No, nothing,' said Bud. 'Oh, she did say that most of the pilots were down with this Sydney flu, and that she had to stay in the Lower Forty-eight for some time, but she seemed vague about when she would return to Alaska, if at all.'

Scott busied himself examining the dog booties that Natû was finishing.

'These are great. Better than the ones sold in the shops,' he said.

Patrick noticed the quaver in his sibling's voice.

'I'm sure Anna will be back soon. She loves Alaska, and she's flying in the Iditarod team.'

'Not so sure,' said Bud, unaware of what Patrick was trying to do. 'She did not seem at all eager to come here. She didn't even ask about the race. Perhaps she's enjoying the novelty of flying down in the lower states.'

'Could be,' said Natû, throwing the last bootie on the pile. 'But I know she was very proud and excited to be chosen as one of the Iditarod pilots. She'll be back in time for the race.'

Scott squeezed his eyes closed.

Please let her come back. Let me have a chance to show her how much I love her.

Patrick crossed to where Scott stood still, pretending to examine the red booties. He squeezed Scott's shoulder.

'Anna will never give up the chance of being an Iditarod pilot,' he said. 'A week before the race, she'll be here. Trust me.'

Chapter Twenty-Four

Anna McInnes strode from the room, leaving the door open behind her.

'I'll resign,' she shouted at the man seated behind the desk. 'I'll fly for Smyth up in Barrow. I'll fly for anyone, but I will not miss the Iditarod.'

'Anna,' he called as he watched her buttocks, encased in stretch jeans, disappear with the twitch of an angry cat's tail.

'Okay, Anna. You win. I will bring Bill down and you can go back to Anchorage. If . . .' He held up his hand. 'If you have dinner with me tonight.'

'It's a deal,' she answered. 'If you bring your wife.'

She stalked from the room as satisfied as a cat settling down to a dish of cream.

Anna let out a long sigh of relief as she looked out of the side window and saw the tidal flats shimmering in silver and pewter like an antique mirror. Dark tussocks of wet grass, as black as the patches tarnishing mirrors which tell of age, pock-marked the shining surface.

Anna felt all the excitement of a child before a festivity at the thought of being close to Scott, but then fear crept in to cloud her joy.

What if he still won't see me or talk to me? she thought, as she watched the flats continue to unfold like grey watered silk beneath the plane.

Make him, an inner voice urged. If you want him, go out there and get him.

In response to the cabin attendant's instructions, Anna raised the back of her seat and lowered her footrest. She had enjoyed travelling as a passenger.

The plane landed with a hard thump, which had the passengers clutching their armrests.

Anna pulled her tote bag from under her seat and moved to the front of the plane.

'Good solid touchdown, Jerry,' she said, teasing the co-pilot who'd made the landing.

'So not only are you a passenger nowadays, you're also an examiner,' retorted Jerry, embarrassed by his bad landing and sensitive to criticism. 'Come up here and see if you can do better.'

'Only kidding, Jerry. I love you for bringing me back to Anchorage. The Lower Forty-eight stinks. I never want to see it again.'

Anna blew him and kiss and elbowed her way to the steps.

'I wouldn't challenge that girl to do better,' warned the pilot. 'I've flown with her. She's a natural. Worked as an instructor for Moroney at Tri Star before she married that fat cat at BP.'

Jerry whistled softly.

'She must be good if she flew for Bruce,' he said. 'That guy accepts only the best.'

'Anna is. She's also part of the elite Iditarod team of pilots.'

Jerry whistled his amazement once again.

'Those guys fly their light planes in conditions which force bald eagles to walk. I've always wanted to be one of the Iditarod team.'

'With a landing like this you'd do well. Plonk it down on ice and make sure it stays put.'

'Okay, enough of that,' said Jerry, gathering his flight papers and cap. 'Let's go.'

The two pilots watched Anna stuff a handful of letters and notes into the side pocket of her tote and stride out of the building to the car park.

'She's received something good,' said the pilot. 'Look at that grin on her face.'

Anna stood in front of the mailbox that was nailed to a post near her cabin, then decided to leave what would only be bills and circulars till later. She needed to open the letters from Scott that were in her tote. The log cabin felt damp and cold when she arrived. Before opening the letters, she tidied it up and built a fire to drive out the feeling of desolation that an unlived-in house acquires, along with dust and the unpleasant odour of mushrooms.

Anna quickly sorted through the letters. The two with Scott's handwriting she placed on the sofa. The thick one with Ted Dawson's scrawl across the front she tossed unopened into the fire. She poked at it with a stick until the tight wad of pages unfolded and blackened into ash.

'I will never see you again, Dawson,' she muttered. 'I did what I had to do to make sure you didn't wriggle out of sponsoring Scott's friends. It's too late for you to withdraw now, so I'm free.'

With eager fingers Anna tore open the first of Scott's letters.

She cursed quietly when she realized that, in her haste, she had torn the letter as well.

Sitting cross-legged on the brown bearskin in front of the fire, she carefully pieced the letter together and threw the envelope into the flames. As she read, tears came to her eyes.

'Thank you God,' she whispered. 'You heard my prayers. Thank you.'

Like most people who live in Alaska, where they are surrounded with beauty so magnificent that the mind has difficulty accepting it, yet is enthralled and entrapped; where winters in the Interior and along the coastlines of the frozen northern seas are so terrifying in their might and darkness that people cower and hope only to survive; Anna knew that a Life Force existed. A force so powerful that it was well beyond the comprehension of man. She, like her fellow Alaskans, knew that God, this Life Force, was part of the heartbreaking beauty and terrifying power of nature in this special country.

Anna had glimpsed the face of God as she flew over mountains dazzling in their whiteness, and fought her way through gales and sleeting snow, when planes and pilots should have been grounded but could not, as someone needed to be rescued.

She came to Alaska a cynic, and had found the reason for life and something to believe in.

'Thank you,' she whispered again, stroking the tears from her lashes as she put Scott's second letter in her lap.

She sat motionless in front of the fire, hugging Scott's words to herself. Tears of happiness now plopped onto the page and smudged the words.

Sensing the wind freshen and tap at the window panes, Anna glanced up. It was dark. Reluctantly she stood up and walked to her kitchenette to prepare a mug of soup and some toast. Carrying the laden tray back to the fire, she stopped to choose a CD.

Roberta Flack's clear voice filled the room with the beautiful words of Scott and Anna's favourite song.

Anna sipped her soup dreamily, and thought of Scott's mouth covering hers.

She listened until Flack's voice faded. She pressed the play button again, and as the haunting melody enfolded her she picked up her tote and fumbled for the car keys. 'I must see Scott now,' she said. 'Even if he can't leave Patrick and Trapper, as the Iditarod is so close. I'll be able to see him, touch him, kiss him hello, tell him I'm here.'

The love song followed her as she ran to her car.

I owe you so much, Patrick, she thought, so very much. You have given Scott back to me. One day I'll do something for you. I swear that I'll repay you. I swear it.

As she neared Bud and Natû's cabin, Anna lifted her foot from the accelerator. The car coasted down the incline to the brightly lit log home.

The huskies heard the car. They greeted her arrival with a shattering chorus of barks and howls.

Muktuk shook his head, but did not remove his finger from the map spread out on the table.

'Pre-race fever,' he said. 'They drive each other crazy. By the time they get to the starting chute they are all plumb loco, out of control and damn dangerous. The force and pulling power of sixteen tough dogs all wild to run is frightening.'

Anna closed the door of the car quietly and tiptoed up to the uncurtained window.

Everyone was standing, peering intently at a map spread out on the kitchen counter. Muktuk was speaking and they were listening intently. Muktuk's words carried to her. Anna stared at Scott, storing up every detail as if she would never see him again.

'Last year two mushers scratched at the start. The one's team belted straight into the crowd, wrapped the musher round a truck. The truck wasn't damaged but he broke three ribs and smashed his sled.

'The second team made the first two blocks. They were doing fine until the first sharp-right turn. Team made the turn; he didn't, hung out the wrong way. Stupid dude was at the end of the dog whip when it cracked, whipped him from the sled and smashed his leg.'

Muktuk laughed, a mirthless sound. 'Took the officials two hours to catch and stop that crazy team. They chewed everything they found, as they raced through the suburbs of Anchorage. I think the final score was three cats, two poodles and a pet goose.'

Everyone laughed, and Anna smiled as she saw Scott's eyes crinkle in the corners.

How I love you, Scott Butler, she thought.

She was about to walk to the door when she noticed Scott fetch a note pad and pen. He jotted down notes as Muktuk spoke and the others nodded.

The mood in the room was suddenly serious and businesslike. Anna stuffed her hands deep into her pockets.

This is not the time to see Scott, she thought. They are

obviously engrossed in final preparations for the race. Scott will have to know exactly what to do as Patrick's handler, or those dogs will drag Scott and Patrick off their feet before the countdown and they'll be disqualified.

She turned away from the window with her shoulders hunched.

When I see Scott, I want to be alone with him. I want him to come to the cabin with me. I can't bear a quick kiss, which is all that I can hope for tonight,' she whispered to herself.

It will be worth waiting a little longer.

I have to fly food and dog drops tomorrow. I'll wait until after the madness of the media start in Anchorage and true start in Knik are over, then I'll have Scott. She paused in her whispering. *It will be worth the wait.*

Chapter Twenty-Five

BUD, NOW completely recovered from his rabies scare, was stunned as he walked into the Sullivan Arena where the mushers' pre-race banquet was to be held. He had not expected almost one and a half thousand excited people all shouting, laughing and drinking. The sea of faces seemed to rise and fall with the level of noise in the room.

Since the Wednesday before the start of the Iditarod, things had spun in an ever-widening vortex. He felt he had lost control and was being sucked in.

At Wasilla on Wednesday, Trapper's team stood behind the Iditarod veterinary officer with bated breath as he examined, weighed and gave each of the sixteen dogs in the three teams an electrocardiogram.

Tourists who were pouring into Anchorage for the race watched the proceedings with interest, and kept the staff busy answering their questions. Visitors to the Iditarod headquarters fondled the dogs and fawned over them, as if visiting a ward of newly born babies. Most of the huskies enjoyed the attention, but Shark took exception to a rotund woman who waddled towards her calling, 'Nice doggie. Come, girl.'

She waited until the woman was within biting range, then launched herself at her outstretched arm.

Muktuk saw disaster looming. He seemed to fly through the air. His shoulder hit the woman and knocked her off her feet before Shark could sink her teeth into the tourist's arm.

Confusion reigned as officials ran to placate the woman, and

Muktuk unclipped Shark from the peg outside the container built onto the truck.

'So you've done it again,' he growled at her as he held her at arm's length. 'Right, back into your compartment till the vet is ready for you.'

He put her into her small, warm compartment in the dog trailer. She immediately rested her paw in the opening and laid her head on it, trying to lure some unsuspecting fan to stroke her.

'Try it,' warned Muktuk. 'Once more, and Delilah is the new lead. The only lead. You can stay in Chugiak with the rejects.'

Shark snarled at him as he turned and strode back to the vet.

None of the dogs were pulled from the race due to heart murmurs, tumours or unnoticed pregnancies. Finally the vet inserted a microchip into a hypodermic syringe and injected it into the scruff of each husky's neck, just under the skin.

'What's that for?' Bud asked Trapper quietly.

'Helps officials scan the device at checkpoints. Gets the dog's medical history quickly.'

'Also stops mushers sneaking in fresh, rested-up dogs,' said Muktuk cynically.

The vet glanced over his shoulder at Muktuk.

'Got that same bad-lead bitch?' he asked.

'Sure. Shark's the best in the race.'

'Tape up her jaws when I examine her,' he said, looking down at his hands.

'Each year I have a new scar. I'm running short of fingers.'

'Comes with the job,' answered Muktuk, grinning.

The vet grimaced, and turned back to Trapper's team.

'Good dogs here. Hope the trail is great for you,' said the vet shaking hands with Bud, Patrick and Natû.

Mad, he thought, as he turned to examine the next team. Anyone who willingly runs this race is crazy. Plumb crazy.

On Thursday, Bud and sixty-odd mushers were at the mandatory mushers' meeting at the Regal Alaskan Hotel. The meeting seemed to be an enormous noisy class reunion, as mushers met, exchanged news, joked and collected freebies given out by the major sponsors. Bud collected a duffle bag and a set of chore gloves, which he then gave to Patrick to add to his stockpile of Iditarod necessities.

Hours passed as roll-call was taken, mushers signed their commemorative cachets, paid their Iditarod Trail Committee dues and listened to speeches given by officials and sponsors. Bud found that the words became meaningless, a drone which lulled him into a doze.

He started as Patrick dug him sharply in the ribs.

'Listen,' he said, 'this is the race manager, he'll tell us about conditions on the trial.'

Bud sat up sharply as if hit by a snowhook.

'Suckholes on Yukon. High winds up on Rainy Pass obliterating trail. River near Rohn is rocky trail and bad.'

'Sounds like a cakewalk,' Bud muttered to Patrick with a wry grin.

'The Iditarod is many things, but never a cakewalk,' said a musher sitting beside Patrick. 'You'll hate it and you'll glory in it, but you'll never make Nome unchanged by it.'

Scott nodded. He shadowed Patrick. He made no comment, but like a sponge absorbed everything. When it was his turn to run he wanted to know as much as possible about the toughest race in the world.

Bud was silent, overwhelmed by the enormity of what he had undertaken. He looked around at the other mushers. They seemed excited but relaxed.

Natû leaned across and squeezed his hand. 'We'll pretend we're on a training run,' she said quietly. 'Remember, we don't have to win, we're not one of the big names. We'll be okay.'

Bud rubbed her fingers, grateful for the contact.

The musher sitting beside Patrick watched Bud and Natû for a few moments, then he said, 'The first time I ran this damn crazy race I was so scared that I almost missed the start. I couldn't stop peeing, ended up running my team to the chute with wet underpants. I dribbled all the way out of Anchorage.'

Bud, Patrick and Scott laughed uproariously. Mushers turned

to look at them. The veterans in the crowd decided it was nervous hysteria; the rookies were impressed that anyone could laugh when listening to a description of what was obviously an impossible trail.

At last the meeting came to an end. Bud stood beneath the stuffed moosehead in the lobby of the Regal Alaskan. He looked up at the huge head with its oversized, bulbous nose and grinned at Scott. 'Looks like Disney's Pluto,' he said.

'Not when you meet a live, aggressive one on the trail,' answered Muktuk. 'You then have two options. Give way and go around it, or shoot it.'

Natû shivered, thinking of her team bolting into the spruce forest to avoid a moose.

'Come on,' she called to Bud, who seemed entranced by the stuffed head. 'We have to be at the banquet at six to draw our starting-position number.'

Bud groaned.

'All I want to do is sleep. These past few weeks have been hell. I feel like I've run two Iditarods.'

Muktuk grinned as he and Trapper followed Bud, Patrick, Scott and Natû from the Regal.

'Pray you draw an early start,' he yelled after them. 'The longer you wait, the crazier your dogs become and your lead no longer knows which sled runners to follow, as some of the bums don't make it out of Anchorage. They run up and down the streets screwing up the snow, which is specially trucked in on Friday so you don't start off on asphalt.'

The visitors standing in the hall and milling out of the meeting room stared at Muktuk. He seemed to be shouting at no one, as the four youngsters were walking in front of him and Trapper, listening but not looking back.

'Another reason to pray for an early start,' shouted Muktuk. 'You'll have good snow, helps hold brakes and snowhooks, asphalt doesn't work as well.'

'Who are you scaring the pants off?' one of the veterans called to Muktuk.

'Just whipping those kids of Trapper's into shape, so we don't have to pick up the pieces on the way to Nome,' Muktuk retorted with a rare smile.

Anchorage was as feverish as a patient whose temperature was soaring out of control.

It was well before dawn on the first Saturday in March. Fans and tourists were trudging towards Fourth Avenue, which lay resplendent beneath its new mantle of thick snow.

Light snow had dusted the city the night before and as they walked, it lifted with their boots leaving dark footprints across the pavements.

Television teams and cameramen from the daily newspapers were already in place. Fans jostled to obtain a position where they could see each musher and his team leave the start chute.

Trapper followed the red tail lights of Muktuk's truck, with the dog compartments built onto the back, very closely.

It was still dark, but the sky held a faint promise of dawn. Street lights and gaudy neon signs sketched vivid colours across the snow.

Scott, Bud, Natû and Patrick sat shoulder to shoulder on the front seat.

The day of the race had finally arrived, and as Trapper followed Muktuk to Fourth Avenue, Bud suddenly felt alone and afraid. The fried bread, eggs and thick slabs of ham he had eaten for breakfast lay oily in his queasy stomach. He now wished that he had taken Trapper's advice and drunk only water at the banquet the night before, but caught up in the air of camaraderie and excitement, he'd lost count of the beers he consumed.

'You were a little over-refreshed last night, Bud,' teased Natû. 'But I'm sure that the good breakfast you ate this morning helped.'

Bud swallowed an oily belch.

'Yeah, it was great, Natû. Thanks.'

Trapper looked out of the window, pretending to study the snow on the road. He did not want Bud to see him smile.

Just like her mother, he thought. She rubs in the lesson while offering sympathy.

'Herbie's made a great job of fitting dog compartments onto the back of the truck,' he said, looking in his rear-view mirror.

Most of the huskies were curled up on the straw in their boxes sleeping, but a few who had run the race before had their heads out of the small holes sniffing up the excitement in the air, plus a thousand other smells that only their keen noses could detect.

Their pink tongues lolled from their mouths and their teeth gleamed in wide grins.

To the passers-by they looked like dogs about to be guillotined. One could expect heads to roll to the ground as the blade came down on the small openings.

Muktuk pulled up at traffic lights throwing bands of red blood across the snow.

Trapper stopped close behind him. In the distance they could hear the sound of trucks and barking dogs approaching.

Suddenly Shark stuck her head out of her compartment on Muktuk's truck, snarled and barked some canine obscenity at Trapper's truck.

It was Clarke, the large white neutered male whose only fault Patrick could find was his constant need to prove that though they had emasculated him, he was better than any other male in the lot. This led to a great deal of growling and threatening. He looked a formidable opponent because of his size, but like most large growlers, he was loving and gentle.

Patrick recognized Clarke's bark answering Shark.

'That should put the little bitch in her place,' he said.

Trapper was about to disagree, when Shark's head disappeared into her box and there was silence.

Patrick loved the large 'grunt' dog, and Clarke returned the love with devotion and hard work. He seemed to want to please Patrick at all times.

Trapper's team heard the noise long before they reached Fourth Avenue.

'Sounds like a mixture of parade day and bedlam,' observed Scott.

'Wait till we get there,' warned Trapper. 'Pack seventy mushers and over a thousand tough dogs into one area and you have . . .'

'The start of the Iditarod,' said Natû quickly. Her eyes were sparkling and the cheek flaps of her fur cap stood up like hare's ears on either side of her head.

Muktuk found a relatively open spot for the two trucks to park. He propped his feet up on the dashboard, unwrapped a hot dog and poured himself a mug of coffee.

He seemed totally unconcerned about the race, the noise and the people. He had drawn number twenty-two, and was in no hurry to hook up his team. Shark would only be clipped onto her tugline a minute or two before the start.

'Yeah,' they heard him drawl in answer to a musher who had stopped at his van to talk to him. 'I'm too old for this damn race now. I'll just lope along, nice and easy like. Aim to let you youngsters break trail.' He took another slurp of coffee, sighed and closed his eyes. The musher shook his head and moved off.

'All show,' said Trapper. 'That old fox can run the boots off anyone in the race. He's been in the top five three times. He may lope, but only when he has finished the race.'

Bud and Natû had drawn numbers thirteen and sixteen. Patrick would leave early at number nine.

The three jumped out of the truck, eager to recheck the ganglines, tugs and sleds, though they had repacked the sleds at least a dozen times.

Each time they had the sleds ready for Trapper and Muktuk's inspection, Muktuk threw off extra items.

'Don't need all this damn city stuff,' he growled. 'Give your dogs all the help they can get. They don't need to drag this extra gear. You're not leaving to discover the North Pole. It's been found already. Rookies would take Mama and the wood stove if they could.'

At last Muktuk was satisfied that they carried what they needed for safety, but were not burdened with unnecessary clutter.

When the dogs saw the Butler boys, Natû and Bud climb out of the Ford, they all stuck their heads out of their boxes as far as they could without strangling themselves. They yipped, yowled and howled, begging to be let out, but mindful of Muktuk's warning, the youngsters left the dogs where they were.

'You'll be hooked up just before the start,' said Patrick, burying his face in Clarke's soft white fur ruff. Clarke licked his cheek in return.

Clarke was one of the 'grunt' dogs used in the middle of the team. He formed the brawn and heart of the team, but Patrick found that he was intelligent and took commands, so he occasionally used him as a lead dog as well. Sockeye seemed to accept the partnership happily.

A deep bond of love and trust had formed between Patrick and the large white 'old-timer', whose Iditarod days should have ended the year before. Patrick had taken the old boy, to teach the rest of his team, but Clarke pulled so well and was so eager to run that Patrick gave him a place in the middle of the team.

'Can always drop him if he tires,' he said. 'I think he deserves the right to try one last Iditarod.'

Muktuk shook his head and rubbed his eyes with his gnarled fingers. 'The Idit. is a race. You can't afford to be held back by an old-timer because you feel sorry for him.'

Patrick set his mouth in the obstinate line which Trapper recognized meant that nothing would change his mind. The boy loved Clarke and Clarke would run.

Patrick well remembered Trapper and Muktuk saying that a dog who had run the Iditarod a few times was invaluable. They remembered the trail, cliffs and canyons years after the race. They would follow their memory trail even when snow and foul weather had changed the landscape beyond recognition.

'You'll soon be out and at the start,' murmured Patrick to Clarke. Clarke seemed to understand, and whined softly with pleasure.

Chapter Twenty-Six

BUD GULPED nervously and glanced down at the passenger who had paid to sit in his sled bag for the start of the race. The man was a big, burly rigger. He had been one of the boys, one of Bud's friends, before he met Natû.

Trapper, who was helping as one of the ten handlers, studied the man. 'We could do with two his size to hold back this team,' he said. 'They've watched all the others go past to the chute and are now crazy. They're wild to go.'

He turned to look at the young handler handling the second sled, which would hopefully slow down Bud's team. The young man looked confident and cheerful. He waved to his girlfriend in the crowd. You're on the end of the tail when these dogs 'crack the whip' around bends, thought Trapper. Hold tight, you'll have quite a ride to Eagle River and the second start at Knik, where Bud has to drop both you and his second sled.

Bud had been fairly relaxed when he watched Patrick leave. It had been a perfect start. The team led by Sockeye behaved as if they ran the Iditarod regularly.

Natû was not as fortunate. An overeager fan stepped from behind the barricade just as the marshal started the countdown. The flash on her camera upset Natû's highly bred lead dog. She spun in the air yipping and barking. Natû was unable to make her voice carry over the noise of the crowd.

Come on girl, she thought. Do it for me. Calm down. Get ready to pull. Oline, make her listen. As if hearing Natû, the dog settled. As the countdown reached one, she was ready.

Natû breathed a sigh of relief. The teams were sent off at two-minute intervals. She did not want to be disqualified because her lead started before the command 'Go' from the marshal.

At times like this she regretted giving Patrick her favourite dog, Sockeye, but he had so little at the time, and she knew that with sponsorship she could have her choice of trained lead dogs. After much deliberation and checking the genealogy of the dogs, she chose a small grey bitch splashed with white. The dog looked as if she had fallen into a pot of paint. She fell in love with Natû instantly, and fought off any other dog who attempted to approach her for a cuddle.

'The bitch sticks to you like oil to a rag,' teased Bud one day. The dog was thus named Oily, and she lived up to her name.

Bud had his team lined up. He walked down the gangline of dogs, patting each in turn. To the spectators it looked as if he was reassuring the huskies. He was trying to calm himself.

Anna pushed her way roughly through the crowd. She elbowed aside a woman sporting a headdress fashioned from the stuffed head of a wolf.

'Damn madhouse,' she groused. 'It gets worse every year. They're not sure whether it's the start of a serious race or a fancy-dress rave.'

The TV camera zoomed in on the woman balancing the wolf's head on her hair, then the cameraman noticed Anna forcing her way around the woman.

He whistled softly and trained the camera on Anna as she found herself a place near the chute.

She had watched Patrick and Scott from a distance. I wonder if I'll ever mean as much to Scott as Patrick does? she thought as she watched the brothers hitch up the dogs and check the sled. Tears came unbidden as Scott put his arms around Patrick and hugged him.

Patrick said something which made Scott laugh, then glance at the crowd.

Anna saw the devilish twinkle in Scott's eyes as he walked back to Patrick, held his head firmly in his hands and kissed him on both cheeks.

Patrick flushed and looked uncomfortable.

'Don't be too long. Remember, I'll be waiting,' he yelled out loudly to his already discomfited brother. The crowd whistled and catcalled the boys.

Anna grinned, and waited until they moved up to the chute before finding a space where she could watch them run the few blocks before they had to turn down a side street to get out of the media-crazed capital and into the trees lining the highways, to meet up with their truck and handlers at the appointed place near Eagle River and drive to the 'new' start near Wasilla, thus bypassing open water on the Knik and Manastuka rivers.

Anna still hugged the idea to herself of a private reunion with Scott.

After they had left, she began battling her way to the starting point.

She saw only the back of Natû and her team as they belted down the avenue, but she was determined to wish Bud luck, as she felt he was the real rookie and needed encouragement.

Anna pushed back the cuff of her parka. Claire had given her the start numbers of Trapper's team, and she had arranged to fly only after Bud had left the chute.

I'll meet up with them somewhere along the trail, she told herself.

The rising sun whisked away the dark mantle obscuring the magnificent mountains that encircle Anchorage. Like a magician it revealed the snow-capped peaks sparkling like spun sugar. The landscape seemed to wait for applause. Bud was blind to the beauty.

'Thirteen!'

Bud froze. That was his number. There could be no going back now.

'Come on,' said Trapper. 'The sooner we get the dogs away from the crowds and music, the calmer they will be.'

Handlers moved in to take up the drag on each dog.

White-out forgot he was a dog with four legs. He pranced to the start on his hind legs, like a circus performer. His tongue hung out of his gaping mouth and his eyes rolled wildly.

The team followed suit. Bud saw the handlers' feet leave the ground as they struggled to hold the dogs in place until the count-down was complete.

Anna smiled sweetly at an official holding back the crowd.

'My brother,' she said, 'his first Iditarod. I need to get a little closer to wish him luck. He won't hear me from here.'

It worked. The official allowed her to walk to where Bud stood frozen to the sled runners.

'Good trail, Bud,' she shouted. 'We all wish you a great time.'

Bud grinned and lifted one hand in a quick wave, but replaced it immediately.

Anna's face was familiar, but his mind was frozen and would not give him her name or connection with the family.

He bent his knees to absorb the shock as the sled hit the street with its light covering of snow.

The plastic runners would swing it behind the dogs like a dry leaf in the winter wind. The countdown continued as inexorably as the march of time. Bud licked his lips nervously.

'Damn wolves,' he said quietly. 'When they are excited they think they're still chasing caribou on the tundra.' He shook his head and tightened his grip on the handlebar. 'Never breed this wild strain out of them, no matter what Natû says.'

'Three,' called the marshal, and the dogs started straining.

'Two.'

Look at that ten-thousand-dollar lead dog of mine. Dancing in circles like some damn trained bear.

'One. Go!'

White-out dropped down and his feet did not seem to touch the ground as he bounded down the avenue. The pulling power of sixteen maddened dogs was terrifying. Bud clenched his teeth and held on grimly. Figures flashed past. Words flew on the wind. He was conscious only of remaining on the sled and leaving Anchorage, preferably on his feet, not dragged down Fourth Avenue on his belly.

He had watched the rookie before him desperately hanging onto his catch rope, until officials could stop and hold his team and he could get back onto the sled.

'Only a few blocks, then a right turn into the side street and watch out for Cordova Hill at Sixteenth Street, also the tunnel at East Twentieth,' he said, repeating Muktuk's instructions as he clung to the handlebars and the dogs ran like ravenous wolves.

Bud let White-out follow the bike trails of Chester Creek green belt and run parallel to the busy Glenn highway, heading to checkpoint two at Eagle River where the dogs would be trucked to the restart near Wasilla.

'I am trusting my lead dog, Trapper,' he said, 'though I must be mad to trust him. If he keeps this up all the way to Nome I'll have to scratch, or they'll prise me off this sled once rigor mortis has set in.' He unclenched his fingers for a second, then quickly resumed his death grip on the handlebar.

'If you can arrive where Trapper and the others are waiting still standing upright, then you'll make the trail,' he told himself as his team led by White-out, whom he now was convinced was brain-damaged, tore along the side paths to the stop before Eagle River.

Occasionally Bud would yell 'Gee', or 'Haw', commands which White-out ignored. White-out glanced back over his shoulder. His eyes still rolled and Bud believed he could see a gleam of wild wolf ancestry shining in them. Bud gritted his teeth and prayed for White-out to ease the gruelling pace he was setting.

'Whoa,' he yelled. White-out's broad shoulders hunched and his legs stretched as he ate the miles. 'Whoa. You mad wolf, you rabid idiot. Whoa!' To his amazement, White-out suddenly responded and slowed down. The tugline went slack and the rest of the team stopped pulling.

Gingerly Bud unwrapped his fingers from the handlebar. He dropped the brake, not trusting White-out to remain still as he massaged the cramp from his hands.

He wiped his eyes with the back of his glove, clearing them of the tears torn from the ducts by the wind. As his vision cleared, he realized why White-out had stopped.

Muktuk, Trapper, Patrick and Natû were busy unhitching their dogs boxes on the trucks. The dogs had been fed and seemed happy to curl up on the straw beds.

'Hi,' shouted Patrick. 'Fun, wasn't it?'

Bud merely nodded, but stopped massaging his fingers.

'Except for the noise and cameras,' said Natû.

She walked across to Bud, stood on tiptoe and kissed him, then whispered in his ear, 'I'm proud of you. Two rookies have scratched already. Three didn't make it out of Anchorage, and we hear that one is in hospital with broken ribs and a suspected puncture in one lung.'

Bud hugged her, then watched as she went and knelt beside White-out. She held the dog's head in her hands and rubbed her cheek along its nose.

'Well done, boy. I knew you would bring the team here safely,' she said.

To Bud's amazement, White-out rested his head on her knee and looked up at her with soft, gentle eyes. Gone was the mad, wild wolf. His lead was behaving like a kitten.

Bud walked past them to greet Trapper and Muktuk, and resisted the urge to put his boot under White-out's tail as he passed him.

'Ham actor,' he said. 'Tell Natû what you really did.'

'What he did was to bring you here,' said Natû, defending the husky.

'You mean I paid ten thousand dollars for the dog to take me on that hell ride?' answered Bud.

'What hell ride?' growled Muktuk. 'That was a cakewalk. Cheer up, Bud, it gets easier after the first thousand miles.'

Bud started to relax, and recounted the run from Anchorage.

'The sled only touched ground twice on the way down Cordova Hill. I closed my eyes crossing the street and prayed that the police had stopped the traffic,' he told Natû. 'My second sled and handler were flying behind like a flag in a high wind.' Natû's high peal of laughter relaxed him completely, and Bud exaggerated the trip to Eagle River.

Everyone laughed, and White-out lifted his lips in a grin as Natû kissed him and called him a lovely boy.

'What is the restart at Wasilla like?' asked Bud apprehensively, chewing a jam doughnut and gulping warm coffee gratefully.

'Quieter,' answered Trapper.

'Easier to run than the jigsaw to get out of Anchorage,' added Natû, noticing for the first time the strain in Bud's face.

I'll run with him to Skwentna, she thought. White-out is probably testing male dominance. I'll help Bud remind the big boy that he has four legs and is part of a team; that he's not in lead place to play power games with his musher.

'Only the most avid fans come to the restart,' she continued. 'It is better.'

'How many?'

'They say ten to fifteen thousand.'

'The remainder stay in Anchorage nursing heads from the party they had the day of the start,' cut in Muktuk.

Bud managed to grin.

'From Knik we're out there on our own. At times you'll long for people and a little noise, if only to keep you awake,' he added.

'You'll also lose your ballast, as your second sled and handler have to stay,' said Trapper, 'but you'll take the heavier sled with all your mandatory equipment and you'll settle down into the rhythm of the race.'

Bud was to remember those words as he struggled to Rohn checkpoint.

Chapter Twenty-Seven

SCOTT NUDGED the truck out of the parking bay and headed for Chugiak and the Damas cabin.

The Chugiak mountains lay on the landscape, a semicircle of baroque pearls gleaming white, cream and pink in the fresh morning light.

Scott felt bereft and lonely, like a child sent back to boarding school after the excitement of the summer holidays.

The cabin seemed smaller and as abandoned as the huskies staked to pegs outside their boxes.

'It's okay, guys,' said Scott in response to their mournful howls when they saw him. 'I know just how you feel. I almost howled at the start when Patrick left with Sockeye. Belt up now, and I'll feed you.'

He ran up the steps and flung open the door expecting to hear Trapper and Muktuk arguing, but only the silence of an empty house greeted him.

He dragged out the bag of dog mash and lined up the pails. On his way to put water on to boil, he bent down and switched on the television set.

'May as well see who left the chute on their arse instead of their feet,' he said, as if talking to himself would bring the cabin to life.

Scott moved methodically between the stove and pails of specially prepared dry mash. Every now and then he glanced at the screaming crowd on the screen. Walking from the stove with a pot of boiling water in his hands, a wolf's head fashioned into a winter cap caught his attention. He paused to look at it more closely. It was grotesque. The wolf's tongue hung down over the woman's forehead, and its white fangs were bared to the heavens.

'Uugh,' shuddered Scott.

He was about to move away and start stirring the pails to cool the food, when a woman dressed in thick black pants and a cherry-red parka pushed her way past the wolf's head.

Anna, breathed Scott. He sat cross-legged on the floor in front of the set. The camera zoomed in on her face. Scott studied every line and curve. A smile warmed his face. The woman he loved had not remained in the Lower Forty eight. Anna was back for the Iditarod. Natû was right: nothing would stop Anna flying for the Iditarod Air Force.

'If she's here I'll see her,' he said, getting to his feet as the camera swung back to the dogs and musher waiting at the chute.

Suddenly the red parka was back in focus. Anna was shouting something to the musher. It was Bud. The huskies were pulling at the handlers as if tearing into ptarmigan they had flushed. Scott watched as Bud raised a hand to Anna, then glued himself back onto the sled. He was still on the runners heading down Fourth Avenue when the camera swung back to the next musher.

'Looks as if Muktuk will lose his bet,' said Scott with a grin.

Muktuk had bet Trapper two fox pelts and a bearskin that Bud would not make it out of Anchorage.

'He seems sure of himself, and his dogs are running like veterans, speedy veterans. Muktuk had better have those skins, as Trapper always pays and collects.'

Scott left the preparation of the dog food and ran to the telephone.

'ITC headquarters, Wasilla,' a woman's voice answered wearily.

There was so much noise in the background that Scott had difficulty hearing her.

He was in the middle of explaining that he was a friend of Anna McInnes, one of the Iditarod pilots, and needed to contact her urgently, when he heard her sigh of exasperation.

*

The volunteer at the Iditarod headquarters had a pile of messages on her desk plus a list of people to phone and her head was pounding. All she wanted was some peace and quiet.

'You seem to be unaware that we are organizing a race here. We are not running a singles club.'

The woman's voice had risen to a shrill shriek. It attracted Claire's attention as she passed the counter in the main room on her way to her office.

'Who is that?' she asked.

'Some young fool looking for one of our pilots.'

'Who?'

'Anna McInnes, whoever she is.'

Claire put her hand out for the phone. 'Hi, I'm Claire, a friend of Anna's. What's the problem?'

Scott breathed a sigh of relief. He had expected to hear the slam of a receiver being angrily replaced.

Claire spoke for a long time, and Scott scrawled down dates and times as fast as he could.

'Things change by the hour here. The info I've given you could be out of date by lunchtime,' said Claire finally.

'Thanks for listening,' said Scott. 'When you see Anna, tell her I'm at Bud's cabin waiting for her.'

'Will do.'

Claire hung up and dumped the armful of folders on her desk with a small smile.

'In your fat face, Double Dick,' she whispered. 'Payback time has come.'

Chapter Twenty-Eight

NATÛ LOOKED at Bud and his team running ahead of her. The snowmobiles had prepared a smooth track running beside the Yentna River.

Bud's team must be hitting nearly twenty miles an hour, thought Natû as she studied how fast her team was running to keep up with Bud.

Natû had dreaded this rerun of the trip she'd done with Patrick, thinking that her memory would put her back in the spruce forest and she would relive the cold, the terror and the pain as the crash wrenched her baby from her warm womb.

But it was a magical day. The sun shone down from a periwinkle sky. For the first time in months she felt that she could touch the silence. In the wilderness there were no cars, no cameras and no crowds – only a handful of mushers spread over what seemed to be half the State of Alaska.

'Thank you, Kiluk,' she thought. 'Without your advice I would have told Bud of my miscarriage, and he would not be as relaxed and happy as he is now. He and Trapper may have tried to stop me running the race this year, and I would have missed this wonderful day.'

At Yentna Station checkpoint they found Patrick. He had already checked in and out to save time, at the tent set up in the unpopulated place, a tip given to them by Muktuk. Natû and Bud went to check in, while Patrick fetched water from the hole he had cut in the river ice.

The three rookies took a short break after checking in and giving snacks to the dogs.

'Bad moose country from here to Skwentna,' said Patrick, not looking at Natû. 'I think I should run in front and let Bud bring up the rear, as we both carry guns.'

Natû merely nodded. Patrick had agreed to say nothing to Trapper or Bud about the moose that had driven Natû's team off the trail.

In the preparations for the race, the incident seemed to have been forgotten. Even Muktuk made no mention of moose.

'I think that Bud and I will take our twenty-four-hour stopover at Rohn cabin,' said Natû as they checked the dogs' tuglines and sleds before leaving the desolate and lonely Yentna checkpoint tent.

'Good thinking. A rest will be necessary after the three gut-twisters, Happy River Canyon, Rainy Pass with Dalzell Gorge to negotiate at the bottom of Rainy, and then on to the checkpoint at Rohn cabin,' he answered.

'I'll see how my dogs are running after the twenty miles of Dalzell. I may go on farther before I take my layover. Wait until they really need a rest,' said Patrick.

'Okay. May meet you at Rohn,' said Bud cheerfully.

'Has anyone seen Muktuk?' asked Natû suddenly.

'Heard on the radio that he is running well and seems like he'll make the top twenty cut-off. He'll be in the money this year,' shouted Patrick as he gave his team the command to move.

Bud laughed.

'Let's roll,' he said.

Patrick, like a husky, seemed to have a memory for trails. He led Natû and Bud straight into the Skwentna checkpoint.

Natû looked up at the Owens's cabin. It seemed old and deserted. The windows were boarded against marauding bears, and no welcoming plume of smoke feathered the cold air. She knew that she would see Kiluk and Herbie Owens in the village of Safety or in Nome, when the town joined the weary mushers in a crazy party of excitement and relief.

But she felt a twinge of nausea deep in her stomach as she remembered her last visit to the cabin with Patrick and Muktuk.

'That's over,' she told herself. 'Now concentrate on the race.'

Bud gasped and stopped his team as they reached the settlement. Ahead of him, guarding the entrance to the Interior, lay the Alaska range. The mountains stood as proud, tall and sharp as sharks' teeth in the clear light.

'Impossible,' he breathed, realizing that this was the formidable barrier to the feared Interior of Alaska and the dreaded cold associated with that word.

'Yes, they are beautiful, aren't they?' answered Natû happily. 'We're lucky, Bud, they were predicting "bottomless trail" around here, but it seems as if we're going to miss the deep snow.'

Hearing Natû's voice, Oily looked over her shoulder and barked softly.

'All right, girl. We'll move on once we're signed in. You're lucky that the snowfall is late. I would lose you in sixteen feet of that soft stuff.'

Natû bent down and fondled Oily, then had to repeat the procedure with the rest of her team. Vega, who was running behind Oily, licked the snow from Natû's balaclava, then ran her warm tongue down Natû's nose. Natû hugged the bitch who had run the team from her wedding party at the Captain Cook to the cabin.

She had followed Trapper's advice and included Vega on her team. The husky ran well, and a bond of trust and love quickly formed between them. Once the pecking order was established Oily accepted Vega, but still demanded to be fondled first.

When they had settled down, Natû found Bud deep in conversation with one of the mushers in the tent.

'Just heard Happy River Canyon is better this year. The snowmobile guys, who break trail, have built up a snowbank on one side,' said Bud as Natû came and put her arms around his waist.

'Better than what? Hell?' queried a grizzled musher sitting on his sled chewing a piece of jerky. 'You're going down that damn chute so fast that you'll roll over that snow wall without realizing it's even there.'

Natû peered at the musher, as stringy and tough as the jerky he was masticating.

'How many times have you run the Iditarod?' she asked.

'This is number seven. Lucky for some, unlucky for others,' he answered sombrely.

'Scares the pants off me, but I love the bitching race. Don't do drugs, don't smoke, but the Idit. is one habit I can't break. Short Seppa is the name,' he said, standing and hitching his pants up around his waist.

Natû and Bud watched as he tucked the half-chewed stick of dried meat into his pocket, patted his dogs and left the checkpoint for the next one at frozen Finger Lake.

'Aim to reach Happy after dark,' Short Seppa advised as he left.

'Why?' queried Bud and Natû in unison.

'Better if you can't see where you're going.'

Natû shrugged. 'We'll be there well before dark,' she said to Bud.

'We could just close our eyes,' he teased.

Natû smiled at him. Once again, she was pleased she had listened to Kiluk. Bud was happy in his ignorance. The vigour of the race was also cleansing her of all guilt.

The highest mountain range in North America looked less formidable in the soft flesh tones of a setting sun. Yet Bud felt his stomach muscles clench as he looked up at the peaks soaring overhead. He fancifully imagined himself and Natû as tiny black ants attempting to climb a starched tablecloth which hung in folds to the floor.

His mind was still occupied with the implausibility of crossing the mountains with a team of crazy dogs, who were still fresh and ready to run. He dropped his gaze from the towering peaks just in time to see Oily vanish. One moment she was pulling, strongly leading Natû's team, the next she was gone. Within minutes the whole team and Natû seemed to disappear as if a lead had opened in sea ice and swallowed them.

'Natû,' he screamed.

The silent, brooding mountains mocked him. They threw back his call unanswered.

'Whoa!' he shouted to his team. 'Whoa!' But within seconds White-out followed Oily, dragging the sled and Bud to the edge of the abyss.

Before dropping into what seemed certain death, Bud looked at the canyon falling in near-vertical sweeps to the river below. The sheer mountains dwarfed the Happy River to a thread of silver cotton winding through the deep cold shadows.

Bud had no time to look for Natû. His feet left the ground as his team fell into the canyon. The dogs scrabbled desperately for footing on the narrow trail lining the edge of a cliff. The wild ride down with two major switchbacks tested Bud's will to remain in the crazy race. He experienced what a first-time mother does when birth pangs begin. Blind terror, coupled with knowledge of the inevitability of the event.

It had started and nothing could stop it. Bud screwed his eyes up tightly and his muscles bulged as he held onto the handlebar. His body bounced off rocks as it swung behind the tumbling sled. He neither felt nor saw the boulders. He only prayed for the oscillating, wild, uncontrolled ride to end.

After what seemed to be an eternity, he lay sprawled on the frozen river with his dogs in a snapping, tearing tangle in front of the sled.

Painfully he pulled himself to his feet and looked up at the five-hundred-foot drop.

'That was some ride, wasn't it?'

Bud swung round to see his wife standing on the runners of her sled, her dogs straining, ready to run.

'Are you hurt?' he asked.

'No. A few bruises probably, but my suit protected me from the worst.'

Natû wondered whether it would be wise to tell Bud that she had watched his free fall in horror, certain that he would be killed.

Listen when your inner voice speaks. She heard Trapper's words clearly.

Her inner voice was telling her not to destroy Bud's confidence, but to let him enjoy the race and believe that he was driving his sled dogs well.

'You negotiated Happy Canyon like an Olympic downhill ski champion,' she said, swallowing back her fear for her husband on the rest of the trail.

'Wonder where Patrick is?' said Bud, trying to control his breathing.

'Probably at Rohn cabin, stretched out on one of the bunks,' answered Natû.

She waited patiently until Bud had sorted out his team. The dogs had to respond to him as the dominant male. She would not interfere. White-out was proving to be a good lead; he was trying to pull the gangline tight as Bud untangled the other huskies, keeping clear of their jaws as they snapped at each other.

'You look like an old lady untangling a ball of knitting wool,' laughed Natû as Bud hobbled up and down the line checking tuglines and putting his team back into their positions.

Bud grinned weakly and rubbed his back.

'I feel like an old woman.'

Natû was immediately contrite. 'We'll get a doctor for you at Rainy Pass check-in,' she said.

And I'm running the rest of the race with you. I'm not going to risk losing you, she added silently, giving away her chance of a placing.

Rainy Pass. The mere name made Bud feel nauseous. Everyone had warned him of the terrors awaiting him on the three-thousand-foot climb up to Rainy Pass, and the infamous twenty-mile ride down Dalzell Gorge. No one had told him about Happy Canyon. They obviously felt that the canyon was not worth complaining about in comparison to the gorge.

The whisper of runners alerted Bud and Natû to the presence of another musher. It was a woman heavily bundled in a primrose-yellow suit.

'You came up so quietly,' greeted Natû.

'Yeah, noiseless as fear in a wide wilderness,' the musher said. 'That's Keats. English. But dead now. I learn poems as I run. It helps keep me awake, and impresses the hell out of my friends,' she shrugged.

Natû studied the petite woman. Even in her arctic gear she looked small and vulnerable. Her eyes were hidden behind dark goggles and her face was red and raw from windburn, but her smile was warm and infectious. If she's running this race she's a tough cookie, thought Natû. It's spirit, not size, that gets you to the burled arch, and this babe seems to have plenty of punch.

'Hi, both of you. Name is Violet. Vi for short,' Vi held out a mittened hand. Natû grasped it and winced slightly as Vi's grip tightened.

Not only spirit with Vi, she thought; she'll have no problem handling a team of huskies, probably picks them up like puppies.

'Hi,' answered Natû.

'Bud and Natû Damas.'

Vi pursed her lips, which were already showing cracks.

'Yeah, heard of you. They were betting whether BP would stake you or not. Pleased they did. I reckon you'll make it.'

Bud and Natû smiled. It was good to talk to someone out on the trail. Vi started checking her dogs and the lines.

'Took me a hour to collect my equipment and repack my sled. I came down Happy like a Christmas stocking being emptied.' She studied Bud and Natû's teams. 'You seem to have done okay,' she said.

They merely nodded.

'Watch out for Rainy. The ascent is worse than the descent, no matter what they say. When you hit Dalzell close your eyes and pray. If you're still there when you open them, you'll know your prayers worked.'

With a wave of one gloved hand she was gone, a tiny yellow figure in the white wilderness.

'Look,' breathed Natû. She pointed to the north where Mount Denali, six times higher than the peaks ranging beside her, held her head up to the sun as if glorying in its setting rays, which streaked her snow scarves of purest white to peach and pale melon.

Bud shaded his eyes as Denali was dazzling.

'I thought she was beautiful framed by the window in our cabin,' he said. 'But out here . . .' He threw his arms open wide, at a loss for words.

Oily barked again, only this time it was insistent.

'Okay, let's go,' shouted Natû, and her team raced along the river as if they had just been released from the start chute.

Bud shook his head.

'You are as tough as they come,' he said admiringly, then tightened his grip as White-out took Natû's command to go to include his team.

Dalzell Gorge appeared like a nightmare in the middle of a lovely dream.

Bud glimpsed Natû careening along a narrow ice ledge bordering a torrent of water which seemed about to uproot the gigantic wet boulders with the inexorable force of an avalanche.

His team appeared to look upon the gorge as a challenge – the switchbacks from one side of the rushing river to the other across ice bridges or single logs didn't appear to bother them. They skidded round thirty-foot-high boulders, slid down the ice ledge that served as a path, their tongues hanging out and tails held high. White-out seemed intent on setting a speed record for Dalzell as he raced his team across a bridge that was only wide enough for half the sled.

As Bud was swung against one rock after the other, he realized why Dalzell was one of the most frequently used words when talking of the Iditarod, though colourful adjectives usually accompanied the word.

'Twelve miles,' he muttered, 'this hell only lasts twelve, or is it twenty miles? Twenty. Twelve. Twelve. Twenty.'

He found that the numbers were a maddening tinnitus. He felt that his brain was exploding, but the numbers would not stop coming.

Suddenly White-out jerked to a halt. Ahead of him, Natû's team was struggling up a snowbank.

'Go on, Oily. Up, my girl,' urged Natû as her lead dog strained to scramble from the freezing water which had suddenly opened beneath their weight under a thin covering of snow.

Bud watched helplessly as Natû ran round the trough of black water and pulled Oily onto firm ground. He was afraid that if he helped her she would be disqualified from the race.

Vega tried to follow Oily, but Natû had placed her in the middle of the team to give her a change of position and rest her a little.

The huskies were frantic to escape the open water, which still had chunks of snow breaking into it. They pulled to reach Natû on the opposite bank, dragging Vega off her feet. She was unable to regain her footing against the combined strength of the dogs, and was hauled up the snow bank with her nose ploughing a deep furrow.

Natû had run round to manhandle the sled onto firm snow.

'Vega,' shouted Natû, fear and horror cracking her voice, 'Vega, girl.'

Natû reached Vega, lifted the bitch in her arms and sat rocking back and forth. She moaned, the mournful lonely song of the polar bear.

Bud planted the snowhook and trudged round the treacherous open water. Natû stared at him as if at a stranger. She had her finger in Vega's mouth, attempting to remove the packed snow, which had choked Vega as she lost her footing and was pulled helplessly across the open water and up the bank.

Bud squatted beside Natû.

'Don't cry,' he said, 'don't cry.'

He realized that words would not ease her pain. She loved the bitch.

Bud wrapped his arms around Natû. He pulled her fingers from Vega's mouth.

'You must warm your hands,' he said.

He crooned to her as she stuffed her now ice-cold hands back into her mittens and curled her stiff fingers round the hand warmers.

The two sat wrapped together as Natû stroked Vega lying across her lap. The husky's clear blue eyes clouded and lost their light as death claimed her. The drone of low-flying aircraft made them turn from the dog and look up.

Anna McInnes looked down at the two dog teams and the open water.

'No,' she breathed. 'Don't let this be the tragedy everyone has been predicting for this year.'

She circled overhead, flying as low as she could without scaring the dogs.

'Go to your team,' said Natû, realizing that if the plane came much lower they might bolt.

She unzipped her sled bag and dragged Vega across the snow. Tears streamed down her face and sobs racked her body. Tenderly she lifted Vega, kissed her on her still warm nose, then tucked her into the bag and zipped it up.

Natû knew that she would be closely questioned about Vega's death. The Idit. committee had stringent rules regarding the care of dogs, but the only thing that worried Natû was the loss of one of her dogs. It was almost as traumatic as her miscarriage. She had not seen the unborn child, but she had loved and fondled Vega and worked with her every day. The husky was part of her. Now the magnificent dog lay in the sled bag.

'Let's go,' she said to Bud. He followed in silence, realizing that there was nothing he could do to help her.

Finally Natû shoved the sled after her team, who were all safely through the open water and trying to roll in the snow.

She was breathing heavily but unclipped each dog in turn and allowed it to blot the water from its coat in the snow.

Bud held his team in check, preventing them from challenging Natû's dogs to a fight.

When Bud gave the call to move on, White-out skirted the open water like a veteran Iditarod racer, then grinned at Natû as he led his team past hers. Oily growled and bared her teeth, but in the infuriating manner possessed by males, he ignored her.

Chapter Twenty-Nine

As THEY approached Rohn checkpoint, Bud felt excitement mounting. They would talk to Patrick and perhaps hear news of Muktuk. For a short while he forgot his aches and bruises.

The log cabin at Rohn seemed to have been lifted from a postcard and set among tall dark pines. A frieze of serrated, towering mountain pinnacles blocked out part of the night sky. Bud threw back his head and stared up at the heavens, slashed by stars, until his eyes watered.

'Come on, we have to sign in and rest the dogs,' said Natû, kissing him softly on the cheek then pulling away as her lips stuck to the snow and ice that was caked on his face.

'You'll get frostbite if we don't warm you up,' she said. Bud rubbed his cheeks hard to restore the circulation and hurried into the hut.

For a moment he reeled back. The smell of wet clothes steaming on lines over the small wood stove, unwashed bodies and coffee brewing was overpowering. Every inch of space seemed to be taken up by an exhausted musher either dozing, snoring or mumbling.

Natû studied the jumbled bodies, then pointed out a small wooden table beneath a boarded window close to the stove.

'Let's rest for an hour or two, then do our twenty-four-hour mandatory farther up the line,' she whispered. 'We'll have no rest here, neither will our team.'

She and Bud stumbled over inert bodies and crawled under the table. They curled against each other as tightly as two spoons packed into a cutlery tray.

*

Patrick had mushed his dogs into Rohn checkpoint the night before. After feeding them and checking their feet, he decided they were still too fresh for the mandatory twenty-four-hour stopover, so he dropped down into the riverbed ugly with rocky shale and no smooth snow to run on.

'Think you can make Ophir, Sockeye?' he called to his lead, who seemed to be taking his position seriously.

'You'll be tired, but we'll get some real sleep there. Rohn cabin is like Fourth Avenue on start day.'

Sockeye merely strained forward and the sled jolted over the cold grey river-washed stones.

Silently Patrick thanked Herbie for building the sort of sled that could withstand the jarring and jolting of being pulled over dry gravel beds and up and down icy riverbanks.

Up on the bank, hidden in the depths of the spruce forest, the wild, lonesome song of a wolf cut the silence.

'Wonder where Bud is?' said Patrick quietly. 'He hates the creatures. Hope Natû has stayed with him. He's tough, but Alaska breaks and spits out tough guys like used toothpicks.'

He grinned to himself in the dark. 'I must remember that one to tell Scott when I'm back in Barrow.'

For the next hour he let his mind dwell on his childhood, the trouble and the fun he and his twin had caused and enjoyed. He then thought of Scott and Anna. His lips tightened as he realized that Scott had now chosen a path they could not walk together. He should hate Anna McInnes, but he liked the little he had seen of her and could not hate anyone who loved Scott.

Patrick was so lost in thought that the past had become the present and he did not notice that they were in the Burn, an enormous area razed twenty years earlier by Alaska's worst forest fire. It now tested the mushers skill and will to continue the race.

Their sleds caught on charred tree stumps every few yards. They chopped through the wood only to find the dogs tangled in another mess of old branches and pieces of charred tree trunk. It was a neverending struggle to free dogs and sleds, and as a dog-sled team does not reverse, the only way through the Farewell Burn was forward, chopping, hacking and cursing.

The area was a jigsaw puzzle of sled tracks as each team sought and could not find an easy way through the remains of a once magnificent forest.

Patrick swore as Sockeye led the team around a sapling growing straight and tall from the bed of tundra and ashes.

'Can't you miss the new trees, Sockeye?' he yelled. 'We have enough problems getting through the old stuff.'

Patrick had run beside the sled most of the way, as jarring over ground with no snow was worse than skiing black runs and mogul fields. His thighs trembled and his muscles burned, but he was determined to finish well ahead of the other rookies.

'Trapper will be proud of me and Mum will realize that she has passed on her trace of Eskimo blood. I love this land, and I'll do well in the Idit. to prove it,' he shouted.

The three hundred and sixty thousand devastated acres of tundra forest and streams heard his boast and ignored it.

The Burn had heard many men and women delusional from sleep deprivation shouting as they stumbled and hacked their way through the Burn, where trail markers are blown down by the wind and buffalo appear, terrifying the dogs, making them deaf to all commands.

Patrick did not realize how he had been pushing himself until he found himself hacking at a non-existent tree trunk. The sharp blade of his axe swung past his head and, meeting no resistance on the downswing, lodged in the side of his sled. He wrestled it out and prepared to swing again when a voice stopped him and brought him back to reality.

'The Burn is bad, but not bad enough to use your sled as firewood.'

Violet mushed her team up behind Patrick's, then walked forward to meet him.

Embarrassed that a woman should find him hacking at imaginary trees, Patrick tried to find an excuse.

'Just a few branches,' he said.

'Yeah, I know. Most people go a little crazy in the Burn. I'm giving my dogs a snack and making coffee. Join me?

Patrick looked at the small figure bundled in yellow and grinned.

'A break would be great.'

They turned their sleds on their sides, making it more difficult for the teams to bolt, though as Vi said, 'Any team that manages to bolt in the Burn will go down in the record book.'

The coffee warmed Patrick, and Vi's companionship dispelled his delusions. His head dropped sideways onto her shoulder and he slept.

Vi watched him for a few minutes. She should move on, but it felt warm and comfortable sitting in the shelter of the sleds, and she found Patrick very attractive.

'I'll let him have an hour,' she said. 'My dogs could do with the break; so can I.'

She closed her eyes. Snow, as soft and thick as an eiderdown, soon covered dogs, sleds and the mushers. They were merely part of the Burn, one of the many white mounds.

Vi stirred, uncomfortable under Patrick's weight. He had slumped over and now lay across her.

'I've slept too long,' she whispered. 'I must move; it's dark and I don't want to run the last part of the Burn at night.'

She tried to shake Patrick, but he was heavy and did not move.

'Patrick,' she shouted, 'Patrick.'

Eventually he grunted and edged himself off her.

Vi could not understand what had happened. The weight was still pressing down on her, yet Patrick had moved.

'Snow,' he said. 'Snowstorm. Buried.'

Patrick breathed shallowly. The thought of being buried alive appalled him, but he did not panic as he had survived a snowfall when out with Trapper on the line. Then they had curled up with the dogs and remained warm and snug until the blizzard was over.

He ran his hand up the sturdy planks of the sled, then wriggled onto his knees. A shaft of light lasered his eyes. He stared at the Burn in amazement. The tangled hell had turned into a white snowfield.

'Vi,' he called, 'look here, can you believe this?'

There was no answer, and he realized that she was still buried under the blanket of snow. He dug at the opening and reached down for her. A strong hand found and held onto his fingers.

'One good turn,' she said.

'Deserves another,' he answered.

They both laughed and brushed the snow from their clothes.

'Now let's find our dogs. If we have any,' said Patrick.

'They'll be enjoying the break,' prophesied Vi. 'See, they haven't moved. They think the snow is a duvet especially ordered for their comfort.'

Patrick and Vi walked along the mounds of snow with only small vents and wisps of steam telling of a dog.

'Sockeye,' roared Patrick.

There was a movement under one of the mounds and Sockeye appeared. He blinked in the daylight like a mole emerging from its burrow. Clarke, the large dog from Tri Star, was the next to emerge. He stood tall, eager to go.

'I love that hunk of a dog,' said Patrick looking at Clarke. 'He's always ready to run and pulls more than his share.'

He trudged up to Clarke and fondled his ears. Clarke immediately stood on his hind legs and rested his forepaws on Patrick's shoulders. Patrick staggered under the weight and tried to avoid Clarke cleaning his face with wet dog licks.

'After the race I'm going to try to buy him from Tri Star.'

'I don't think you'll have much luck,' said Vi. 'He is one of Tri Star's best dogs.'

'Yeah, I know. I was lucky she let me have him for this race.'

'Diana has a heart as big as a husky's,' laughed Vi.

One by one the other huskies roused themselves and shook off the snow.

'Next stop, Nikolai,' said Vi, stretching and flinging her arms wide as if to encompass the now beautiful Burn. 'It'll be good to be in the native village and have some decent food.'

'Yeah, they seem to think that the race is Christmas and each musher, Father Christmas,' grinned Patrick. 'Oh, thanks for the coffee last night. I could have put that axe through my leg or head. I didn't realize how quickly one can start hallucinating.'

'No problem,' answered Vi with a grin. 'It's one area where women have a small advantage in the race.' Patrick looked puzzled.

'Sleep deprivation,' she said. 'Have babies and you get very little sleep. The sleep you do have is broken.'

'Do you have children?' asked Patrick, suddenly aware that he did not want her answer to be 'yes'.

'No. Dogs are my children. I haven't found the time or the man.'

Suddenly Patrick felt relieved.

'Let's share the run to Nikolai,' he suggested.

Vi studied him for a few minutes in silence. 'Where are you taking your twenty-four-hour stopover?' she asked.

'Ophir. They tell me that it's quiet. Dogs are really tired and rest properly. Very few other mushers around.'

Vi nodded. 'That was my plan. I'll run it with you. Then we leave Ophir as competitors again.'

'Done,' said Patrick with a wide grin. He realized that he enjoyed this woman's company.

The enforced rest beneath the covering of snow seemed to have revitalized Patrick and the dogs. The run into Nikolai was perfect, though later, anything would seem perfect after fighting through the Farewell Burn.

Patrick and Vi were infected by the enthusiasm and warm hospitality which greeted them in Nikolai. They did not stay long, but left for McGrath checkpoint in high spirits. The run to McGrath was relatively easy as the route followed the river almost all the way.

A few hours out of McGrath, the river looped as if it suffered severe stomach cramps. Patrick found it frustrating to see the lights of McGrath but still not reach the town.

He switched off his headlamp as he found that dogs often saw better in the dark. Suddenly his team stopped and milled around, yapping and pulling wildly at the tugs. He put on the lamp, trained it on his team and for a moment did not realize what had happened.

'Dog down,' shouted Vi.

A finger of ice slid down Patrick's spine. It was an open, easy run. How could he have a dog down?

He ran to the front of the team. Sockeye was all right: he was snarling at the dog behind him.

'Whoa, Sockeye, and quiet,' yelled Patrick.

In the gloom he saw one of his 'grunt' dogs lying on the snow.

'Don't let it be Clarke,' he whispered, as he and Vi both ran to the dog. Clarke had more heart than any dog he had seen or worked with.

'Hold your light on Clarke, Vi,' said Patrick, still uncertain as to what had caused the dog to collapse.

The yellow beam flickered over Clarke and came to rest on the line knotted round his neck, choking him. His tongue lolled loosely from his mouth and faeces splattered the snow where his bowels had voided in death.

'He's dead,' said Vi sadly. 'I'm so sorry.'

'No,' said Patrick. 'I won't let him die. No. He's too good a dog.' It was obvious that the big dog had slipped, the team had pulled on and the line had wound round his neck, choking him.

Vi stood by, training her light on Clarke as Patrick whipped out his leatherman, snapped open the knife and cut the line from Clarke's neck.

The dog did not move. Patrick knelt beside him in the snow and started mouth-to-snout resuscitation.

To Vi watching, it seemed to go on for hours; a man crouched over a dead dog determined to bring it back to life.

Suddenly Patrick pumped the air in a victory sign, then put his ear onto Clarke's mouth.

'He's breathing,' he whispered, his voice ragged after all the effort to blow air into Clarke's lungs. 'Clarke is alive.'

Vi swung her headlamp onto Patrick's face, then back to Clarke when she saw the tears on his cheeks.

'I must get him into the sled bag and have the vet check him at McGrath.'

Clarke weakly resisted being zipped into the bag. He made his intentions clear – he wanted to be back in his place on the line.

'Clarke, you can't run with the team,' said Patrick sadly. 'I'll probably have to dump you at McGrath and you'll be flown back to Tri Star.' He put his arms around the husky's neck, 'I'll miss you when we run under the burled arch, but remember, your strength helped us over the worst places.'

As he talked he manhandled Clarke into the sled bag and zipped him in. He then checked the tugs on the other dogs. He walked back to where Vi stood waiting.

'Thank you,' he said. 'You could have gone ahead and had a longer rest in Ophir.'

Vi merely shook her head, then said very softly, 'We agreed to run to Ophir together. That means all the way.'

The lights telling of the settlement at McGrath seemed to loom up as Clarke started struggling to get out of the bag. When Patrick refused to unzip the bag, the husky added a mournful wail to his pleas. He soon had some of the other dogs howling. Patrick looked back at Vi's team and decided that the howling could affect her dogs.

He stopped Sockeye and the team stood still, listening to what Clarke was saying.

Patrick jumped off the runners and opened the sled bag. He was rewarded with a warm, wet tongue slapping his face. Clarke jumped out and loped to his position.

Patrick shrugged.

'What do I do?' he shouted at Vi. 'Clarke wants to run.'

'Any dog who comes back from the dead should know what is good for him,' she answered. 'Let him run.'

Patrick was uncertain, but gave in when he saw Clarke's obvious delight to be out of the bag and back with the team.

He breathed a sigh of relief as they ran into the checkpoint.

'A vet,' he said to the first checker. 'I need a veterinary officer urgently.'

A woman in a padded red parka with a balaclava to match turned from the table where she was pouring coffee.

'Patrick,' she said.

He stared at her blankly, his mind occupied with Clarke and the possibility of still losing the husky.

'Anna McInnes,' she said. 'We met at Skwentna. I dropped Scott there and collected Natû.'

Suddenly Patrick saw the woman crying in the cockpit, begging him to tell his twin her story.

'Oh, of course, Anna. I'm sorry. I was worried about not finding a veterinery officer.'

Anna smiled.

'It's okay. I understand what the race is like. I've just brought Paul into McGrath. He tells me he had to certify one of Natû Damas's dogs as dead. She is apparently distraught.'

'Bud and Natû,' said Patrick. 'How are they doing?'

'Fine. Decided not to take their twenty-four-hour mandatory at Rohn. They are having a short break and taking the mandatory later.'

Patrick wanted to ask Anna more about Natû's dog, but a deep male voice boomed out, 'Hear I'm needed. Well, here I am.'

Patrick spun round, and soon the two men, Vi and Anna had formed a ring around Clarke.

'Nothing wrong that I can see. Heart's fine. Lungs working well. If the two of you weren't there when he fell I'd say you were hallucinating. Clarke can complete the run to Nome, and I hope I'll be there to check him as he finishes the race.'

The vet hurried off to check another musher who had just arrived, leaving the three of them looking down at Clarke.

'You're a miracle dog, Clarke,' said Patrick.

'You weren't too bad with your mouth-to-snout,' said Vi with admiration.

'Let's go inside and find some coffee,' said Anna, eager to know how Patrick had managed to make Scott listen to him.

242

'I'll be with you in a moment,' said Vi. 'I need to speak to Paul about one of my swing dogs.'

Patrick and Anna nodded and walked back to where Anna had been pouring coffee for the mushers.

'Tell,' said Anna. 'How did you make Scott listen?'

'Ran him till he could hardly breathe, that way he wasn't able to argue. Then sat him down to a pepperoni pizza and coffee. The combination worked. A man with his mouth full can only nod.'

Anna put down her mug and flung her arms around Patrick. 'You don't know what this means to me,' she said. 'Thank you, Patrick.'

'I thought my kid brother was too young to be serious about a relationship,' he said, still holding Anna in his arms. 'But it seems he knew what he was doing. Good luck, Anna. Scott is a great guy. The best.'

Vi watched Anna enfolded in Patrick's arms, and found to her surprise that she wanted to separate them.

Watch it, Vi, she warned herself. You're enjoying your life and your freedom. You settle down with a guy and you won't run the Great Race again. Your exercise will be cleaning the cabin, cooking and probably changing a baby's nappy. You really don't want to change your lifestyle. Be sensible. Alaska is crammed with lonely men.

She continued checking her dogs and tugs, but found that she kept Anna in view.

'Vi, come and finish your coffee before it gets cold.' Anna's voice rang out across the snow, and Vi had no excuse to ignore the invitation.

'Here, I brought some fresh doughnuts from Anchorage.'

Chapter Thirty

DELILAH AND Shark tacked instinctively as the wind, armed with needles of snow, hit them hard in the face. The team followed obediently, happy not to run directly into the wind.

'Travelling by dog sled is like sailing,' said Muktuk loudly. He talked to himself to keep awake. 'Sled creaks like the wood in a rolling ship. I lean away from port when the sled rolls to starboard, or lean starboard when we're on a port roll to stop the sled tipping.'

He shook his head, covering his shoulders in a flurry of ice and snow. 'Ships and sleds. My father and grandfather sailed the waters of this coast in whalers, and here I am sailing the waves of the snow.'

Muktuk snorted. 'Getting old, Muktuk Peters,' he chided himself. 'Put your mind where it belongs, on the race, not in the past. As Trapper says, "The past is for those afraid of the present and shying from the future," and he is an okay, wise old guy.' Muktuk smiled as he thought of Trapper. They were of an age, but he would be offended if anyone referred to him as an old guy.

Muktuk pulled the fur flaps of his cap well down over his balaclava. He tightened Patrick's brightly checked scarf under his neck warmer. His face was red and tender where the wind had peeled away his skin. His lips were puffed and blistered. He neither felt nor heeded the discomfort as he made slits of his eyes and tried to discern any movement in front of his dogs.

'All the damn wind and cold in Alaska drops into the Yukon,' groused Muktuk.

Suddenly he lifted the ear flaps of his cap. The sound of screaming snowmobile engines filled the night.

Muktuk did not even look behind him. He pulled his team over to the high snow bank on the left side of the great river of ice.

Two snowmobiles, racing each other along the river ice, roared down on him. He turned, swinging his headlamp onto them, warning them of his team.

'Idiots,' he roared after them. 'How many accidents do they need before they kick your butts and your bitching machines off this river? No place for dog teams and 'mobiles, driven by crazies at seventy miles an hour. Get out of it. You and all your stinking, noisy machines.'

His curses followed the bikes up the river until they rounded a bend and were lost to sight.

The noise did not recede. There was a sudden abrupt silence, followed by the sickening crash of metal and the shrieking of dogs.

Muktuk raced round the corner. A sled lay overturned on the ice. The musher was trying to lift his heavy swing dog plus a 'grunt' dog in his arms.

The 'grunt' dog howled piteously. Its intestines curled onto the ice as the musher tried to lift it. They froze immediately. It seemed as if the musher and the ice were waging a tug of war with the dog's intestines.

Muktuk pulled his revolver from his suit and ran at the young men on the snowmobiles. 'Bloody murderers,' he yelled. 'Now I have to shoot dogs which have given all they had to reach the Yukon. I should shoot you bitching fools.'

Two shots rang out and the men disappeared, zigzagging across the river, terrified that the bullets would find their mark.

Muktuk ran to where the musher knelt trying to stuff the insides back into his dog. He was murmuring to it incoherently.

Muktuk checked the swing dog. Its head was crushed. Blood filled its eyes. It looked up at him in mute appeal through the red mask.

Muktuk patted it gently, then placed his revolver behind its head. His finger tightened on the trigger. The dog slumped silently on the silver ice at his feet. A pool of black solidified beneath its head, cushioning it like a velvet pillow.

Muktuk walked to the musher, who flinched as he watched Muktuk approach.

'Not both of them,' pleaded the musher.

Muktuk stopped. He recognized the voice.

'Short, Short Seppa?' he said.

Short nodded. 'My dogs, Muktuk. My dogs,' he said. 'I was running with my light off. My lead sees better without the shadows thrown by the lamp.'

'Short, you can't let your dog suffer like this. Listen to him,' said Muktuk gruffly. 'I have to shoot him.'

Short bowed his head. A loud retort cut the silence. Two huskies lay sprawled in death.

Muktuk pocketed his revolver and walked down his team, calming them. Delilah tried to reach his face and lick him.

Shark lunged at them, not particular as to which one she managed to bite.

'Did you see what happened, you stupid dog? Keep up this nonsense and you'll probably end up the same way. Dead. Very definitely dead.'

Shark ignored the warning as she did all of Muktuk's threats. She growled at Delilah and was in turn ignored.

Muktuk then patted Short roughly on the shoulder. 'Let's turn your sled over. See if it'll make Kaltag and get off this son of a bitch of a river.'

Seppa nodded mutely.

'I'll run behind you to Kaltag and help with the report on the dogs and snowmobiles,' Muktuk offered.

Seppa looked as if he was about to cry.

'Now race me to Kaltag, Short. I expect you to be in before me. I'll carry one of your dogs in my sled, you take the other.'

Muktuk waited until Short Seppa was out of sight before he picked up the heavy dog from the ice, wrapped it in a thermal blanket and tied it down onto his basket.

He followed Short warily into Kaltag, expecting other drunks celebrating the Iditarod to come racing out on their machines, but all was still.

As Muktuk drew close to the village, he saw Short sitting on his sled with his back to the wind, rocking back and forth. His dogs were curled into tight balls of fur and did not stir as Muktuk approached.

To Shark's dismay they did not respond when she offered to fight the lead, not even when she extended the invitation to include the whole team.

'Hi there! You okay, Short?' yelled Muktuk as his dogs, with the exception of Shark, skirted the seated musher. Shark, unable to resist the opportunity, lunged out and sunk her teeth into the musher's arm, ripping open his suit. Blood seeped into the fuchsia pink cloth.

The grizzled man looked up. Despair etched his face and fear clouded his eyes.

'I've run this bitching race six times. On my seventh I have to hear them. Bad luck. Yup, that's what it means.'

'Whoa,' shouted Muktuk to Shark, who was about to fly at Short again. 'I'll kill you, you miserable bitch,' he yelled at Shark. 'Now I have to stop. Can't leave the guy bleeding when it was you who bit him.'

Short Seppa continued talking as if he did not know that Shark had ripped his suit and he was bleeding.

'That's what I told that young couple at Skwentna,' continued the musher. 'Seven is lucky for some, unlucky for others. Seems my luck has been decided here near Kaltag.'

Short looked up at Muktuk. 'Have you heard the voices?'

'Sure.'

'How many times?' asked Short.

Muktuk had a convenient fit of coughing.

'What you need is black coffee,' said Muktuk. He was not interested in ghostly voices.

But Short Seppa continued to rock his body, seemingly unaware of what Muktuk had said.

'Can't you hear them?' he asked suddenly, straightening up and peering into the fog of swirling snow. 'Listen – now they are clapping.'

Muktuk shrugged. 'You probably need sleep more than coffee,' he decided.

The old man's eyes brightened and he stared at Muktuk as if seeing him for the first time.

'The missionaries,' he said clearly. 'Remember the massacre of the missionaries near Kaltag? Those about to die hear them. Don't you hear them whispering and calling?' he asked piteously, hoping that someone else could hear the ghostly voices.

'Everyone hears them,' lied Muktuk, eager to corroborate Short's story about the dogs and snowmobiles and continue with the race.

'See how their blood has stained the snow red.'

'Reflection from the sky,' Muktuk muttered gruffly.

'Look at the sky. Their blood is pumping out of their veins. The heavens saw it happen and now they show us how the blood ran in the snow at Kaltag,' said Short Seppa, refuting the explanation.

'Northern lights usually pulse and dance in the sky,' said Muktuk. 'It's not blood. One finds the northern lights everywhere, not only at Kaltag.'

For a moment it seemed as if Muktuk's logic would work.

'God's watercolours, they call them in other places,' said Short Seppa, 'but here, they are to remind us of what happened. You have heard them. You said so and you're still running.'

'Sure,' said Muktuk, eager to be on his way but unable to leave the musher alone in his misery. 'Come on, let's fix that arm.'

He rummaged in his suit and brought out a bag of ointments hanging round his neck, resting them on his thermal underwear to stop them freezing solid.

Muktuk pushed the cold tube of Betadine into his gloved hand to warm on the hand warmers.

'Okay,' he said as he massaged the tube, 'seems soft enough to squeeze. Let's see your arm.'

Short held out his arm obediently and watched as Muktuk rubbed the brown ointment well into Shark's teeth marks.

'It'll have to be cleaned up at Unalakleet,' he said. 'Sorry about Shark. Only reason I keep the troublemaker is because she smells trail and open water under six foot of snow.'

'No problem. A good lead is what wins the race in most cases.'

Muktuk looked at the old musher with the tear in his sleeve and felt guilty. He had lied to him. Shark had savaged him, and now his suit was no longer windproof. The old man also believed that he was going to die as he had heard the slaughtered missionaries.

Muktuk felt responsible for the musher. Showing a compassion which the inhabitants of Skwentna would not believe possible, Muktuk lifted the musher to his feet.

'Here,' he said, fumbling around his neck, 'let me tie this scarf round your sleeve. It'll keep the wind out until we reach Unalakleet. Let's make the run there together, but let's move before the wind gets up again. Then we can separate and meet again in Nome.'

Short's dogs uncurled, stood, stretched, then fell in behind Muktuk's team.

Shark barked, gloating at them.

'Quiet,' roared Muktuk. 'You're in the lead to find trail, not trash-talk other dogs. Next stop, Unalakleet,' he shouted.

'Unalakleet, the place where the east wind always blows,' said Short. 'Bitching wind. Who can understand a wind that holds snow parallel to the ground for ten miles, or pulls at two hundred mph when it's not gusting? They call it a hurricane down in the Lower Forty-eight when it's only seventy-three mph. Bitching wind. Come on, let's go,' he called to his dogs.

'Right on,' said Muktuk, happy that Short had dropped the subject of ghostly voices and bad luck. 'Wind? Remember that climbing party who were blown off the top slopes of Denali and never seen again? If they want to talk wind and cold we have it all here. Best goddamn place in the world.'

Short nodded, happy to have found someone who agreed with him about the weather, and relieved to have company from Kaltag to Unalakleet.

'I was on Denali,' he said. 'I was with the party who established that there was a windchill factor of a hundred and forty-eight degrees below zero.

'Cold like that would take your damn finger off like a bandsaw if you held it in the wind. The bitching wind claimed four toes and two fingers. All amputated when we returned. That's when I turned to dog-sledding. Here you can run with your dogs and warm up. Can't run up a mountain, unless your dad was a Dall sheep.'

Muktuk grinned, but was silent. He kept watching for signs of slacking in his dogs.

Entering the coastal Eskimo settlement of Unalakleet was like going from solitary confinement to a ticker-tape parade in New York. Sirens shrieked, church bells rang and a jostling, cheering crowd gathered outside the Unalakleet Lodge.

Muktuk and Short checked in. They refused invitations to party, and Muktuk left Short in the care of a veterinery officer. The woman who checked them in offered to sew the tear in Short's snowsuit.

'You'll have to do something about that dog of yours,' warned the veterinary officer. 'Her reputation precedes her like the flu.'

Muktuk merely grunted. Shark had saved him many times by refusing to run where he wanted her to go, or tiptoeing with her tail straight, warning him of thin ice.

'See you in Nome,' he said to Short, and clapped him on the shoulder. 'Good trail. Sorry about Shark.'

'Good trail to you too. Thanks for the company. It sure helped.'

Muktuk wanted to ask for the scarf that he had tied round Short's arm. He had found it wound into the bare branches of a shrub beside the trail near Skwentna. He had wrapped it round his neck to return to its owner sometime.

Scott had given the bright orange and green scarf to his brother as a twenty-first birthday gift and Patrick used it constantly, wearing it as the Inupiats wore amulets for good luck in health or hunting.

The old musher looked so tired as he sat on a box with his shoulders hunched, watching the vet probe the wound in his arm, that Muktuk simply yelled, 'Short, bring the scarf to Nome. It's not mine. Belongs to a friend.'

Short nodded, and lifted a hand in a farewell salute.

Chapter Thirty-One

NATÛ AWAKENED with a start from a sleep as deep as death. Adrenalin rushed through her veins making her nauseous as she fought to remember where she was.

Bud grunted as she tried to stretch her legs in the cramped space.

As Bud threw his arm over her body, she realized that they were at Rohn and were to enjoy a few hours' rest.

Natû cuddled back into the hollow of Bud's body. They could check the sleds, replace runners, repack the supplies and examine the dogs later. But Natû found that the sounds of teams arriving and leaving made her impatient to be up and working with her dogs.

She crawled out from under the table, leaving Bud asleep.

Another ride down Dalzell Gorge is the only thing that would wake him now, and perhaps not even that, she thought. As Natû opened the wooden door and slipped out, a blast of icy air took her breath away. It also made her realize that she needed to relieve herself. She trudged through the snow and sleeping dogs to the two toilets. They consisted of wooden box seats placed over deep pits, but on the trail were a luxury.

Natû contemplated the freedom of dropping her suit pants and sitting down for a few minutes.

'Damn,' she groaned as she approached the two plank cubicles. Sticks were jammed into the soggy snow, keeping both doors closed.

'It's back to the HEET can, I guess.' She walked to her sled and rummaged in it.

'Good, I thought it was near the top,' she said as she held up the front section cut from a bright yellow can of HEET.

'Not the normal use for this,' she said as she stood behind a large pine and unzipped the lower part of her snowsuit. 'But the spout works well. Beats dropping my pants and getting wind rash.'

A musher, his moustache and beard glued with icicles, drove his dog team into Rohn checkpoint. A checker showed him where to bed his dogs. He signed in, then looked round for a pine tree.

'Hell, sorry,' he said as he saw Natû behind the tree trunk. 'Saw yellow snow and thought it must be some guy.'

'Works the same way,' grinned Natû.

Natû glanced over her shoulder as she heard a wooden door creak and groan.

'If you're quick, you'll be able to sit down. It's warmer in there.'

'Thanks,' he shouted.

'No sweat.'

Natû shook the droplets from the plastic yellow spout and eased the HEET container from her suit. She zipped up quickly and walked over to the sleds.

Oily stirred as Natû approached, but did not remove her nose from the warm cushion of her fluffy tail.

Natû tucked her makeshift urinal back into her sled. She breathed in the crisp air deeply. On the way back to the cabin she stopped and stroked the crudely carved figure of an upright bear. She was unwilling to leave the clean air and return to the cabin sweating with humanity.

'Yogi,' she said as she ran her fingers along the bear's nose. 'You have it right. The woods and rivers are your home, or what we've left of them.'

'Coffee is up inside,' growled a musher coming out of the cabin. He fumbled with the zip of his suit and ran for the trees.

'Guy must think I need it if I'm standing talking to a log of wood carved in the likeness of a bear,' said Natû, turning to go to the cabin.

As Natû pushed the heavy door open Bud turned from the table where he and three mushers were talking in low voices.

'Sorry about your dog,' said one of the men.

'Yup, bad to lose a good dog this early in the race,' added another.

Natû nodded. Vega's death was still too fresh; she did not want sympathy.

'Any hot water?' she asked. 'And how did you hear?'

'Anna McInnes flew over you and Bud just after it happened. She landed here to drop off a checker and pick up a vet for McGrath.'

'Anna says the weather at McGrath is "severe clear" again, not a cloud in the sky, and you need to be a polar bear to be comfortable in the cold,' grinned another musher as he handed Natû a mug of coffee.

Natû shook her head. 'No thanks; no caffeine for me when I'm running dogs. The down isn't worth the up. I'll have some seal oil to warm me for McGrath.'

'Uugh,' grimaced the musher and took the mug for himself. 'Don't know how you swallow that rubbish.'

Bud looked at Natû, ready to rush in to her defence if she took umbrage at the remark, but she merely smiled.

'My ancestors have swallowed it for thousands of years, and they live where few others could survive. When you're freezing your butt off on the Yukon try some, then eat a chocolate bar to stop yourself puking.'

The mushers laughed at their friend's discomfiture.

Bud put an arm round Natû.

'Let's do the dogs,' he said.

'Tough babe,' said one of the three mushers as the door closed behind Bud and Natû.

'She is Trapper Jack's daughter,' said another.

'Heard he trained them and that godson of his for the race. Interesting to know what placing they'll get.'

'Don't you mean that it'll be interesting to know if they finish the race?' said the one Natû had told to eat chocolate if he was unable to drink seal oil without throwing up.

'They'll finish, bet on that. The Damas guy is an ex-rigger. Those riggers can move mountains. Sleds and dogs will be easy meat.'

'But not blizzards, white-outs and the Yukon cold,' retorted the one still smarting from Natû's remark.

Natû and Bud dropped down the steep riverbank and their sleds hit the grey shale with a sharp jolt.

'This should do the new runners a lot of good,' said Bud sarcastically as he looked at the few patches of snow nestling between glare ice and shale. In the distance 'pyramid mountain' seemed to block the end of the river.

'We won't worry about that until we've done the Burn,' said Natû. 'It's a great day. Let's run and wait until we're out of the Burn before we worry about the sleds' runners again. These orange-V quick-change runners will be great for the Burn. At Nikolai we'll find out what the trail conditions are like, and if there is good snow we'll feed the dogs snacks and put on the XH black again. I know they are soft,' she said, forestalling Bud's objection, 'but they have low resistance and the dogs can pull the sled easier.'

Bud nodded. Natû had more experience mushing than he had, and she had certainly read more on the subject.

'I suppose steel strips covered with plastic are better than wooden ones plastered with mud or ice,' he teased.

You're a funny little Inupiat, my love, he thought as he followed Natû into the Burn.

You feel the land and can draw topographical maps correct to the smallest river, from memory. You understand and discuss the most modern technology in sled-building and arctic wear.

Ultra-high molecular-weight polyethylene. High density polyethylene. Radian-Tex, Gore-Tex and Thinsulate are not merely words. You understand more than I do about them, yet you refuse to let Edwin show you how the computers work in MOC on the North Slope oilfields.

But I love you more than I believed it possible to love anyone.

Natû was silent as they entered the Burn.

'Someone has been kind to us,' she said as she surveyed the field of snow, its whiteness broken only by the odd black branch or stump pushing up like a flagpole.

'If this is the dreaded Burn, let's get through it before the wind strengthens and all the snow vanishes,' said Bud.

'Plus the markers with their fluorescent tags,' added Natû.

Later, Bud stopped his team close behind Natû. They dropped the brakes and looked back at Farewell Burn.

'Wonder how often the Burn is that kind to mushers?' said Bud.

'Not often. We've made excellent time. Let's use the time the Burn has given us and hit the trail hard to Haiditarod. We'll do a run-rest-run, programme for the dogs.'

'Great. We'll be halfway to Nome when we hit Haiditarod, won't we?' said Bud happily.

Chapter Thirty-Two

TRAPPER JACK plastered his moustache along the sides of his lips until it met and mingled with his beard.

Kiluk Owens studied him while pretending to knead dough for fresh bread. The room filled with the warm smell of wet flour and yeast. Trapper was worried. He usually sat as motionless as one of the carved bone Eskimo figures sold to tourists, but today he was restless. His fingers ceaselessly wove his wispy beard into plaits, then unwove it.

The radio made talking difficult. Kiluk and Herbie kept it on all day. Scott listened most of the night. They had pinned a map on the wall and Scott moved markers to pinpoint where Patrick, Bud, Natû and Muktuk were on the trail.

Trapper, Scott and the Owens had arrived in the village of White Mountain the week before. Kiluk's aunt and uncle had a home in the small settlement barely eighty miles from Nome.

The mushers had an eight-hour mandatory break there before crossing the infamous Topkok Hills with their brutal, changeable weather.

The mushers knew that they could be trapped by terrifying storms on the barren, seemingly endless, rounded hills. They were dangerous because most of the contestants lightened their sleds at White Mountain and dropped dogs they didn't consider fast enough for the final sprint to Safety and then into Nome.

Scott turned from the radio. Kiluk, Herbie and Trapper looked up at him expectantly.

'I think Bud and Natû have grown wings,' he said.

'What's happened?' asked Kiluk anxiously, immediately associating wings with angels and therefore death.

'Why are you looking so worried?' asked Herbie, alarmed at the sudden pallor in Kiluk's face.

'Blondies have angels with wings guarding the graves of their dead. I've seen pictures of angels flying up to the stars with those who have died. What has happened to Natû?' she wailed.

'Kiluk, I'm so sorry,' said Scott, putting his arm around her shoulders. 'Flying is only an expression I used to say how fast they have crossed the Burn. They are really moving.'

'Race isn't over yet,' warned Trapper. 'Many mushers have made the mistake of relaxing too soon. They still have the Yukon, Topkok Hills and the sea ice on Norton Sound. All treacherous. All bad.'

But he had a satisfied grin on his face as he returned to his chair and stared out at the falling snow.

'They have crossed Farewell Burn, checked in and left Nikolai. Apparently they've said that they intend stopping at Haiditarod.'

'But there's nothing there. Hasn't been since the gold ran out. Fourteen million dollars of it,' protested Kiluk.

'It now has something more important,' said Trapper, easing himself from the wooden chair and moving across the room to study the map of the trail.

'Rest. Undisturbed rest. They can sleep.'

Natû had listened when they worked out the potential strategy for running the race. The village of Haiditarod was not mentioned as a possible stopover. Trapper was worried when he heard that Bud and Natû were at Rohn, as he thought that the loss of Vega, plus the rigours of Dalzell Gorge, Happy River and Rainy Pass were too much for her and Bud. They were obviously tired. He had hoped that they would run farther before taking their mandatory stopover.

Trapper said nothing to Scott and the Owens, but prayed quietly to Oline and asked her to make Natû restless and eager to leave the cabin at Rohn.

Now as he watched the wind twirl the snow, he whispered, 'Thank you, Oline. Thank you for being her mother and for still looking after my child Natû.'

Scott saw the smile dance round Trapper's mouth and relaxed. Trapper was happy with the way the race was progressing. He turned back to the radio to hear if there was any news of Patrick.

Trapper watched Scott punch the buttons on the radio for a few moments.

'Don't worry about Patrick, Scott. He is running like a veteran, not a rookie, so is the woman running with him,' said Kiluk.

'What woman?' asked Scott, abandoning the radio. 'Patrick is running alone.'

'Was. He now has a veteran with him in a bright yellow suit.'

'How do you know?'

'Whispers,' said Kiluk laughing. One of the mushers who stopped in at White Mountain earlier had told a friend of Kiluk's that he had passed Trapper's godson and a woman in a yellow suit on the trail.

'Native whispers,' added Kiluk mysteriously.

Chapter Thirty-Three

As PATRICK and Vi left the small village of Takotna behind them and started their run to Ophir, where they had agreed to separate, Patrick experienced a pang of regret at losing Vi's companionship.

She was an expert on mushing and dogs, and loved the country. She ran beside the dogs for as long as he did, and lack of sleep did not seem to bother her.

For the first time Patrick admired a woman for her accomplishments and not her physical attributes. To his surprise she showed no interest in him as a man, merely as another competitor. Patrick was accustomed to women clustering around him; Vi was a refreshing change.

They ran the two teams along the state highway, which was built when the DEW line was installed as an early-warning system during the Cold War with Russia. The trail then led through the once famous gold country surrounding Ophir.

Vi was leading as they entered the ghost town of Ophir, named after King Solomon's fabled gold mines.

Patrick and Vi bedded the dogs down and examined their paws for cuts or ice balls which may have formed between their toes.

The huskies lay in the snow with their eyes closed, and merely lifted up each paw in turn as Vi and Patrick worked over them.

'They'll sleep well,' said Patrick, looking around the deserted area they had chosen for the stopover. 'I'll fetch water and we can prepare their food.'

'Plus our own,' said Vi. 'One of the main reasons for hallucinating and making mistakes on this run is that mushers care for the huskies and forget to feed themselves. They tire, their brains become sluggish and instead of reading the warning signs the weather is giving them, they blunder on, usually into disaster.'

'Right on,' said Patrick, trying not to smile at the serious expression on Vi's face as she lectured him.

'You at least eat Eskimo food,' she continued as if Patrick had not spoken. 'Seal oil and whale blubber are marvellous for keeping you warm and your energy levels up, especially when that Yukon cold saws into your bones.'

'Is the mighty Yukon really that bad?'

'Worse.'

Soon Vi and Patrick had eaten, unzipped their sleeping bags on the sleds and pulled the outer covers over their heads. The dogs were curled into tight balls and were already asleep. Patrick sighed contentedly. The thawed and warmed chilli moose had been good. He closed his eyes and dropped into the deep, dreamless sleep of exhaustion.

Vi lay awake for a while, warming her hands between her thighs. A picture so vivid that she wondered if she was hallucinating filled the darkness of her double-zipped sleeping bag. It was Patrick, with tears streaming down his cheeks as he cradled Clarke in his arms.

'Yes,' she whispered, 'if ever I decide to change my wild and wonderful life, it will be for you, Patrick Butler, or someone like you.' Her eyes closed and the two mushers and their huskies slept undisturbed.

Something awakened Patrick. He sensed rather than heard noise or movement. He lay still, listening. Wolves foraging for food? Moose, or a bear who had been disturbed from his semi-hibernation?

No, it was something moving close to him. He strained his ears to catch any familiar sounds. Suddenly he recognized what had dragged him from sleep: it was the sound of a dog team being fed and hooked onto the gangline.

'No,' he whispered. 'We said we would run to Ophir, then separate, but not like this.'

He struggled to unzip the double zips on his sleeping bag and clamber from the sled to talk to her.

'Damn,' he cursed as the zipper slipped from his fingers. 'Vi wouldn't sneak out without saying goodbye.'

He felt nauseous as he remembered a conversation when they were in McGrath. Vi's words now resounded like a death knell to the feelings he was developing for her.

'This race is a drug, but there is no rehab centre to cure the addiction. One has to keep running it until one reaches journey's end.' She had smiled mockingly. 'That is Dryden, Patrick.

'I have to run the Iditarod, which means I need money, and that comes from sponsors. They only hand over money and equipment to those who place, so I must be somewhere in the top twenty.'

As he remembered the conversation he also remembered one of her many quotes, 'silent as shadows'. He thought she said it was from one of Coleridge's poems.

'She has probably moved out as silent as one of her damn shadows,' he muttered, still battling to open his bag.

Patrick unzipped his bag and stared over to where Vi and her team were resting.

He expected to see only snow with a few tufts of scrub breaking through, but there, stretched out, were sixteen huskies and a sled with the cover still zipped closed.

Patrick breathed a sigh of relief: Vi had not run out on him. As he climbed out of the sled, Sockeye stood up and stretched, awakening the rest of the team as well as Vi's huskies.

Patrick watched the yellow and orange sled cover rise and fall as Vi wriggled from the bag to emerge sleepy-eyed. She stretched, yawned and seemed surprised to find Patrick up and watching her.

'Hi,' he said cheerfully, pulling out the aluminium box that held the quart cans of HEET, cooking alcohol, to make the dogs' food.

Vi watched as he threw the frozen slabs of meat into one pot, then poured boiling water over it from the pot on the stove. He then stirred in the dry ingredients.

'Neat,' she commented. 'Who taught you that trick?'

'Natû told me about it. She reads everything anyone writes on the Iditarod. It stops the taste of sour or burned meat polluting the dogs' meals for the remainder of the run. Beats using one pot for everything.'

Vi nodded and rummaged in her sled, emerging with similar cooking equipment plus the coolers to hold the extra food and save cooking further down the trail.

'Well, this is where we agreed to become competitors again,' she said, as she surveyed both teams clipped onto the ganglines and the neatly packed sleds.

Patrick swallowed hard. He had expected something more in the way of a farewell, but Vi was obviously eager to continue the race.

'Good trail, Vi. Thanks for the company,' he said, forcing himself to smile, though he was unable to make it reach his eyes.

Vi raised a hand in farewell.

'Let's go,' she shouted, as she jumped onto the runners.

Patrick watched as her team climbed easily into Beaver Mountains.

'Come on boys, let's get through the big country before the wind gets up and leaves us with no trail,' she said.

Patrick gazed round their mandatory stopover. It was very empty without Vi. The twenty-four hours had passed as swift as a sudden blizzard, and like the blizzard had taken everything with it, leaving him with nothing.

Patrick shook himself mentally. 'You're becoming maudlin,' he said. 'Concentrate on the race, like Vi does.'

'Go, Sockeye,' he yelled.

Sockeye, the scent of Vi's team strong in his nostrils, set off as if he was on a mission to overtake Vi and her huskies. He found one of the bitches in Vi's team very interesting, and wanted to further his acquaintanceship.

'You're pulling like a star, Sockeye,' shouted Patrick, unaware as to why his lead was showing such enthusiasm and energy.

Chapter Thirty-Four

SCOTT CAME into the cabin stamping the snow from his boots and flinging his arms across his chest to warm himself.

Trapper and Kiluk looked at him in silence.

'What news?' asked Herbie, who was not blessed with the patience and acceptance of adversity possessed by his wife.

'Muktuk has chosen not to leave Shaktoolik and cross the sea ice,' said Scott in a monotone. 'There is a strong east wind blowing. Some of the permanent land ice is already breaking away and moving out to sea. Leads are opening. The other mushers have also taken the advice of the natives in Shaktoolik and followed the shoreline, choosing to add an extra fifteen miles onto the trail rather than risk the ice pack of Norton Bay.'

Scott crossed to the map and moved the peg marking Muktuk's position.

Trapper sighed.

'Sea ice is an animal to be feared. It growls, groans and grinds its teeth. Every year it eats many of those who attempt to cross it.'

'Our young women can be widowed three or four times before they are twenty-five,' agreed Kiluk. 'The sea ice swallows their husbands when they venture out to hunt.'

She shook her head and opened the door to the oven, allowing a flush of hot air to warm the room.

'One's pulse and heart beat differently when one is on the ice,' said Trapper, repeating an Eskimo saying. 'Muktuk has chosen wisely. But there will be those who will be blinded by the desire to win or receive sponsorship, and they will take their teams onto the ice.'

'What about that crazy story of the musher who ran, fed and bedded his team for two days on a section of snow-covered ice pack which had broken away from the mainland?' said Scott, turning to Trapper for confirmation or denial of the tale.

'Not a crazy story but a true one,' answered Trapper seriously. 'He only realized what had happened when they reached the black open water of the Bering Sea. Luckily for him the wind changed and the ice drifted back to land. They say he went down on his knees and kissed the land.'

'Now I understand why one's heart has a different beat when on the sea ice,' said Scott. 'I wonder if that's how many of the young women's husbands vanished?' he mused. 'I can think of nothing worse than to be out on what seems to be land-fast ice and suddenly find it's a floating island.' He shivered at the picture he had painted in his mind.

'Something worse would be to find that a polar bear out hunting was drifting on the same section of ice,' said Herbie. 'I have nightmares at the thought of being hunted by a hunter who is as clever as man and is certainly better equipped for living on the ice in the Arctic.'

No one laughed. They held bears and their hunting skills in high esteem.

Trapper stared out at the snow until his eyes watered. Once again he saw the crumpled figure of Oline huddled on Pingkok Island, waiting for grandfather Nanuq, the mighty polar bear, to find her and tear her apart as easily as he would a small seal.

'Yes,' said Trapper softly to himself, 'it takes great courage to face a hunter as strong and devious as the polar bear.'

'Didn't one of your . . .?'

Herbie did not finish the sentence as Kiluk, moving surprisingly quickly for a lady of her girth, stood in front of him making signs which he recognized meant he was to keep quiet immediately.

'Yes,' said Trapper, answering the unspoken question. 'Yes.'

Scott suddenly turned up the volume on the radio. He listened intently, then turned to Trapper.

'Do you know a Short Seppa?' he asked.

'Yeah. He's run the Idit. for years. Why? He's a great guy, always ready to help a rookie. He gives good advice, doesn't try to mislead or kill them like some I can name.'

'Shark, Muktuk's lead, took a piece out of his arm.'

'Sounds like that mean bitch,' said Herbie.

'Muktuk cleaned the bite and ran with him to Unalakleet, where he left him in the care of a veterinary officer.'

'Muktuk?' everyone said in amazement.

'No,' said Kiluk, 'they have the wrong guy. I know Muktuk. He wouldn't stop for anyone or anything. Shark tears into whatever moves, Muktuk is used to it. No, it's not Muktuk, they mean someone else.'

Herbie and Trapper nodded in agreement.

'When Muktuk runs he does it to win. He does not go for the humanitarian award.'

Scott did not disagree. He merely turned his attention back to the radio.

'One meets many mushers along the trail,' said Trapper. 'Some become friends, others you never see again. That's part of the race.'

Chapter Thirty-Five

BUD AND Natû stood on the runners of their sleds looking at the ghost town of Haiditarod.

'The rest-run-rest routine that Natû had set all the way to Haiditarod helped the dogs, but Bud was light-headed. He felt nauseous from lack of sleep, and the calls of a pack of wolves hunting a heard of caribou, which seemed to have followed them from Ophir, upset him more than he cared to admit. The abandoned rusted tin buildings rattled in the wind and seemed to float above the ground in the silver-blue light that preceded the dawn.

'Haiditarod, the Indians named it. A Far Distant Place,' said Natû. 'We've made it. Isn't it beautiful? It looks like the inside of an oyster shell.'

Natû saw only the pastel colours she loved. For her, the howling wolves added to the beauty of the deserted spot.

'What do we do with the dogs' food with those damn wolves so close?' asked Bud, trying to peer into the dark scattered trees behind him.

'They're interested in hot meat on four legs,' said Natû. 'They'll keep to the edge of the caribou herd until they find one that is tiring or weak, then they will single it out from the herd and bring it down.'

Bud listened, gaining comfort from the thought that the wolves would remain near the caribou.

'I'll go down to the river and cut out a hole in the ice to get water for the dogs,' said Natû.

She was worried about Bud. The pen of weariness had etched

deep lines in his face and he swayed where he stood on the sled runners.

'No. I'll do that,' he said.

Natû was about to argue when she realized that his pride needed pampering.

'Thanks, Bud. That pail does get heavy when it's full of water.'

She watched him walk away towards the river.

'I'm so proud of you, Bud Damas,' she said as she unpacked the pots and cooking boxes to prepare the dogs' food, plus some warmed-up stew for herself and Bud. 'You're running like a veteran. I think Trapper will be proud of both of us. That red lantern hanging from the burled wood arch in Nome will not be presented to us for being the last to finish the race.'

As he stepped onto the ice Bud froze. In the trees, something moved with the stealth and intent of a hunter. He squeezed his eyes closed. When he opened them, the creature seemed to be glaring at him. As he stared, it moved aside to let another join it.

A wolf is the only animal to recognize a motionless man by sight alone.

Bud struggled to remember where he had heard that information. Trapper or Natû? He shook his head, and as he did so the wolves seemed to grow in size.

'Their jaws crack bones even grizzlies can't. They swallow chunks of meat the size of a man's fist.'

Bud turned from the river, but in his feverish fear he turned away from Natû and the dogs. He started running. To his horror, the wolves came towards him. Their eyes were flat and yellow. Their tongues hung from their open mouths and pieces of bloody meat were wedged between their teeth.

As he ran a flash of yellow light between the trees caught his attention. It was a small log cabin. Outside hung a widow's lamp to guide and welcome weary travellers to safety in the overwhelming wilderness of Alaska.

Instinctively he turned and ran towards the lamp.

'Perhaps the sight of human habitation will stop them following me.' As the hope of rescue ran across his mind, the cabin door opened. A woman with a smile warming her face beckoned. Bud stumbled up to her and tumbled into the room.

'No,' he screamed.

The room was filled with wolves fighting over the carcass of a caribou. He ran to the door. The woman grabbed his arm. 'Stay,' she said. 'It's all right, they aren't hungry any more and won't harm you.'

Bud flung her from him and fled. The picture of gleaming teeth and the stench of blood brought him to his knees.

Wolves streamed from the cabin's open door towards him. The male leading the pack streaked ahead. When Bud could smell his foetid breath he screamed. He covered his throat with his hands.

Natû heard the scream. She dropped the pots in a ringing clatter and stopped only long enough to pull the revolver from Bud's sled, then she ran to the river. She followed his footsteps and found the empty pail standing on the ice.

'Bud,' she shouted. The wind whistling through the derelict buildings and the cacophonous clatter of rusted iron sheets was her only answer.

'Bud! Where are you?'

There were no footprints on the ice for her to follow, so she climbed up on the bank.

A long, lonesome howl rang down the river, as chilling as the sounding of the last post.

'Good; they are moving away,' she said quietly. 'Bud will be relieved. He pretends not to worry, but he's been jittery ever since we saw the caribou and heard the wolves hunting.'

Bud pounded the snow, throwing fistfuls into the air.

'Get,' he shouted. 'Get out of here. If you come for me I'll die fighting like a man.'

Natû shaded her eyes. Her sharp eyesight caught the movement of what looked like a minor blizzard. Snow flew wildly in all directions, but only from one place.

Cautiously Natû approached the spot, wondering what animal would cause the snow to fly up.

Must be in its death throes, she thought.

'Bud,' she whispered in wonderment as she recognized her husband kneeling in the snow, mumbling obscenities to creatures she could not see.

'Bud?' she touched him on the shoulder. He shrank from her touch.

'No. I won't come back to your cabin to be fed to your wolves. No, I'd rather kill you,' he shouted, and pushed Natû away so violently that she stumbled and slid down onto the river ice.

'Oline,' said Natû. 'I need your help. He is too strong, I cannot force him to return to the sleds. Whatever he saw he believes is real. While he is hallucinating he could kill me. Tell me what to do. Help your child.'

Suddenly Natû felt the same sense of peace creep into her which always came when she spoke to the spirit of her ancestor.

'Bud,' she screamed. 'I have the pail. Where is the water? The dogs must be bedded and fed. Get up and help me. I can't carry this on my own.'

The list of everyday chores seemed to bring Bud back to reality.

'Natû?' he said groggily, looking down at the frozen river. 'The wolves. The woman and the cabin with the lamp?'

'Sleep,' ordered Natû. 'I can't keep my eyes open. White-out and Sockeye were snoring before I left. A pail full of water and we can hit the sack. We have twenty-four wonderful hours to rest.'

They filled the pail and walked back to the dogs, swinging it between them. The huskies heard them, but merely snuggled their noses deeper into their thick tails.

'The wolves, Natû?' said Bud as they put down the pail.

'Gone,' answered Natû warily, not certain as to whether he was still hallucinating.

'Now sleep. We'll talk about them when we wake up.'

She waited until she heard Bud snoring before she climbed into her sled bag and wriggled into the warmth of her sleeping bag. With a soft, satisfied grunt she closed her eyes.

The wind strengthened but it did not disturb the exhausted teams and mushers. The pale sun had clawed her way to her zenith and was sinking when Natû finally peered out of the bag. The dogs were still curled up tightly, but as she watched, Oily stood up, walked in a circle sniffing her bed and prepared to lie down again.

'Time to feed you all,' said Natû as she struggled from the sled. The cold wind acted as a shower, refreshing her and driving away the last traces of sleepiness.

Happily she poured out half a mug of seal oil for Bud. She chuckled as she imagined his face as he tried to swallow it. She added a bar of chocolate to mask the aftertaste. She stuffed jerky into her pocket to chew as they ran. Four frozen hamburgers were laid on the grill beside the can of water boiling for the dogs' food.

'That should set you up until we reach Anvik, where we'll stop and fill up for the run on the dreaded Yukon to Kaltag,' she said, talking to a still sleeping Bud.

Sensing that they were about to be fed, Bud's huskies barked greetings and a few insults to Natû's team. They were well rested and hungry.

The noise awakened Bud. He appeared from his bag looking relaxed and normal.

Natû waited for him to mention wolves and the hallucinations of the previous night, but he crossed over to where she was cooking and nuzzled his face in her hair where it escaped from her caribou fur hat.

'I love you, my little Inupiat wife,' he said. Natû swung round to face him. Their breath steamed and mingled in the evening cold and their mouths were hot and urgent.

'Think we could both fit into your sled bag?' asked Bud, his voice hoarse and ragged.

'No,' said Natû pulling herself away from him and temptation. 'Remember the race. We don't want to lose the time the Burn gave us.'

'Right on,' said Bud. 'From now on, "Nome is Home". We stop for nothing or no one until we reach that arch across the front street.'

'Drink this, Bud,' said Natû handing him the seal oil. 'Next check-in we hit river ice, and we'll run into the wind in the middle of the Yukon until we reach Kaltag,' Bud shivered at the mention of the Yukon River.

'You only know what the word cold means when you're on the ice in the middle of the river facing temperatures of sixty below, with headwinds screaming at fifty to sixty miles an hour,' said Natû, watching Bud grimace as he swallowed the seal oil and held out his hand for the chocolate.

'It's also cold enough to "wee and sit on it". All the cold in Alaska settles into that damn Yukon valley. We'll have to get out of there as fast as we can or we'll freeze our butts off,' Bud continued, running his tongue around his mouth trying to clean it of seal oil.

'Every musher hates the Yukon, Bud. I reckon they have good reason. We'll have to be prepared to run with the dogs; that way we'll keep warm.'

Natû grinned at him. 'I know a few things to keep you warm, Bud Damas,' she said.

Bud laughed, then became serious.

'Natû, about yesterday. I really saw the log cabin and the wolves. I can still see them.'

'I know, hallucinations are frighteningly real and can last for weeks. But believe me, I was on the river. There were no wolves or cabin.

'But several mushers have seen a blinding white light which guides them out of tough spots. They are usually the ones who pray for help. Our ancestors help us when we appeal to them. I believe that there is a Life Force way beyond our comprehension, and if we can connect with it, we receive help.'

Bud smiled and blew Natû a kiss. 'Thanks for understanding. Sorry for knocking you over, but it was really that woman in the cabin.'

'Okay. Do it again and I'll floor you, Damas.'

*

'Whoa,' shouted Natû. Sockeye pulled to a halt just behind Bud.

Nothing Trapper or Muktuk said had prepared Bud for the enormity of the Yukon. He knew it started in Canada and flowed almost two and a half thousand miles to empty itself in a three-mile-wide flood plain and into the icy Bering Sea. Bud threw his arms wide in disbelief.

'Numbers mean nothing until you see it,' he said.

Natû nodded.

'Let's get on down there. Once we've crossed to Anvik on the other side, we still have a long run to Kaltag.'

Chapter Thirty-Six

PATRICK WAS whistling as he ran. He was almost off the Yukon. He had negotiated the islands before Eagle Island. Sockeye stayed on the trail in spite of the tributaries branching off the Yukon. They were now on the twenty-two-mile stretch before Kaltag that most mushers found monotonous.

The sameness of the river, high winds, glare ice and severe clear weather tired them and tried their concentration. They had to take care not to have delusions or fall asleep and tumble from the sled, risking losing their team and everything they needed to stay alive.

Patrick hardly noticed where they were going. All his thoughts were of Vi and the possibility of a future with her.

His attention swung back to the river as Sockeye barked a loud, urgent bark.

Patrick studied the team ahead, which had attracted his lead dog's attention. His eyes smarted into the wind as he lifted his goggles and tried to confirm that the musher was wearing a bright yellow suit.

'Yes,' he shouted, pumping his arm in a victory sign. 'Yes, it's her.'

'Sockeye,' he shouted. 'Go get them, boy. Don't let that team outrun you.'

Sockeye looked back over his shoulder and barked again, but this time it was a defiant 'we'll beat them or kill them' bark.

Patrick watched the husky's shoulders bunch as he strained forward, and knew that they would soon be level with Vi.

'Dogs passing,' he yelled as Sockeye drew level with Vi.

Without looking round she mushed her team over, though it was not necessary to give way on a mile-wide river of ice.

As his sled drew level with Vi, Patrick yelled, 'Hi there,' intending to follow his greeting with a cleverly couched invitation to run together again. But the words stuck in his throat as she turned to face him.

Cotton wool was wadded beneath her goggles where they rested on her cheeks. He studied the bruises, as purple and black as an Arctic winter, which spread across her swollen cheeks. Then his eyes rested on her nose, once thin and straight, now knobbed and bent like that of an unsuccessful boxer.

'Vi?' he said. 'Were you ducking sweepers?'

'Not many trees with low-hanging branches growing in the middle of the Yukon,' she whispered with a hint of sarcasm.

'No, I hit a real sweeper on that miserable trail through the woods just out of Shageluk, but it was my fault, I wasn't paying attention to the trail. Our twenty-four-hour mandatory stopover at Ophir must have dulled my senses. I've never done this before.'

She attempted to smile, but the swelling pulled her mouth into an ugly rictus.

Patrick looked away. He could not bear to see her once pretty face so disfigured.

'I know we agreed to part at Ophir and run to Nome as competitors,' he said. 'I now see that I can't trust you to leave the trees alone. You'll probably be the only person to find sweepers in the Yukon. I'm taking you to Kaltag where we'll find someone to set that nose, unless you enjoy impersonating a boxer, a beaten-up boxer,' he added.

Vi was about to protest, then she nodded. The run up the Yukon was hideous. She had been unable to keep the cold from her nose. It seemed to seep through her skin and burn like blisters rubbed raw when she breathed it in.

The cold plus the wind made the temperature plummet to where it was not only dangerous but lethal.

Vi tried running with her dogs to keep warm, but the thumping of her feet on the ice pounded in her head until she threw up.

She covered as much of her face as possible with a scarf when she checked in and out at the checkpoints. She was not going to scratch from the race, certainly not because of a sweeper.

Patrick was worried about Vi. He was certain that her nose was broken. He kept his team close behind hers, much to Sockeye's disgust. He was being kept behind the bitch he fancied in Vi's team.

'Don't give me that cross-eyed look,' Patrick warned Sockeye, as he ran to the front of his team and then back to the sled, to warm himself.

Sockeye was now well into the spirit of the race, and felt that it was demeaning to be kept behind a slower team. He continued to show his displeasure every time Patrick jogged along the line of dogs.

As they moved up the river of ice to Kaltag, the northern lights played around and over them, throwing sheets of pale pink and mist green over the snow and ice. The heavens were alive with pulsing colours.

'This is like running in a rainbow,' said Patrick looking up at the sky.

'My heart is like a rainbow shell / That paddles in a halcyon sea,' she answered.

Patrick looked bemused.

'Shakespeare?' he guessed.

'You say that for all the poems. It's Rossetti. Christina Rossetti.'

Silently Vi completed the verse,

> My heart is gladder than all these
> Because my love is come to me.

Patrick was relieved when they reached the village of Kaltag. He noticed that, cold as it was on the Yukon, Vi did not run to warm herself.

'Let someone be here to help her,' he whispered as they mushed the dogs up the sixty-foot bank from the river to the village.

The checker answered his prayer.

'Yes, Anna McInnes dropped Paul yesterday. As you know, he started his training as a doctor, then decided he preferred working with four-legged animals. I'll ask him to have a look at Vi.'

The checker bustled away to find Paul. Patrick was left to tell Vi that he had arranged for her to see Paul. To his surprise she did not argue.

'But I expect you to stand beside me if he wants me to scratch. If I have to crawl to Nome I'll do it. I'm finishing this race. Do you understand, Patrick?'

Her eyes flashed. Savannah, his sister, had taught him early in life not to argue with a woman when fire shows in her eyes. The anger of determination which fans the flames comes from deep within and is not to be trifled with.

'Sure thing, Vi. Sure,' he said.

Patrick stood outside the door, listening to the raised voices.

At last Vi emerged triumphant clutching a bottle of tablets.

'Painkillers,' she said in answer to Patrick's unspoken query. 'My nose can always be re-broken and set after the race if I don't like the look of it once the swelling goes down.'

Patrick walked with Vi to where they had left their teams.

'Thanks, Patrick,' she said. 'You did good. I owe you.'

'No – this is payback for the Burn.'

He put his arm around her in what was meant to be a brotherly gesture. Her tiny body fitted snugly beneath his shoulder. Without thinking, he dropped his head just as she raised hers. He met the query in her clear, heavily lashed eyes by covering her lips with his mouth. Her lips softened in response, and he tightened his arm around her.

'Hey there, handle that patient gently.'

Paul stood watching them, framed in the light of the doorway. His hands were on his hips and his feet astride.

'Beats me how you Butler twins find two of the best women in Alaska and take them out of the market, when guys like me advertise month after month in the *Alaska Men* magazine for someone, anyone, to love us.'

Vi laughed at his woebegone expression, and the moment with Patrick was broken.

Ease up, girl, she warned herself. He could become as addictive as the race. Remember your freedom.

She turned away from the men to give snacks to her dogs and snap on the tugs. With a soft whistle to her leader, the sled runners whispered as they slid over the snow on the way to Unalakleet.

'See you in Nome,' she shouted back at Patrick, as he and Paul watched her vanish into a spruce forest.

'Watch the trees. Good trail,' Patrick bellowed.

'Great girl,' said Paul. 'Trouble is, no one can get near her. Dogs and racing interest her, not men.'

Patrick smiled. He could still feel the softness of her lips responding to his.

He nodded. 'I've a race to run and I'd prefer the Iditarod brass belt buckle to the red widow's lamp for being the last rookie into Nome,' he said as he prepared to follow Vi.

Chapter Thirty-Seven

TRAPPER LOOKED away from the window sharply. His face crinkled as it made room for a wide smile. He eased himself up from his chair.

'Sit,' said Muktuk. He filled the doorway like a hairy grizzly. The wolverine fur on the hood of his parka stood out as if blown by a blizzard. Icicles fanned out his stringy beard, and his moustache was a block of ice beneath his nose. His eyes were ringed red with weariness.

'Close the door. Come in and warm up,' invited Herbie.

Muktuk nodded, shrugged off his parka, stamped the snow from his boots and went to stand in front of the stove.

'Here, sit,' ordered Kiluk, placing a large round bowl of moose stew in front of him. She tumbled hot sourdough rolls on the table beside the bowl.

Muktuk lowered his head over the bowl and did not lift it until he had mopped up the last of the sauce with a piece of sourdough.

'Thanks, Kiluk. You make the best chilli moose in the country,' he said, holding out his bowl for a refill.

Everyone waited in silence for Muktuk to finish eating.

'Bitching Unalakleet, had to break trail for the dogs.'

Everyone nodded. They all knew the back-breaking work of snowshoeing in front of the team, to give the dogs a path to run on in deep snow.

'Bitching Skaktoolik, birthplace for blizzards, couldn't see my hand in front of my face, couldn't even see Shark. That little bitch runs on radar, she has a trail memory stored in her horrible head that keeps her alive.

'Bitching Norton Sound. Kept off the sea ice. Natives in Shaktoolik said it was bad, they should know. Live beside it. Hunt on it. Die on it. Blizzard is covering the new ice with snow so it looks good, but being bitching salt water it freezes slowly and unevenly.'

Muktuk was becoming agitated, his arms windmilling as he spoke.

Kiluk handed him a mug of coffee heavily sweetened with sugar.

'We natives have over two hundred words to describe different types of snow,' she said, offering him doughnuts to dunk in his coffee.

'I can add a few more to those,' muttered Muktuk darkly.

'But none which could be used in a dictionary,' said Scott.

'Wait till your turn comes, you pup,' growled Muktuk.

'My favourite word,' said Kiluk, as if there had been no interruption, 'is *quanik*, "snow in the air".'

'I hope Patrick has the sense to keep off the sea ice,' said Scott suddenly. 'He must be nearing Shaktoolik. Perhaps the blizzard will have died down.'

Muktuk grunted. 'Bitching blizzards.'

Patrick reached Shaktoolik. He was weary after running the dogs up and down the switchback of mountain ridges that separates the cold Interior of Alaska from the Bering Sea coast.

Trapper had warned him to rest and give the dogs snacks in the lee of the hills before dropping sharply onto the flat, frozen marshland which would take them to Shaktoolik.

As Patrick forced Sockeye to ignore the old village of Shaktoolik and climb up onto a higher spit of land to the new village, he was pleased that he had listened to Trapper.

'A resort for storms,' snorted Patrick, as he was buffeted by the wind whistling down the streets. He looked up at snowdrifts towering over the houses.

'It's no wonder the natives call themselves Inupiats, the Only People. Living here, they must feel like the only people on earth.'

He soon found the small government house where he was to make his stopover. The welcome was warm and the food delicious, but the other mushers who had been assigned to the same house were strangely quiet. They seemed intent only on checking and repairing their gear and their clothing. Patrick missed the jokes and gruesome stories which mushers usually tossed around, especially if they wanted to terrify some rookie.

'I hear Muktuk decided not to cross Norton Sound this time,' he said to break the silence.

The mushers merely grunted, but one lifted his head and looked at Patrick.

'Blizzard has slackened somewhat since Muktuk checked in. But I swear my heart stops beating when I first step onto that heaving ice. It only starts up again when I reach Koyuk. It's thirty-five miles of death at each footstep. Unless you have a lead dog who can feel new ice, keep off the goddamn stuff.'

He was silent after his long speech, and looked around the room as if expecting to be berated for taking so much time talking to a rookie. One of the mushers shrugged and opened the door.

'Safe ice,' called the musher who had spoken to Patrick. The departing musher did not answer, but they heard his dogs whine in anticipation as he left the house.

'I've come this far and I'm damned if I'm trusting that ice. I prefer to add the extra miles and run into Nome. I don't want to be carried in dead and frozen as stiff as an ice sculpture,' continued the loquacious musher.

Patrick thought of the time he had lost in Kaltag waiting for Paul to attend to Vi.

'Trapper taught me to fish and hunt on the sea ice,' he said. 'I'm used to the sudden opening of leads, the wind building up pressure ridges and the risk of moving on new green ice which looks safe under its coating of thick snow. I think I'll go for the short cut. I'll take the Sound.'

The musher shook his head.

'In this race death comes in many disguises.'

Vi ran her dogs into Shaktoolik after dark. Now that she was away from the intense cold of the Interior and off the Yukon, her nose felt a little more comfortable.

She was assigned to the same house as Patrick. When she saw his name on the list she grinned. It would be good to see him, though she had decided that they would only be friends. The race confirmed her decision to retain her freedom.

'Patrick Butler?' said one of the mushers, making room for her at the table. 'He left at dawn. Decided the wind had dropped enough to try Norton Sound, even though the natives say that the sea ice is unstable with an east wind blowing. Boy says Trapper Jack brought him up on the ice. He certainly seemed confident when he left.'

'If I want to check in at Koyuk before he does I'll have to hit the trail,' said Vi.

'Say,' called one of the men as she walked to the door. 'What does the other guy look like?'

Vi fingered her nose tenderly.

'The tree is a bit battered and bowed, but it'll survive,' she answered, and closed the door behind her.

The men's laughter rang in her ears as she left the village and dropped from the beach onto the ice pack of the Bay.

Vi hated running on sea ice. It groaned and cracked beneath her feet as the waves from the open sea rolled in under the ice, causing it to heave and move like a sea monster in pain.

The blizzard had opened leads in the ice, and many of the ITC's stakes with fluorescent orange markers had fallen over or been washed away.

Vi moved cautiously, even when the lights of Koyuk appeared. She knew that it would take five to six hours before she reached the village.

All the time she searched the ice for another dog team. She knew that Patrick was ahead of her. She hoped to catch him before Koyuk.

'He's a rookie. This is his first time on Norton Sound,' she told herself. 'I've crossed it many times, therefore I should overtake him.'

But Vi mushed her team into Koyuk without finding Patrick. She refused to allow herself to be concerned.

'Perhaps he was right, and Trapper Jack's training allowed him to cross the ice with no problem,' she comforted herself.

When she inquired at the check-in to see if Patrick had checked out, the checker looked surprised. 'We know he signed in and out of Shaktoolik, but we've heard nothing since,' she said.

'He crossed the sea ice ahead of me and should be here,' insisted Vi.

'I'll send out an alert for anyone about to cross Norton Sound to look for him. Don't worry, he could have lost the trail. We hear a lot of the markers were blown down.'

Vi pursed her lips. She knew how hard the supervisors worked and how difficult it was to keep track of every musher. But this was Patrick.

'Will you organize a plane search if he doesn't check in within the next few hours?'

The checker looked at Vi's face as if seeing her for the first time.

'Sure, but one of the guys out of Shaktoolik is certain to find him somewhere on the pack. Don't worry. The best thing you can do is carry on to White Mountain, where you have an eight-hour layover. He's sure to meet you there.'

Every instinct of Vi's told her to stay in Koyuk and press for a plane to be sent out to search for Patrick, but the thrill of danger and finishing the race heated her blood to fever pitch.

She nodded at the checker.

'When he checks in tell him to catch me before White Mountain. If he can.'

The checker grinned and gave Vi the thumbs-up sign. She admired the women who faced danger and possible death running the most relentless, gruelling race in the world.

Short Seppa checked his dogs and fed them snacks before flinging open the door of the house he had been given to rest in, prior to crossing the shifting sea ice.

'Hiya Short,' one of the older mushers greeted. 'How ya doing?'

'Good. Good,' answered Short, sitting down to enjoy what the Inupiat family had to offer him.

'Ah, seal oil,' he said, tearing apart a sourdough roll and soaking it in the foul-smelling oil.

'This'll keep out the cold on the ice.'

'You crossing the Sound?' asked the Inupiat woman, refilling the plate with oil.

'Yeah. I've done it six times, why miss it on my seventh run?'

'The hunters say the sea ice is bad today. The east wind blow the shore ice away from land. There is much green ice. Maybe better you go round by land for number seven. The ice she not like the wind. Take two, three day before she ready for big man, heavy sled and dogs.'

Short laughed and nodded.

'You must mean Muktuk. He is bigger, heavier and older than me, and he went in the blizzard. The sea ice can't be that bad.'

'Can't trust sea ice. Two men go over. She eat number three. When she is hungry ice opens like wolf trap. No escape.'

As Short held up his bowl for more stew, he remembered the wailing of those slaughtered near Kaltag. He shivered.

'You cold? Here, put on.' The woman flung a caribou parka belonging to her husband over Short's shoulders. As she fastened it under his chin she untied Patrick's scarf.

'No. No, that belongs to a friend. I promised to give it to him in Nome.'

'Okay. Here, I put in your pocket. that way you can't forget. Leave coat with checker in Safety. We have many friends there.'

'Thanks. It sure is warm.'

'The best.'

The woman smiled, but there was a strange look in her eyes as she watched Short pull the tugs and set out for the beach and the ice on Norton Sound.

Short whistled softly as he ran his dogs along the beach. He felt the familiar movement of waves under the ice as he and the team dropped down onto the ice pack, but his lead husky was showing no signs of distress. His tail was straight and he trotted easily.

Short looked around and breathed a sigh of happiness. The blinding blizzard seemed to be resting. The sun appeared briefly held in a pale blue slash across the grey sky.

The bright light bounced off the glare ice and snow leaving shattered diamonds, too brilliant to look at. Light this intense was like breathing pure oxygen, and Short wanted to scream out his joy and contentment.

'This is Alaska. Where else can a man find land, ice and snow with not a living thing in sight? They can keep their stinking cities. Traffic, where a guy wants to kill you because you pull into the lane in front of him. Advertisements all day long, urging you to spend the money you work from eight to midnight to earn.

'Bitching cities should be blasted off the earth. We should live like the Inupiats and Alaskans. Take only what we need. Respect the land the Great One gave us. Yeah, that would be good.'

Short turned behind to look at the expanse of glittering whiteness. He felt that he was caught in the centre of a gigantic crystal. He missed seeing his lead dog's tail whip upright and the large dog try to tiptoe on its claws. The dog's hair stood out, as if pulled straight by static electricity.

Short swung back to watch his team. The smile was still on his face, but the whistle faded and was carried away by the wind as his lead howled. The dog's weight plummeted it through the thin, new ice.

Short flung himself onto the ice face down to spreadeagle his weight.

The huskies, howling in terror, were dragged beneath the ice, tangled in their tuglines.

Short tried to cling to the ice as the heavy sled tumbled into the frigid black depths, but he felt himself being dragged inexorably to the abyss which had drowned his dogs.

In a last desperate attempt to survive, forgetting that he had only a few minutes to live once the black, seemingly bottomless water closed over his head, he scrabbled for Patrick's scarf in the outside pocket of the caribou parka and threw it towards one of the fluorescent markers. 'There, Muktuk. Thanks,' he whispered hoarsely. His body spiralled down with the sled and huskies, their mouths open in silent howls of terror.

'Unlucky seven,' he thought, before the cold deadened his senses and killed his brain.

The ripples settled on the Stygian water, hiding the watery grave.

Light puffs of the east wind scudded along the ice. They lifted Patrick's scarf, but the sharp edges of the metal marker tore the fabric and held the scarf in place.

The wind strengthened, winding the orange and green checked scarf even tighter round the trail marker.

The easterly wind started closing the lead where Short Seppa and his dogs moved lifelessly to the will of the currents beneath the ice pack.

Muktuk lifted the phone on the first ring. He listened, grunted and replaced the receiver.

He avoided Scott's eyes and turned to Trapper.

'Doesn't sound good. None of the guys saw Patrick on the ice. Most have checked into Koyuk already. That blasted easterly is blowing again, though not as strong as it was when I left Shaktoolik. Mushers report bad conditions, open leads, new, unstable ice.'

Trapper said nothing. Scott thought he could read Patrick's death in Trapper's heavy-lidded eyes.

Kiluk and Herbie exchanged a long look. Kiluk crossed over to where Scott stood transfixed in front of the map. He was slowly and methodically scratching out Norton Sound and Shaktoolik on the map.

Even when the pencil tore through the paper, he kept ripping at the two names which he was certain had taken his twin.

Kiluk put her hand over his to stop the pencil gnawing at the map, as hungry as a rat in winter.

White-out and Sockeye ran across the frozen marshes easily. The easterly wind was strong but not enough to hinder them.

Bud and Natû had chosen not to cross the sea ice.

'We have over one hundred words to describe ice,' said Natû when Bud queried why they were not taking the short cut across the sea ice.

'Salt water doesn't freeze like fresh water, Bud,' she said. 'A man can stand on three inches of frozen fresh water, but needs six inches of frozen salt water. Crossing sea ice is like walking through a minefield. We can find Grease Ice, New Ice, Young Ice and of course the Old Ice with pressure ridges up to fifty foot high.'

Bud nodded and acceded. As he ran behind Natû and her team he mentally drew a map of the remainder of the trail into Nome.

'Only five check-ins before Nome,' he told himself cheerfully. 'Never thought I'd get this far.'

Rainy Pass, Dalzell Gorge, the Yukon, Ophir and the wolves all seemed nightmares, which one forgets when daylight brings back courage.

But he was to learn that the wilderness is merciless, and that no racer can relax until he is standing beneath the arch spanning Front Street in Nome.

Scott heard the knocking on the door above the sound of the wind.

'Patrick,' he shouted and pulled the door open.

A small figure in a stained yellow suit was caught off balance and stumbled into the room.

Scott looked at the yellow suit and it seemed to hold all the hope of sunshine.

'Is Patrick with you?'

'No. He crossed the sea ice well ahead of me. I asked them to send out a plane if he didn't check in within a few hours. Do you have any news?'

'No one saw him on the ice,' said Trapper soberly.

'And the pack is bad,' added Muktuk. The blood drained from Vi's face and she swayed.

'Sit,' invited Kiluk, pity softening her usually sharp voice.

'Okay,' said Vi, and sank onto one of the chairs thankfully.

'I'm Vi Vickers. Patrick and I ran part of the trail together.'

'We know,' said Scott, bitterness edging his voice.

Vi looked up sharply. 'Native whispers, I suppose?' she said.

'You are Scott, his twin. He spoke about you a great deal. If he shaved off that bushy beard he's growing, you'd look alike.'

Scott scowled at her. She had been the last person to talk to his brother and he disliked her for it.

As if reading his thoughts Vi said, 'I couldn't persuade him not to run on the pack. He'd left Shaktoolik before I even arrived. I ran it hoping to find him.'

'In this bitching race each musher must do what he thinks is best,' growled Muktuk. 'You cannot be responsible for someone you meet on the trail.'

As he spoke, he suddenly wondered how Short Seppa was doing. Somehow he felt responsible for the grizzled musher.

'Just phoning to see if Seppa has checked in at Koyuk yet,' he said. All eyes followed him to the phone. Muktuk spoke in a low voice, then turned as if his back would stop the people in the room hearing him.

Scott froze, and he left the room as he heard Muktuk say, 'A search. Looking for a pilot to land on sea ice. Yes, I understand. Yup. Two people?'

No one spoke as he turned back to the room. The time of waiting had arrived.

Anna McInnes was at Unalakleet, counting the dogs that had been dropped by the mushers because they were not considered fast enough for the final run to Nome.

Most were trussed in bags, making it safer in the plane. No pilot needed to deal with a dog fight plus bad weather.

Anna was consulting a clipboard, trying to juggle the leapfrogging of vets and checkers with the flying out of dropped dogs, when she heard someone shouting her name.

'Have you had any experience landing on sea ice?' asked the male checker.

Anna nodded. She had plenty of experience of landing on iced rivers and lakes and Bruce had taught her the dangers of sea ice, but the few times she'd had the controls Bruce had been in the cockpit with her.

'Nods aren't good enough. You have to know what you're doing out there. Moroney has left for Granite Mountain, and we need a plane out to search for the Butler boy.'

'Patrick?' whispered Anna, clutching the board until the edges cut into her palms.

'Yes. He was reported missing. An alert was put out, but no one crossing the Pack saw him or his team. He may of course be on a slab of ice which has drifted away from the land-fast ice.'

'Or he may have gone through bad ice,' said Anna quietly.

'Yes. We don't have the time to wait for Bruce, as the weather is unpredictable on Norton Sound. But if you leave now before it closes down completely . . .'

Anna thrust the clipboard into his hands before he finished speaking.

'Get someone else to do this,' she said. 'I'm on my way.'

'Anna,' he shouted. 'Be careful out there.'

'It's Patrick. Don't you understand? Patrick.'

The checker shook his head. He was perplexed.

'Patrick? I thought she had a thing going with the other twin.'

Anna swung into the cockpit and ran swiftly through the pre-flight checks.

Sorry, Bruce, she apologized silently, but I have no time to waste.

'We also need to search for Short Seppa, he hasn't checked into Koyuk yet,' shouted the checker. But his words were spun away by the whirl of the propeller blades and the roar of the motor.

The wind swirled the Cessna 180 as if she was a snowflake, but Anna kept her on a steady heading for Shaktoolik. Approaching Shaktoolik, she radioed in to say that she was starting a search on the sea ice.

'Wind estimated at thirty miles per hour with a ground blizzard,' a disembodied voice advised her. Anna groaned. She would have to quarter the area at three hundred feet up; that would give her slant visibility of almost a mile, enough to pick up a dog team. But once she descended into the blowing snow, she would be lucky if she could see a few feet ahead.

Time seemed to stretch beyond eternity. Anna's eyes ached as she stared at the seemingly endless pack ice.

Something appeared at the periphery of her vision. She rubbed her eyes vigorously. It had not moved, but she could not identify what the object was.

As she changed direction and flew towards the dark smear on the snow, her face was transformed from a mask of worry to one of hope. It was a dog team. She was unable to identify the driver. She circled a few times. She set the instruments up to maintain a constant descent and tried to remember the instructions Bruce had given her during her training for landing on sea ice.

'Trust your instruments, because when you descend into a blizzard it's like closing your eyes. Wait till the plane hits the ice. Try not to bounce but stay on it and plant it.'

Anna sat waiting as the dog team vanished, and she descended into a featureless white cloud.

She was landing on sea ice in a white-out.

'If you hit anything you'll never know.'

Suddenly Bruce's words seemed ominous, and Anna wanted to get out of the swirling whiteness.

'Please help me,' she prayed, forcing herself not to panic.

The aircraft hit the ice hard and slewed. Anna fought it back, breathing heavily. She sat still for a few moments, waiting for the dreadful feeling of descending as the Cessna sank through the thin ice and settled on the bottom of the cold ocean.

When nothing happened, Anna wiped the sweat from her face and hands. She searched frantically for the plastic-lined bag and was violently ill. She snapped the top of the bag closed, cutting the sour smell of vomit from the cabin. Anna realized that she needed to find the dog team. She had fixed their position and knew that they were moving towards where she had landed.

As she sat waiting, listening to the wind buffet the plane, her eye caught the flash of one of the fluorescent markers.

The musher must be running with his headlamp on, and it had picked up the marker.

Anna studied the marker, thinking that the spruce trees the natives used to plant in the ice made far better markers.

Suddenly the marker moved. Anna rubbed her gloved hand across the side window. It was not the marker that moved, but the end of a piece of cloth wound around it.

A flashlight lit up the marker again and Anna recognized the orange and green check scarf that Patrick had given her to dry her tears.

With a small cry she struggled to open the door. It opened and the wind dragged her out, throwing her onto the snow.

She scrambled to her feet and inched her way to the marker.

It was Patrick's scarf. She unwound it and held it tightly in her hand, as if holding it would keep Patrick safe.

'Perhaps his scarf blew off a few metres away, and this is his team approaching,' she whispered. 'He'll be glad to have it back.'

'Hi there! Looking for Short Seppa?'

It was not Patrick. A musher with a large beaky nose resting on an upper lip thatched with pale ginger hair mushed to a stop beside her.

'Short Seppa?' asked Anna in surprise.

'Yup. Said they had sent out a plane, asked us to keep a lookout as well. Unless you fell over him you'd never see him in this damn stuff.'

'I was told to find Patrick Butler,' said Anna, 'but now I'll watch for Short as well.'

'What's that?' he asked, pointing to the orange and green scarf flapping in Anna's hand.

'Patrick's scarf. I found it wrapped round that marker and recognized it.'

'Probably blew off and he didn't notice it. See no reason for him to tie a good warm scarf round a marker.'

The musher looked ahead to where his lead dog was attempting to turn the team back. The husky held its tail as straight as a marker pole and was trying not to step on the ice.

'Unless he was trying to warn us of the same thing Blizzard is. Thin, unstable ice.'

The wind dropped for a few moments. In front of them lay a lead, the open, dark water as ugly and lethal as a poisonous black snake.

'Patrick? Do you think . . .?'

Anna could not complete the sentence.

'Possible. It could have been closed and snow-covered when he hit it. The edges will probably drift together again in an hour or so.'

Anna started walking towards the open water.

'If he went in there, he'd be dead in a few minutes or seconds, I can't remember which,' said the musher sombrely.

'Come here,' he yelled as Anna continued to walk slowly to the deadly water.

'This blizzard has blown away all tracks. You'll never find any trace of sled runners or prints now. It was luck that the scarf was caught and wound tightly around the marker.'

Anna felt numb and as cold as the frigid sea water in the lead.

'You'd better get out of this if you're looking for Short,' he said. 'He's an old veteran who has often crossed the Sound. I'll look for him as well.

'Search for a man dressed in a bright fuchsia pink suit. He says it reminds him of the northern lights. No lights I've ever seen are that colour. Sunsets maybe, but not the dancing lights.'

Anna hurried back to the Cessna, eager to leave the scene of Patrick's death, afraid to take off on ice she now knew was probably unstable in front of her.

'Good luck,' shouted the musher as he and his team prepared to circle round the lead.

'Thanks,' muttered Anna, busy in the cockpit. 'I'll need it.'

She wound Patrick's scarf round her neck. 'Scott! How am I going to give you this scarf instead of giving you your brother?' she whispered. 'Why do I have to tell you that his grave is under a floating pack of ice?'

Anna was so distraught at the discovery of Patrick's death that she went through the routine of a short field take-off without thinking of the sea ice.

'Ice which is always on the move, opening and refreezing, as salt water does not freeze easily,' she muttered. 'Damn all sea ice.'

As she broke through the white-out she saw the musher driving away from the markers, skirting the open water.

'Good luck,' she shouted, and dipped a wing, hoping that he was looking up. But his attention was focused on his lead dog and the ice. Death has the effect of making one appreciate life.

The musher was shaken at the thought that sixteen powerful huskies, a sled and a musher could vanish, leaving only an ugly black lead of water sliming across the ice. He now wanted to cross Norton Sound as quickly as possible.

At each groan and movement of the ice under his feet his stomach knotted. He clenched his teeth, determined not to think of the tangled dogs anchored to the sled swinging in the tide like a grotesque pendulum, and the musher probably dragged to the bottom by the weight of his waterlogged clothes with his boots acting as lead sinkers.

There were no smiles in the cabin at White Mountain. Trapper had finally persuaded Muktuk to continue the race to Nome.

'You cannot help Patrick by sitting here,' he argued. 'Remember, this is a race.'

'You're getting soft,' added Kiluk. 'First you stop for Short Seppa, now you want to wait for news of Patrick.'

'He'll probably be hard on your heels into Nome,' said Herbie. 'Go on. Pull the tugs and try the Topkok Hills again.'

'We'll send word to you in Nome as soon as we hear.'

Muktuk nodded and strode from the room. His dogs barked when they saw him. They had been fed, had rested and sensed that the end of the trail was near.

Shark launched herself at him, but Muktuk sidestepped her and her teeth clacked harmlessly together.

'You want to bite again? Remember Topkok? You sailed like a kite out of control in that wind, silly bitch. Try biting that gale, my girl.'

Shark looked at him and bared her teeth as if she knew he was mocking her.

Muktuk checked his sled again. He had already discarded everything he could to lighten the sled. But he had run the Topkok Hills before, and knew what brutal weather could be faced side-slipping through the barren, wind-scoured hills.

He did not want to have his dogs lifted off their feet as they crested the summits, or be pinned down by a sudden storm. It was only necessary to sign in and out at the village of Safety before arriving in Nome.

Cursing beneath his breath, he packed some of the discarded items back into his sled.

'Bitching hills with its wind and storms. Race never lets up. Think the last seventy-odd miles of the Iditarod could be decent trail, but no. It still has the "Topkok Blowhole". They should use that bitching wind funnel to test astronauts.

'Take some of the piss out of you, Shark,' he yelled.

A defiant bark was his only reply.

Muktuk and his team of huskies battled their way through the rounded hills and valleys of Topkok. The hills rang to the music of Muktuk's colourful curses.

Shark eventually led the team to the checker in Safety. Muktuk scrawled his name across the pad, eager to leave for the last hard sprint to Nome. Shark looked back at him over her shoulder. Her eyes mocked him for doubting her ability to find her way through the hills.

Muktuk met his lead dog's stare.

'You were lucky. Wind hadn't even started blowing. Wait for a blizzard on the hills. That'll quieten you down.'

Shark barked her displeasure.

'Lovely dog,' said the checker, walking up the line of dogs.

'No!' shouted Muktuk. 'She's a mean-minded bitch, but clever.'

The checker turned back to remonstrate with Muktuk, but he had already grabbed his finisher's bib and was on his way to Nome.

A few miles from Nome, Muktuk saw spectators sitting on snowmobiles, along with crowds of camera crews and reporters.

'Get back to Nome with your stinking machines and cameras,' he yelled, but his voice was lost in the hubbub.

'Let's go back to the open spaces where a man can breathe, back to the Big White, Shark!' he shouted. 'Who needs this bitching nonsense?'

Shark knew that the run up the ramp from the beach meant the end of the race.

Like a marathon runner she was tired but happy. Once again she had followed the trail safely and led Muktuk to Nome.

As they ran beneath the burled arch and the crowd roared, like thunderous waves crashing down on rocks, Shark turned and bared her teeth at Muktuk. But it was a smile, not a sneer. Delilah held her head high as if for the camera crews.

Chapter Thirty-Eight

'ANNA! ANNA McINNES!' Paul struggled to catch up with Anna, who was battling through the crowd to reach Muktuk.

She pushed through the camera crews and photographers. She was intent only on speaking to Muktuk. She wanted to tell him about Patrick's scarf and to ask if Scott was still at White Mountain with Trapper. She stumbled as she broke through the tight knot of media personnel ringing Muktuk, and landed beside Shark.

'How does it feel to be in the money?' asked a reporter, holding a microphone under Muktuk's chin, while the photographer blinded him with the flashlight from the camera.

'Not as good as it feels to be in Skwentna, away from all this bitching noise,' growled Muktuk.

The reporter backed away, looking surprised.

'That was Muktuk Peters, an Iditarod veteran. He came in at number twenty today. We all congratulate him. I think what he meant to say was that to finish the Iditarod is to win.'

Anna grinned at the look of disgust on Muktuk's face as the roar of snowmobiles approaching Nome mingled with the blizzard of noise on Front Street, announcing the arrival of other mushers.

Shark looked at Anna's leg clad in bright red beside her. She could not restrain herself. She sank her teeth into Anna's calf and shook her head in glee.

Anna's scream catapulted Paul to her side.

'Muktuk,' he roared. 'Do something about this cannibal. I spend more time stitching up people Shark has savaged than I do looking after the sled dogs.'

Muktuk bulldozed his way through the crowd. He swung Shark up from the ground and held her at arm's length.

'You have your photo taken and think you're the new Dracula. Stupid bitch,' he muttered under his breath.

'Anna,' said Paul, looking down at the tear in her suit. 'I've been looking for you everywhere. I have news.'

'Paul! Paul, we need you urgently,' a member of the ITC tugged at his arm.

'I'll be back,' he shouted to Anna.

'It's okay. Her teeth have only scratched the skin. She didn't know how many layers of clothes I was wearing,' retorted Anna. 'Take your time.'

As Bud and Natû chose not to cross the ice pack, they were not asked to look for Short or Patrick. They continued on to Elim, then Golovin and White Mountain with mounting excitement, unaware that Patrick was missing.

'We won't be in the top twenty, but neither will we be in the bottom twenty,' said Natû.

'Wonder where Muktuk and Patrick are?' mused Bud as they crossed Golovin Bay.

The Damas couple ran on the river for a short while, then rounded a corner and saw White Mountain village nestling at the foot of a hill.

'Well, here we are,' said Bud. 'Trapper, the Owens and Scott will all be waiting. Muktuk and Patrick are sure to be in Nome.'

'And we have eight wonderful hours to fix our gear, check that we keep only the fastest dogs and sleep,' added Natû.

They burst into the Owens's family home in White Mountain laughing happily. They stopped short, as if confronted by a pressure ridge on the ice pack.

Their smiles faded as they studied Scott, Trapper and the Owens. The family sat as motionless as corpses. 'Did you cross the sea ice?' Trapper asked quietly.

'No. The Inupiat said it was bad so we chose to run along the coast,' answered Natû, puzzled by the sombre atmosphere.

'Any news of Patrick and Muktuk?' asked Bud. 'Are they placed yet?'

'Patrick's missing on the ice pack,' answered Scott shortly, and turned back to the map.

Natû stared at Bud speechlessly, then dropped her head on his shoulder while tears soaked his sled suit.

Trapper caught Bud's gaze and shook his head pointing to Scott.

'Sshh,' whispered Bud in Natû's ear. 'Your crying won't make it easier for Scott.'

He pulled a large red cloth from his pocket and handed it to her. Natû wiped her eyes, blew her nose loudly and wadded the handkerchief into her sleeve.

'Come. I want to check your dogs and sleds with you for the Topkoks ahead and the final hard sprint into Nome,' Trapper said. Natû looked at her father in surprise. They could accept no help on the trail except from another musher, and only then in special circumstances. She nodded and beckoned to Bud.

Once outside, Trapper stood behind the house to shelter from the wind.

'We've heard that Anna McInnes found Patrick's scarf wound round an ITC marker fifty yards from an open lead. There was no other sign of him or his team. But we are hoping that he is alive and will live to see many great days' dawns.

'You two must finish the race. Behave normally around Scott. Tears tell of Patrick's death. Be cheerful, let him feel that you are certain Patrick is alive.'

'Are you?' asked Bud quietly.

'I do not know. I can only hope. Life is harsh, it chooses those it takes at random. Go safely. Take no risks. No part of this race is easy. If it was, everyone would run it. Sudden blizzards can hold you down for days on the Topkoks. Winds can break your dogs' hearts and their will to run.'

Trapper put his arms around Natû and Bud. 'If the fates have taken Patrick from me, I don't want them to take you.'

Natû burst into tears and buried her face in Trapper's neck. Bud swallowed hard to mask his feelings. Trapper was always quiet and withdrawn. He was unaccustomed to hearing his father-in-law being emotional.

'Now I'm going inside to tell them you are repacking your sleds to run the Topkok Hills.'

Bud and Natû watched Trapper walk into the house in silence.

'We must do as he says,' said Bud sombrely. He started sorting out gear which he felt could be left behind.

'Sure.' Natû walked across the snow to where her dogs lay sleeping. Oily lifted her head and gave a weary wag of her tail in greeting, then dropped her head with a thump and fell asleep again.

Natû chose two dogs that were not running as well as the others and staked them in a protected corner of the house.

'Any dogs you want to drop, bring them over here and I'll find a place for them until they can be flown out,' she called to Bud.

It took them almost three hours to tend to the dogs' paws, re-boot those who needed booties, feed them and decide what gear they could do without.

When they walked back into the house, Kiluk had plates brimming with food on the table.

'Eat,' she said. 'The Topkoks are tough.'

They all sat at the table. Bud told stories of his early days as a leaner driller. The haunted look did not leave Scott's eyes, but his lips lifted occasionally in a weak smile. Eventually their eight-hour rest period was over.

Everyone crowded into the doorway to wave goodbye.

'Pat the burled arch in Nome for Patrick,' called Scott.

'No way. He'll be there to pat it himself,' shouted Bud.

Scott smiled, and Trapper was relieved to see that it was a genuine smile.

Thank you, Bud, he said silently.

Trapper closed the door, said a silent prayer to his ancestors for Bud and his daughter's safety and moved across to the map as if seeing it for the first time.

A loud smashing of fists on the door broke Trapper's concentration and he turned, but Scott reached the door first.

Scott screamed, then was silent. As Trapper ran to him, visions of bears, wolves or an inebriated native with a knife flashed across his mind.

He could not lose both boys.

Scott had run outside by the time Herbie, Kiluk and Trapper crowded into the doorway. He was laughing and crying as he hugged a tall, bulky figure.

'Patrick,' whispered Trapper, and rubbed his eyes roughly. Kiluk sobbed unashamedly while Herbie hugged her.

At last Scott led his brother into the house. Tears had frozen on both boys' faces, but Patrick's smile was radiant as he hugged everyone and quickly recounted his experience on the ice pack.

'That ice cost me almost two days. I had to go round a lead which kept opening like a suppurating wound. The detour took us into an area of thirty-foot pressure ridges. We then had to find our way back to where I thought the markers were staked.

'Sockeye may not have run the Iditarod before, but he knows ice. He smelled the other teams and led us back to the ITC markers, then finally to Koyuk. They called off the search. We ran as if Nome was in sight. I'll tell you all about the ice pack when we are in Nome. Now I must feed and check my dogs and prepare myself for the Topkoks.'

'You need a few hours' sleep,' said Kiluk, tears of relief and joy still running down her face.

While he was talking, Kiluk was busy stirring pots on the stove.

'You also need a hot meal,' she said.

Scott stared at Patrick as he ate as if he was imprinting his image on his mind for ever.

*

300

Bud and Natû reached the east side of the infamous Topkoks, running easily. They passed the small A-frame cabin when the first puffs of wind warned them of the blizzards for which the barren hills were notorious.

They had encountered stronger winds during the race, and thought these mild in comparison when White-out, running in front, crested one of the hills. The wind lifted him off all four feet and shook him as easily as a fox shakes a mouse, then dropped him in a crumpled heap. The big dog growled and snapped at the wind in frustration, but the wind would not allow them to crest the hills. They had to submit and side-slip.

Natû hung onto the handlebar of her sled with her legs flying out sideways like a torn flag.

Halfway through the Topkoks, the wind carried the first signs of a bad blizzard.

'Go away!' screamed Natû helplessly. 'We were doing so well; now you want to hold us down in this forsaken place.'

Bud and Natû battled the wind, trying to keep the dogs away from the cliffs which they knew they had to go down but couldn't see because of the blowing snow.

The trail markers were lost in the blizzard, and Natû sensed that the dogs were losing heart. They were crabbing against the wind which hit them relentlessly, pushing them towards the cliff edges. They needed encouragement and love, but she dared not leave the sled as the wind would tumble her down the hills and Bud would never find her in the white-out.

Without protection she would not survive for long. Natû managed to move her team to the west side of the next hill and waited for Bud to follow. It seemed to take for ever. She was about to go back and look for him, when he and his team edged round the hill.

'What's wrong?' asked Natû, worried by the sudden pallor of his face.

'Nothing,' lied Bud. He was not going to tell her that the wind had smashed him into the handlebar of his sled and that he was still having difficulty breathing. He tried to take a deep breath, but pain doubled him up as it had when the handlebar had hit him across his ribs with all the force of a sledgehammer swung by a giant.

I will not scratch. Natû and Trapper will be proud of me. It's probably only cracked ribs, and those have to mend on their own. Nothing anyone can do, he told himself.

Suddenly the thought of the cracked bone breaking and piercing a lung painted a different picture. Bud could imagine his lung collapsing, leaving him with only one and the chance of that one collapsing as well. He concentrated on taking shallow breaths. It was the only thing that made the pain bearable.

'We can't keep this up,' he said to Natû. 'White-out has had enough. If he stops my whole team will have a sit-down strike.'

'We'll have to stop here and tough out the storm,' said Natû through cracked and bleeding lips.

'Never make it,' said Bud. 'Wish we hadn't passed the Nome Kennel Club shelter cabin at the bottom of those damn hills. I don't know whether I'm walking backwards or forwards in this white-out. The dogs don't like it either, they're suffering from disorientation too.'

'We're only a little over forty miles from Nome, Bud. We'll do it the same way Riddles did it, step by step in a blizzard, the year she was the first woman to win the Iditarod.'

Suddenly Oily's ears stood up and she barked loudly, an excited, frenetic bark. Natû looked round. She could see nothing but swirling snow. Her eyes widened. What was approaching, masked in the thick ermine of snow? Something only her dogs could sense.

'Oline,' she said, 'Oline, be with us.'

A black figure which seemed to be floating behind a line of wavering black dots gradually neared.

It was a man, but Natû did not recognize the face masked by a bushy beard and a thick balaclava.

He mushed close to them but kept his team away from her dogs.

His lead dog was behaving very strangely. He was almost strangling himself to reach Natû. Eventually unable to pull the team up to her, he sat and howled. Natû recognized his howl.

'Sockeye!' she shouted. She dropped the snowhook and stumbled across to the lead dog. Tears rolled down her cheeks which she blotted in his soft fur.

Sockeye? If Sockeye is here, then that musher must be Patrick, she thought.

She staggered through the blizzard to where the two men were standing with their arms on each other's shoulders, laughing hysterically. Patrick slapped Bud across the back. Bud gagged and slumped forward. Patrick held him and lowered his head to hear Bud's words.

'Ribs. Don't tell Natû. Promise.'

'Patrick, Patrick, we thought you were dead,' she said. 'Oh, it's good to see you.'

Natû flung her arms around him and kissed him.

'Scott?' queried Natû, wondering how he had reacted to the appearance of the brother he thought was dead.

'They will all be in Nome to meet us,' said Patrick. 'We cannot let a Topkok blizzard stop us. Can we, Bud?' he asked, trying to make Bud understand that he would keep his secret. 'Three is a good number to battle the storm. We'll let Sockeye lead. He looks upon the wind as his personal enemy and attacks it with all his strength. Watch him.'

'Sure you can run, Bud?' asked Patrick, running his hands over Bud's ribs, making it appear to Natû that he was checking Bud's outer clothing shell.

'Sure.'

'Okay. Stop if it gets worse and I'll try to strap you up tight. It's all they usually do unless the rib is broken and they think it may puncture a lung.'

'Promise you won't tell Natû,' pleaded Bud again.

'Of course not.'

Sockeye, accustomed to dragging whale and bear carcasses

across the ice, dropped his head, hunched his shoulders and dug his claws into the ground. Patrick's huskies followed Sockeye's lead. Sockeye seemed to sense the trail. He had been out on the trapline with Trapper through so many northern winters and blizzards that he ploughed his way through the storm pulling his team behind him.

Bud and Natû followed with their teams, grateful that Sockeye was tough enough to challenge the blizzard.

Sockeye took the three teams down the long decline to sea level, and they ran on towards Safety.

Here they stopped only long enough to drop a few dogs that had tired on the Topkoks and to pick up their mandatory finishers' bibs. Patrick watched Bud closely, but he did not seem to be in any worse pain. He was masking it well.

The dogs raced out of Safety as if sensing that the end of the trail was near. They wound their way round Cape Nome with enormous blocks of ice towering up like skyscrapers on the bay.

The relentless coastal wind calmed. Soon they saw the first signs of Nome – spectators and snowmobiles.

As they were about to drop onto the short stretch of sea ice and onto Front Street in Nome, Natû stopped her team.

Bud was behind and had to stop too, but he was puzzled as to why Natû would halt her team almost in sight of the burled arch with the widow's lamp burning brightly, swinging from it.

'Let Patrick run in ahead of us,' she said softly. 'If he had not caught up with us in the Topkoks we would still be there, or we would have had to scratch from the race. White-out was tired. Oily is not strong enough to bulldoze through those blizzards, though she has enough heart for ten dogs.

'It was Sockeye and Patrick who led us through. It's only fair that they should have the glory of running under the arch ahead of us.'

Bud caught Natû in his arms gingerly and winced as he kissed her. The pain seemed to have become worse now that he had stopped running. 'Another reason I love you, my little Inupiat,' he said. 'You have enough heart for a team of huskies.'

Natû smiled as she saw Patrick disappear in a crowd of photographers and reporters.

The bite in Anna McInnes's leg was beginning to hurt, yet Paul had not returned. She and Muktuk were standing near the burled arch where Paul had left them.

'I wonder what news he had to tell me?' she thought. 'I suppose it can wait until he returns.'

She turned to Muktuk.

'Muktuk, have you heard any news about Patrick?' she asked.

The screech of sirens shredded his answer. 'Only that he has just checked in under the arch,' replied Muktuk when he could make himself heard.

Anna screamed. 'It's not possible. He's dead. He is under the ice pack.'

She was jumping up and down, trying to see over the spectators' heads.

'Pick me up, Muktuk, I must see him,' she pleaded.

Muktuk looked at his hands and then at Anna. Gingerly he clasped her round the waist and lifted her above the crowd as easily as he lifted Shark.

'It's him. It is Patrick,' screamed Anna.

A tall young man with his back to them stood beside Patrick. He seemed to hear her voice above the noise of the crowd. He turned to see Anna in her red suit rising above the crowd like a totem pole.

'Scott!'

'Anna!'

'You want to be there?' asked Muktuk gruffly.

'Please.'

Muktuk rested her on his shoulders as if she was a child.

People looked round in surprise and stepped out of Muktuk's way.

'Bitching crowds, bitching noise, bitching people,' he groused. 'Wonder why I run the race when I have this madhouse at the end.'

When Muktuk and Anna had reached Patrick and Scott, they found Trapper and the Owens were there too.

Anna ran to Patrick first and burst into tears.

'Now, now, I didn't make the first twenty, Anna,' he joked, hoping to stop her crying.

'Oh, Patrick, when I found your scarf and saw where you had drowned, I felt so helpless. I knew that all I had to take back to Scott was a scarf, not you.'

Patrick held her, looking puzzled. He looked over Anna's fur-lined hood to Scott, but Scott shook his head. He was as bemused as his twin.

'What scarf?' said Muktuk, more gruffly than he intended.

'The orange and green scarf that Patrick . . .'

Anna stopped speaking. She did not want Scott to know that she had pleaded with Patrick to intercede on her behalf with him.

'. . . always wears,' she ended lamely.

'Where did you find the scarf?' Muktuk continued.

'Wound round a fluorescent marker near an open lead on the ice pack,' she replied.

Muktuk coughed and spat in the snow.

Thinking she had upset him, and a little in awe of his notorious temper, Anna continued with her explanation.

'They needed a plane to search the sea ice as Vi Vickers reported you missing, Patrick. I left immediately but there was a ground blizzard. I was lucky to land near the marker with the scarf.'

'Damn lucky you didn't land in the lead,' growled Muktuk. 'Needs experience to land on sea ice. Surprised Moroney let you go.'

'He didn't know. I still have to tell him.'

'You sure that scarf was orange and green?'

'Yes. I have it here.' Anna pulled the scarf from her pocket.

'Yeah, that's the one. That's what I used to tie round Short Seppa's arm when Shark tried to take a piece out of him.'

Anna paled.

'There was an alert out for Short Seppa on the ice.'

'Short Seppa. Then that lead . . .?'

Muktuk nodded.

'He probably bought it on his seventh run. Short was hearing voices near Kaltag. Tried to convince him there was nothing, but the old guy said they were warning him of death.'

To their surprise, Muktuk bowed his head. 'Wherever you are, Short – probably up in the northern lights in your fuchsia suit – you were a damn good musher. You went doing what you loved best, running this bitching race. Good trail ahead for you.'

Vi Vickers stood outside the circle that had gathered round Patrick, watching Anna once again cry on his shoulder.

'She knows how to do it,' she thought with grudging admiration.

Suddenly Patrick looked up and recognized the bright splash of yellow behind Scott.

'Vi,' he called.

'Have you been placed?'

'I think about thirty-second,' she answered.

Scott turned round, ready to be polite now that Patrick was safe. 'Congratulations. I'll be happy if I can be placed in the thirties when I run this race.'

Patrick held out his had to Vi.

'Come,' he said. 'Herbie and Kiluk have rented a house near Nome. There's plenty of room for all of us.'

Vi hesitated.

'Sure,' said Kiluk. 'Always happy to have another woman in the house.'

'Thanks. I can sure do with a clean-up.'

Scott and Anna moved towards each other like magnets forcibly held apart and then suddenly released.

'I've missed you,' she whispered in his ear.

'We'll make up for it,' he promised.

There was no wind, yet the small Cessna 180 was rocking on the flat-topped hill.

Two hunters laden with heavy backpacks and hunting rifles looked at the aircraft in amazement.

'*Spirit of Iditarod*,' said the one, reading the inscription on the fuselage. 'It's one of the Iditarod Air Force planes, but what's it doing here?'

'Broken down?' guessed his friend.

'And rocking on a windless day?'

'Probably a bear inside, looking for food. Let's go see.'

Anna and Scott were unaware that the hunters were nearing the Cessna. They had been apart too long. Anna had planned to stay overnight at Rohn cabin, but flying over the strip they saw an aircraft to the side of the runway.

'Probably hunters,' said Anna. 'They use the cabin frequently.'

She turned the Cessna back towards Nikolai.

'Why aren't we going to your cabin?' asked Scott.

'Because certain things can't wait, Scott,' she said, 'and I know a hill where no one ever goes.'

Scott's mouth was hot and his hands urgent as he fumbled with the zip of Anna's suit. She lifted her buttocks as he slid off her pants. Anna sighed as she parted her thighs and guided Scott deeply into herself.

'I never want to be without you again,' Anna whispered huskily.

'Nor I you.'

Scott's movements became more vigorous, and Anna's whispers changed to whimpers of pleasure.

The one hunter nudged the other in the ribs. 'All in the spirit of the Idit.,' he said, as they moved quietly away and made for the comfort of Rohn cabin.

*

Bud and Natû waited for a few minutes.

'This is a race. Let's break that up now and give Patrick a chance to be with Scott and Trapper,' said Natû, watching the reporters still hanging round Patrick, as thick as mosquitoes along a trout stream.

She and Bud mushed their teams up the ramp to the ear-splitting screech of sirens and thunderous applause from the crowd.

White-out and Oily behaved like well-trained circus performers, and ran under the arch in a perfect tie.

As Bud followed them, pain doubled him over the handlebar. He hung there loose and limp as a rag doll. His feet remained on the runners, and the dogs carried their semi-conscious musher proudly past the television and camera crew, but Bud was aware only of the searing pain.

'Bud!' screamed Natû, but her voice was lost in the hubbub of reporters who left Patrick and converged on them.

Patrick suddenly appeared at Natû's side with Paul in tow, and extricated Bud from the mob. Natû looked up in surprise. Patrick gestured for her to remain where she was.

'Talk to them, Natû, Bud will be okay,' he shouted at her.

Paul disappeared with Bud.

Paul felt Bud's ribs carefully and listened to his shallow breathing.

'You will have to go to a hospital for a check,' he said gravely. 'I suspect that one of your broken ribs may have punctured a lung. How you kept running is a miracle. But I have seen this race cause dogs and mushers to perform unbelievable feats. Crazy. The Iditarod turns sane people crazy.' He shook his head as he studied Bud.

'You are certain to be awarded the Rookie of the Year Award at the banquet in Nome,' continued Paul.

Bud winced. 'Must be an easier way to win one and a half thousand dollars and a trophy,' he said with a wry grin.

'Coming up to the arch is the husband-and-wife Damas team. Rookies. Sponsored by BP.'

'What's it like out there?' a reporter asked, pushing a microphone under Natû's chin.

'What's it like out there?' echoed Natû in response to the reporter's question. She wanted to be with Bud, but trusted Patrick.

'You will only understand once you have run the Iditarod, once you have been there. It's hell. It's heaven. It's marvellous and it cleanses your soul. It's dreadful and fills you with the sort of fear you can taste. And there is nothing on earth to compare with it.'